Why the Garden Club
Couldn't Save Youngstown

Why the Garden Club Couldn't Save Youngstown

 THE TRANSFORMATION OF THE
RUST BELT

SEAN SAFFORD

HARVARD UNIVERSITY PRESS
Cambridge, Massachusetts, and London, England   2009

Library of Congress Cataloging-in-Publication Data

Safford, Sean, 1972–
   Why the garden club couldn't save Youngstown : the transformation
   of the Rust Belt / Sean Safford.
      p.   cm.
   Includes bibliographical references and index.
   ISBN 978-0-674-03176-0 (alk. paper)
      1. Youngstown (Ohio)—Economic conditions.   2. Allentown (Pa.)—
   Economic conditions.   3. Industries—Ohio—Youngstown.   4. Industries—
   Pennsylvania—Allentown.   5. Deindustrialization—Ohio—Youngstown—
   History.   I. Title.
   HC108.Y68S34 2008
   330.9748'27—dc22   2008026029

Contents

Why the Garden Club
Couldn't Save Youngstown

CHAPTER ONE

Cities That Worked

In 1975 Allentown, Pennsylvania, and Youngstown, Ohio, could be considered of a piece. Both were midsize industrial cities dominated by the manufacture of steel, automobiles, and electronics. Over 45 percent of workers in both communities were employed in manufacturing occupations—a remarkably high number even in the context of an economy in which manufacturing was still the most important economic driver. By 1983 that manufacturing employment had dropped by over 12 percentage points, and both cities had taken on the moniker of the *rust belt*. The term *hollowing out* came to describe the prospects for places like these as companies shut down operations in search of cheaper labor, and skilled prime-age workers departed for better opportunities elsewhere.[1] Communities feared they would become shells of their once prosperous pasts.

Some, however, foresaw an alternative future—one that might build on the legacy of the past to establish an economically and socially viable postindustrial future. "High-road" approaches called for the transformation of surviving companies by incorporating technology and workplace flexibility through integrating production, innovation, and industrial relations.[2] Others called for the resurrection of clusters of small entrepreneurial companies that had historically proved to be the base from which dynamic new industries had emerged and on which a more competitive future might be created.[3] The remaining option—the so-called low-road approach—promised only to force workers and communities to scrounge for whatever low-skill, low-paying jobs they could manage to attract.[4]

Today it is clear that Allentown and Youngstown[5] have proceeded on divergent postindustrial paths. Articles in the *New York Times* appearing within months of each other in 1999 and 2000 give an indication of the differences. In one, a reporter trumpets Allentown as a "rust-belt phoenix," which rode the economic boom of the 1990s to prosperity.[6] It highlights local companies such as Agere, a high-technology micro-electronics manufacturer that has prospered through a close alliance of engineering, production, and technology. The article also discusses the emergence of entrepreneurial clusters in optical electronics and biotech-nology in the city. A picture accompanying the article shows a construc-tion worker erecting steel beams for a building that would soon be home to a successful biotech startup. The beams frame Bethlehem Steel's famous blast furnaces, which loom, rusting but still majestic, in the distance.

A series of articles on Youngstown appearing several months later paints a sad contrast. It focuses on the city's fight against corruption in the face of the continuing exodus of "good" factory jobs and the succession of scandal-ridden attempts at bringing prosperity back to a once-proud community. The tableau is capped by reports of an investi-gation that would eventually topple Youngstown's U.S. congressman, James Traficant, on charges of racketeering. It is punctuated by a pic-ture of Youngstown's empty and decaying downtown.[7] More recently Youngstown leapt back into the national news because of an innovative plan to reduce the city's footprint: an acknowledgment that its best days are past and that its future lies in making do with diminished cir-cumstances.[8]

The data support what these journalists could hardly have failed to ob-serve. Allentown has emerged as a community that has somehow found itself on the high road, while Youngstown has emerged as the poster child for postindustrial decline and hollowing out. In 2007 Allentown's unem-ployment rate was 4.7 percent compared with Youngstown's 6.2 percent.[9] Average wages in Allentown were 10 percent higher than Youngstown's at $37,440 and $33,960, respectively. Thirty-one entrepreneurial compa-nies in Allentown garnered $1.8 billion in venture-capital funds over the course of the 1990s compared with just fifteen firms and just $780 mil-lion in Youngstown. Allentown's population has grown by 35 percent since 1980, while Youngstown's has fallen. Youngstown residents' average age—about equal to Allentown's at about thirty in 1970—is now nearly forty. Allentown is better educated, with 17.4 percent of the population holding bachelor's degrees compared with just 12 percent in Youngstown.

The regions' tax bases and rates of poverty follow a similar pattern. In the post-9/11 economic downturn, Allentown managed to retain many lucrative jobs, as firms have consolidated operations *into* the region, while production jobs in Youngstown slipped away to the American South, Mexico, and China.

But while the differences between these two places are clear today, an observer in 1983 would have been hard pressed to predict them. Then both cities were in the top 5 percent nationally in the percentage of the workforce still employed in manufacturing, as well as in the percentage of manufacturing workers who had recently *lost* their jobs. Workers who managed to keep well-paying jobs were employed in industries that were clearly on the downturn. Politically, both were highly fragmented, with two primary cities, two rival counties, and two U.S. congressmen competing for scarce political capital. Both were strong union towns with histories of contentious labor-management relations, and both were located far from either the defense industry–laden West Coast or the educational and financial powerhouses of the East, which attracted the most exciting industries and workers. The question that drives this book is how could these two places, which shared so much in common before the 1970s, have taken such divergent paths?

The Crisis of the Rust Belt

It is not clear when the term *rust belt* entered the American lexicon. But at least one account suggests that its widespread use came during the presidential campaign of 1984 when Walter Mondale criticized Ronald Reagan for turning the industrial Midwest into a "rust bowl."[10] Reporters covering the campaign picked up on the term, transforming it in the course of that campaign into the "rust belt."[11] Referring to an area of the United States spreading from New York through Pennsylvania and Ohio and on to the shores of Lake Michigan, the region became known for a proliferation of rusting factories, declining home prices, population losses, high unemployment, and general economic malaise. Freed of the restrictions that had kept industrial activity geographically concentrated, capital began to move out of the region, imposing substantial hardships on the communities left behind. Commentators fretted over the possibility that the country's major industrial cities—cities that had been the engines of American prosperity up to that point in history—would hollow out as the most skilled workers made their way to the coasts, while low-skilled workers decamped along with production jobs to the South and West.

In the 1920s, of course, the region was not called the rust belt. It was referred to with considerably greater enthusiasm as America's manufacturing belt.[12] Industrial manufacturing had emerged on the coast earlier, but it spread to the interior and midwestern part of the country during the second industrial revolution of the nineteenth century. Between 1860 and 1900, the states bordering the Great Lakes (excluding New York and Pennsylvania) increased their share of national manufacturing from 14 to 26 percent, bringing them into line with manufacturing already in place along the East Coast.[13]

Layoffs had been a regular part of life throughout America's industrial heartland for all of that time, and policies enacted in the wake of the Great Depression at both the state and the federal level—in particular, unemployment insurance—were designed to mitigate the social effects of cyclical downturns. But by the early 1980s, it was becoming clear to politicians, workers, managers, and academics alike that the factories that were closing down were not likely to return. Competitive pressures—both domestic and foreign—mounted, and industrial companies that had occupied the upper strata of America's economy began to falter. As Daniel Bell had predicted nearly a decade earlier, America was entering a new phase of its economic development in which mass production accomplished by men with "big shoulders" took a back seat to the "untraded dependencies" of knowledge and service industries.[14]

As it was occurring, the economic downturn of the 1980s was seen by most as simply a particularly bad recession. In hindsight it is clear that it was more than that: it was the end of an era in America's economic history and the beginning of the transition toward an entirely new way of organizing the economy.[15] The institutional regime that had prevailed in the Northeast for much of the twentieth century is sometimes referred to as *Fordist*. Its central feature was the large bureaucratic company, itself organized within large industrial complexes. Industries were defined by their core products (steel, autos, textiles, and so forth). Manufacturing output was oriented predominantly toward mass production. Frontline workers were represented by labor unions organized, not by craft or occupation, but rather by industry. Economic policy was oriented toward social stability, with Keynesian fiscal programs aimed at achieving full employment and a welfare state that mitigated the social impact of cyclical layoffs. The federal government—

particularly following the Second World War—took an active role in regulating a number of key industries, particularly transportation, communication, energy, and banking.

The demise of this way of organizing the economy—leading to an extended period of what economists have referred to as a "structural adjustment"—produced the crisis of the rust belt. Others have written more eloquently and knowledgeably about the economic and political circumstances that gave rise to the set of institutions associated with Fordism and which led to its decline.[16] I will not rehearse those debates here except to point out one aspect of the Fordist system which is generally overlooked: the close interrelationship that existed between industries and the communities they inhabited. It is in examining this relationship more closely that I believe we can find an answer to the question of why some places have fared better in their postindustrial trajectories than others.

The cities and towns in the interior of America's Northeast and Midwest grew hand in glove with industrial production. The very identity of cities like Akron, Detroit, and Pittsburgh—each of which became a "capital" of an industry—was tied directly to the industries that resided in them. The economic and social organization of industrial regions was tightly interwoven. As the Lynds showed in their great ethnographic account of Muncie, Indiana, in the 1920s and 1930s,[17] the leaders of industrial companies occupied prestigious places in the social circles and exercised powerful influence within the machinery of local government. They (and their wives) populated the boards of directors of symphonies, museums, hospitals, and churches. The location of factories dictated settlement and transportation patterns of incoming workers in many neighborhoods. Rhythms of everyday life revolved around the factory whistles and board rooms of these cities' most important industrial companies.

When those companies eventually declined or evolved to compete in a global economy, it touched off an emergency for the communities they had called home. The immediate impact was easily observed: an acute loss of jobs, a rapidly declining tax base, and the exodus of young and highly skilled residents. But beyond the immediate suffering, these places experienced a deeper civic and social crisis. Once "places that worked," they were now set adrift into a rapidly changing economic and political environment in which their future role (as communities and as individual actors within those communities) was uncertain.

The Place of Rust-Belt Communities in a Global Economy

How exactly to characterize the "new" economic model that communities needed to adapt to is the subject of some dispute, but the bold strokes are not in doubt. The economy we live in today is less oriented toward mass production and more focused on specialized goods. Customers, suppliers, collaborators, and intermediaries with which companies interact are much less likely to be found locally than nationally or globally. Services are a much more important part of the economy than before. Production processes are less likely to be contained within organizational boundaries and are instead marked by collaboration across firm boundaries and the imperatives of the capital markets toward achieving higher rates of return through a combination of greater efficiency or innovation. To survive, companies that were organized in such a way as to compete in an industrial world have had to adapt to these and other related conditions of the modern economy.

The changing terms of competition for companies have important implications for regions. In the mid-twentieth century, the economic structure of industry was tied directly to geography. But one way in which this shift is manifested is in the way that industries have been restructured and, in the process, decoupled from the places they had inhabited.[18] In many areas, a hub-and-spoke system predominated. Major industrial companies were surrounded by a local coterie of suppliers and other specialized actors whose production was oriented primarily toward the major local industrial concerns.[19] Economic restructuring in the last thirty years has fundamentally altered these patterns. Large bureaucratic industrial firms have downsized, spinning off ancillary operations into separate concerns. Production has been transferred from large manufacturers to their smaller suppliers, and this decoupling has fueled the geographic dispersion of production as manufacturers seek out lower costs.[20] To survive, companies that in the past would have survived on a largely local—or at most, regional—basis have had to reach out nationally and globally to find customers, suppliers, and collaborators.

Product markets and supply chains have gone global, but, perhaps paradoxically, the importance of localities has not diminished. Indeed, the role of regions as a unit of organizing and regulating the economy has increased over the last several decades. Regions have emerged as major loci of policymaking, with politicians and academics alike touting the virtues of "clusters" and local systems of innovation.[21] And where unions once provided a strong voice for the relatively powerless, communities and community organizing have become equally—if not more—salient axes around which people organize to assert their economic interests.[22]

This is partly a result of a fundamental shift in the locus of economic policymaking in America. The early twentieth century saw policy makers in the United States and elsewhere build up the role of national government as savior and protector of citizens, particularly in the face of the pain that often accompanies economic turbulence. But with the election of Ronald Reagan as U.S. President, the tenor of policy in the United States changed.[23] Reagan sought to push responsibility for economic and social policy down from the federal government and into states and communities. It is sometimes suggested that Reagan ushered in an age of individual responsibility. This interpretation is undoubtedly true on a philosophical level. But on a practical one, it seems too extreme. An intermediate reading is that the Reagan revolution was a rejection of the notion that the federal government could or should attempt to solve social and economic problems through state intervention. But this does not necessarily imply that individuals bear the only or indeed even the primary responsibility for addressing problems or, indeed, opportunities. It was instead a reinvigoration of the role that communities and networks play in addressing common economic challenges. And accordingly, the divergent trajectories regions have taken in this period of structural and societal adjustment can be traced to how well communities responded to these responsibilities.

Toward an Institutionalist Interpretation of Regional Economic Change

Drawing on a historical comparison of the common development trajectories, simultaneous crises, and subsequent divergence of Allentown and Youngstown, this book makes three separate, but related, arguments about why some communities were up to the challenge and others were not.

The first is that the key to rebuilding mature industrial regions lies in whether and how they have reknitted the fabric of civic participation. The challenges facing mature industrial regions are uniquely difficult. The civic and economic structures of many regions with which they compete—initially in the American South and West and then in the rising economic regions of the developing world—have developed in the context of a global economy and, as a result, they are more closely adapted to the current rules of competition. But the roles, rules, routines, and identities in which individuals and organizations in mature industrial regions were embedded emerged earlier and were therefore wedded to a very different set of economic circumstances. These constitutive elements of society could not simply be replaced. They have had to adapt over time. What separates Allentown from Youngstown is that, in Allentown, the roles, rules, and identities of organizations and individuals have adapted with more agility than has been the case in Youngstown.[24]

The second argument is closely related to the first. While the roles, rules, and identities affecting all kinds of actors in rust-belt communities have come up for scrutiny and fundamental redefinition, one category of actors in particular—that of major companies and their leaders— has experienced the most fundamental shift. In the industrial era, the individuals who ran major industrial companies sat at the very center of the regional social structures. They enjoyed the highest status and exerted the most influence over local affairs. Their power and centrality were largely a function of the rules of the game by which industrial society operated in that era, which tied the interests of companies directly to the interests of the regions that sustained them. But the rules of global competition have served to disconnect the interests of companies and their leaders from those of regions. Yet their involvement—and in particular, the personal involvement of top leaders of key businesses within regions—has proved vital to regional success. Allentown owes much of its postindustrial success to the fact that it has retained a strong, central role for the business leaders. To be sure, the roles and identities these leaders have with respect to their community are very different from those of the past. But their participation has helped to ensure that opportunities are recognized earlier and that collective action to realize those opportunities has been implemented effectively.

The final argument concerns what made Allentown so resilient. Many would chalk the difference up to "leadership." But—as we will see— both regions were blessed with leaders who were equally committed to the success of their communities. I argue that what separated Allentown and Youngstown was not leadership per se, but rather the social structural context in which that leadership was exercised.

Regions can be characterized by the complex layers of identity and affiliation along which individuals and organizations are connected to each other. A crisis may erupt within one of these layers, but it is unlikely to undermine all of them equally. When confronted with a deep crisis—that is, a crisis that calls into question not only the rules of the game, but also the identities of the actors—people draw on adjacent social structures to guide their actions. Allentown's economic resilience owes much to the fact that the social structure of its civic interactions connected key constituencies who needed to cooperate in the face of the region's crisis. Those networks were absent in Youngstown, and as a result the leaders who faced the crisis in the late 1970s and early 1980s were confronted with a deeply fragmented social landscape. This led to a lack of dialogue and interaction across salient divisions in that community, which blunted the processes by which new roles, rules, and identities might have emerged. Instead, efforts to lead the region to a more competitive footing were consistently stymie, and outmoded identities became even more deeply entrenched.

The first two arguments are developed in greater detail in Chapter 5 and lead to a series of policy implications outlined in Chapter 6. But this third argument has more general implications for the way sociologists should think about societal and institutional change. It is developed primarily in Chapters 3 and 4. But it requires a bit more explanation to set the stage.

The argument of this book can broadly be characterized as "institutionalist"[25] because it is rooted in an assumption that complex challenges and opportunities require cooperation and that cooperation requires rules. Sometimes these rules are written down in formal documents that define terms and delineate the roles and responsibilities of various parties. But formal rules constitute only a small portion of those that govern daily interactions. For instance, language is inherently a system of rules. But these rules are not defined by statute; they exist simply in the usage. When someone speaks in a way that breaks widely taken for granted patterns of acceptable usage, they quickly find that no one understands them and thus learn to make adjustments to conform to prevailing patterns. The same can be said for any number of human interactions, including the ways that industries and communities are organized. These are social systems in which roles, identities, norms, and rules shape prevailing and accepted patterns of interaction.

Communities typically experience long periods in which the roles and rules governing patterns of interaction remain relatively stable. Indeed, they can be so stable—so deeply entrenched—that they become oppressive. Yet new technologies emerge, new populations arrive, market conditions change, and new competitors enter the arena. Each of these changes is likely to present a challenge to the established patterns. For the most part, addressing these problems is an incremental affair. The actors remain the same, but the roles and rules governing interaction among actors are adapted. Some changes, however, are more fundamental. They are *crises* in the sense that they challenge not only the rules that govern interaction, but also the identities of actors within a community.[26]

The crisis that occurred in Allentown, Youngstown, and other rust-belt cities in the late 1970s and early 1980s was a fundamental crisis because one of the most crucial members of the community, the large industrial firm, ceased to exist in its earlier form. Diminished, downsized, rationalized, and globalized, industrial firms—and their leaders—no longer played by the same rules when dealing with their communities. And because so much revolved around the industrial firm, the redefinition of its identity within communities rippled out to affect the roles and identities of every other actor in these places as well. Unions and universities, local government and civic organizations, supplier companies and banks, society matrons and working-class stiffs all derived their identities to one degree or another from the role they played vis-à-vis the large industrial companies that had come to occupy a central and overarching role. The withdrawal of those companies forced a fundamental realignment of economic identities, roles, and responsibilities in affected regions. And it is in analyzing this process of realignment that we will find the answer to why Allentown has fared relatively well in its postindustrial pathway and why Youngstown has not.

Crises (big and small) require individuals to improvise, and it is through those acts of improvisation that change is realized as old patterns are modified and new patterns are established. While some would suggest that fundamental individual needs take over (thus driving people and organizations to behave solely in their own personal interest) the fact is that cooperation remains imperative, particularly when the problems are as complex and vexing as those that confronted rust-belt communities. The question is not really whether one can or should cooperate in the face of such challenges. Cooperation is imperative. The question is with whom to cooperate, and according to what rules.

Gernot Grabher and David Stark, writing about the trajectories of post-Communist pathways, have argued that when faced with fundamental crises of this kind, actors refuse to commit to any one path, since a false move could ultimately undermine their position in the socioeconomic order that will inevitably emerge. Instead, they argue that actors made provisional moves.[27] Testing the waters and investing in multiple possible trajectories, these provisional moves slowly take on a form and pattern as actors reach bilateral understandings. Bilateral understandings eventually give way to more general patterns as innovations diffuse, and eventually a new social order is achieved and new institutional orders come into focus.[28]

I agree with the thrust of Grabher and Stark's argument, which I take to be that actions are not simply oriented toward achieving material or symbolic goals. Actors are acutely aware that their actions simultaneously have implications for building and maintaining social standing as well. This is heightened at moments of social instability, which provide both pitfalls and opportunities for social advancement. What I take issue with is the implication that crisis returns society to a primitive state in which all paths and trajectories are possible. The provisional, local, and robust actions that actors make in the wake of fundamental crises do not happen in a social vacuum. Societies are thickly layered with intersecting dimensions of identity and affiliation. And while a crisis may affect one or more of these layers, it is unlikely to undermine all of them simultaneously and with equal effect. When faced with acute crisis along one dimension of social interaction—for instance, in the definition of roles, rules, and identities associated with economic interactions, as was the case in Allentown and Youngstown—actors fall back on the nearest stable set of ties to inform the tenor of their provisional moves.[29] To take a somewhat extreme example, the invasion of a country may destroy its political system, but that does not mean that social structures have ceased to exist. Religious, clan, and ethnic relationships remain, and people turn to these layers to suggest whom to cooperate with and according to what rules.

Developing a deeper understanding of the multidimensionality of social identities and affiliations within regions reveals what seems at first to be a chaotic process of rebuilding relationships from scratch to be an ordered—indeed, somewhat predictable—process in which submerged identities and affiliations form the context in which new rules of the game are negotiated. The trajectory societies that have undergone acute change take in the aftermath of such a crisis can therefore be predicted to some degree by analyzing the way that submerged layers of affiliation and identity shape action in the immediate aftermath of the crisis.

Ann Swidler has written about "cultural tool kits," which is to say that the culture provides a range of repertoires about how to interpret and make sense of the world.[30] But the actual range of interpretations may be wider than that which any individual can access because their worldview is limited by the culture they live in. Culture does not determine one's actions, but it may limit the possibilities. The argument here is related, but it adds a structural dimension. When confronted with a crisis as deep as the one faced by people in rust-belt communities, certain kinds of cooperation would seem apparently beneficial in addressing common problems. But the possibility of building those relationships is limited by the tool kit of relational dimensions to which actors have access.

To preview, the key difference between Allentown and Youngstown was the fact that when economic crisis struck it undermined the system of meanings, roles, rules, and identities that linked actors associated with an economic plane of interaction. But actors in Allentown had access to an alternative and independent plane of interaction that linked actors together along a civic dimension. The civic dimension created a context that allowed actors to cooperate despite deep divisions rooted in geography, class, and ethnicity, and it was in the context of that cooperation that new identities were negotiated. Actors in Youngstown did not have access to a similarly cross-cutting system of meanings and, as a result, when crisis came, the region splintered and ossified into opposing factions. Without a context for cooperation, actors in Youngstown have struggled to redefine themselves.

Beyond Allentown and Youngstown, what this suggests is that individuals and organizations that are confronted with acute uncertainty in the external environment fall back on preexisting relationships. Closer relationships trump weaker relationships. Relevant relationships trump irrelevant relationships. But weak irrelevant relationships will trump nonexistent relationships regardless of whether such a relationship might make more sense from an objective point of view. An observer might look at the situation and suggest that it makes sense for leaders of two groups to meet and cooperate in order to overcome a common and shared problem. Yet relationships don't work that way. Relationships are cultivated, not created from whole cloth. This is particularly true at moments of acute uncertainty.

Who cooperates with whom at a moment of acute uncertainty is crucial because it is in these micro-moments of sense making and pragmatic negotiation that new identities, new roles, and new rules are negotiated. But the crucible in which those patterns are shaped is itself shaped by the intersection of cross-cutting, possibly submerged layers of identity and affiliation. New rules of the game will eventually emerge in the wake of fundamental crises, but they will not be crafted from whole cloth. They will emerge from interactions and negotiations shaped by the tool kit of existing relationships available to those who are affected by the crisis.

The Evolution of Civic Leadership Institutions in the Rust Belt

The rules of the game that this book is concerned with have to do with the civic and social leadership of rust-belt communities. A long tradition in urban economics has focused on what Logan and Molotch referred to as the "urban growth machine": the coalition of local elites with practical (typically financial) interests in the use of land and buildings who build their wealth by managing government and cultural institutions in ways that promote growth.[31] But when large companies receded as the economic engines of these regions, they simultaneously withdrew from the central role they had played in the civic life of the communities as well.[32] The leaders of major industrial companies and of the banks with which they were most closely associated were the core of the elite "growth coalitions" that (for all intents and purposes) presided over the development of industrial communities in the nineteenth and twentieth centuries.

The composition and intentions of those elites were the subject of an intense and long-standing dialogue among urban sociologists, with those such as Robert Dahl, who saw essentially benign and enlightened intentions of elite governing coalitions,[33] arrayed against those such as G. William Domhoff, who came to see community economic elites as engaged in bald political attempts to exert over and extract value.[34] But those debates, I argue, have been rendered partially moot because of the fundamental transformation that has taken place in the organization of American society and its economy over the last half century. Prior to the 1980s, leaders of the important locally based companies were typically very active and central members of local growth coalitions. The reason was apparent: to the extent that these major companies depended on the locality for necessary infrastructure, some forms of short-term financing, an educated workforce, and labor peace, it was in their best interests to ensure that their views were heard and respected by local government. But social and economic forces have conspired over the last thirty years to change that. The evolution of the American economy toward global supply chains, customer bases, and financing; the emergence of national markets for labor, talent, and financing; and the willingness of communities to compete against one another to provide tax breaks and infrastructure improvements have cleaved the economic interests of business leaders from their civic interests.

The "coalition" that once brought such leaders into common cause with local landowners, locally based nonprofit and civic associations, and local government and into conflict with the leaders of labor and other community interests no longer exists. In many communities, all that remains of the old growth coalition are the social, civic, and governmental actors. From the perspective of these civic groups, economic organizations—and in particular the leaders of large companies—have become essentially customers or clients: people to be catered to rather than the integral participants of the local leadership coalition which they once were. By the same token, from many companies' perspectives, the communities they inhabit have become just another group in need of public relations management.

That is a problem not least because those economic leaders bring personal talents and resources (*social* as well as financial resources) that other kinds of community leaders do not. And so communities that lack their participation suffer from a chronic inability to reach and implement decisions of vital importance. Challenges and opportunities, when confronted, will not be acted on as effectively. And places where there is not strong personal participation among economic leaders will find that the corporate decisions those leaders make will tend, on average, to have more damaging implications for local economic outcomes than would be the case otherwise. Community growth coalitions need the talents, connections, energy, and resources that the leaders of major companies provide. And it is through interaction with the community that those leaders are encouraged to make decisions that might benefit both the company *and* the community. The upshot is this: communities that were better able to rebuild their civic leadership—and importantly, to rebuild it in a way that establishes a role for economic leaders within their civic networks—have seen better economic outcomes during the subsequent period of adjustment.

This much seems apparent from the story that a comparison of Allentown and Youngstown has to tell, as the following pages—and in particular Chapter 5—will show. In Allentown, the rules of the game governing the local civic leadership have been rebuilt in a way that maintains a central role for business leaders, and this rebuilding has had demonstrable effects on the ability of Allentown to adjust to the new rules of global competition. But if the lessons of what has happened in these two cities—and in the rust belt generally—are to have value beyond simply explaining history, we must also probe into the mechanisms that explain why certain coalitions emerged at a particular place and time and why others did not.

In a sense, this book builds on a long series of books and articles examining the transformation of postindustrial production networks and the impact this has on regional outcomes.[35] That literature contains valuable insights that are largely complementary to the argument presented here. But the key message of this book is that even the best-laid plans for adjusting and responding to economic crises are lost if the social context in which to implement those plans is flawed. And so this book seeks to understand how the social and civic networks of industrial regions have evolved, what impact variation in those networks has had on their postindustrial trajectories, and—more broadly—what explains the resilience of civic infrastructure (and by extension the region more broadly) in some instances and not in others.

Social Structure and the Trajectories of Allentown and Youngstown

Differences in the nature of multiplex networks between Allentown and Youngstown explain the cities' post industrial divergence.[36] The origins and impact of these differences are developed in greater detail in Chapters 3 and 4. To preview, civic life in Allentown came to revolve around two separate but intersecting networks, one economic and one civic. In Youngstown, economic and civic networks were practically one and the same. This difference had momentous consequences for how leaders of each community responded to the steel crisis of the 1970s and 1980 as the region's leading industrial companies faltered. The cities' economic networks were directly implicated in this crisis, and as a result they provided little basis on which to establish cooperation. Instead, the response took shape within the context of the cities' civic networks.

Given the patterns of interaction that existed previously, one might expect a similar fate to have unfolded in each place, with parochial interests coming to dominate within the patterns of social stratification that prevailed. Allentown, indeed, might have been expected to fare worse, given the deep internal divisions across small localities and ethnic groups. But this was not the case.

For reasons discussed in more detail later, a few key organizations in Allentown came to occupy brokerage roles linking the disparate parts of the community. These brokering organizations were essential to creating a context in which improvisation in the face of the acute crisis confronting that community took place; its structure created possibilities for collective action among the region's leaders which in turn shaped the kinds of decisions that were made and the ability to actually implemented those decisions. And it was in this context that new patterns of interaction and, indeed, new identities linking economic and civic organizations within the community were reforged.

No such bridging mechanism was in place in Youngstown. In Youngstown, community leadership had been heavily concentrated among a central core of economic elites. From a structural perspective, what this implies is that economic networks overlapped directly with civic networks; the two were practically indistinguishable. The impact of this dense interconnection across the two layers of the community was disastrous: it meant that the collapse of the economic core took the civic network down with it. With the core economic and civic leadership of the community absent, the community became deeply fragmented. Collective action was not possible in this environment because there was no social structural basis on which to base it. The response to the crisis was foisted on the shoulders of a severely disabled civic infrastructure that struggled to cope, but at a significant disadvantage.

As Chapter 5 shows, the implications of these differences are today readily apparent in the way that economic leaders participate in the cities' civic networks. In Allentown improvisation in the face of acute economic crises has led, with time, to the emergence of new patterns of civic participation. Business leaders play a central role in these patterns, albeit ones that are very different from the roles they played previously. The region has benefited from a productive interaction of economic and civic leaders. Youngstown's local leadership, on the other hand, is fragmented. Its business leaders are conspicuous by their absence from key conversations.

The key contribution of this book is to suggest an answer for why this is the case. The difference lies in the way that different layers of these places were invoked in the midst of crisis. Allentown has more effectively adjusted in the face of globalization because the submerged networks to which actors had access in the midst of that crisis provided a platform in which key constituencies gained access to each other. As they improvised in this context, they developed new rules and new identities that reknit the social fabric. In contrast, the alternative networks to which actors in Youngstown had access were deeply fragmented. Where new identities and new rules of the game emerged in Allentown, the fragmented nature of Youngstown's networks produced multiple, competing factions who ultimately retreated into separate—balkanized—camps. Their response was to cling to outmoded identities and outmoded rules of the game. The social structure evolved, as it inevitably must, but in ways that undermined the ability of that community to adjust to globalization.

This, finally, points toward the more general lessons taken up in Chapter 6. It has become commonplace for politicians and pundits to call for "strengthening communities," and this is by no means the first book to lament the decline of business leaders' involvement in civic affairs. What is unique here is the diagnosis of why some places have had an easier time reknitting the fabric of civic leadership and the lessons the stories of Allentown and Youngstown yield about how to go about the work of strengthening that fabric. I turn, soon, to telling that story in some detail. But it is useful to begin with an empirical puzzle: the divergence of Allentown and Youngstown.

CHAPTER TWO

The Empirical Puzzle:
The Postindustrial Divergence of
Allentown and Youngstown

The trajectories of Allentown and Youngstown must be seen in the context of their histories as minor centers of production within the larger industrial complex known as the American manufacturing belt. Cities and towns like Allentown and Youngstown were established toward the end of the eighteenth century, born out of the general westward expansion of the United States that followed the Revolutionary War. In this very early period, the little manufacturing that existed was oriented toward local—mainly agricultural—customers. But the onset of the Second Industrial Revolution in the later part of the nineteenth century quickly transformed these communities by incorporating them into a broad industrial agglomeration stretching from the coalfields of eastern Pennsylvania to eastern Iowa.[1] Specialized production centers emerged, such as the steel industry in Pittsburgh, the transportation hub at Chicago, and later, the automobile industry in Detroit.

Allentown and Youngstown became secondary production centers tied to the broader mosaic, first by the construction of a network of canals in the 1830s and 1840s and then by the railroads that sprung up in the 1850s and 1860s. Subsequently, as industries began to consolidate, the entire region took on a set of institutional and interorganizational arrangements characteristic of Fordist modes of production, marked by the centrality of large, mass-production-oriented firms that employed considerable and largely blue-collar workforces, which produced and marketed durable goods to end customers.[2] Such firms became the central, and in many cases dominant, organizational actors within middle-sized production centers like Allentown and Youngstown.[3]

The turn of the twentieth century brought extremely rapid growth as workers streamed into the region, first by internal migration from the American hinterlands, then subsequently by immigration from Eastern Europe and the American South. The flood of new arrivals led to massive social strife in the 1920s and culminated in the rapid spread of industrial unions in the 1930s.[4] The success of these organizing drives ensured labor peace during the Second World War; after the war, they opened the way for workers' entry into the expanding ranks of the middle class, which fueled the continued growth and expansion of industry. American industry entered a period of economic hegemony, expanding rapidly domestically as well as internationally. But that period of hegemony proved fleeting. Just as the Second Industrial Revolution had tied together the myriad cities and towns of the America's industrial heartland, the rapid reconstruction of Europe and the rise of newly industrializing countries in Asia began to coalesce into a global system of tightly interrelated firms. By the 1970s elements of that global system had developed to the point of challenging America's economic leadership. By the 1980s the mosaic structure of the manufacturing belt began to break down. Massive structural adjustment ensued as the region began to "equalize downward" into a declining region within the global capitalist system.[5]

The crisis began in the mid-1970s, broke open in the late 1970s, and reached a peak in the recession of the early 1980s, when unemployment levels spiked to over 20 percent in some particularly hard-hit regions. Many theories were advanced to make sense of the problem and formulate strategies to counter it. Companies blamed the decline on high-wage union workers and an undesirable business climate, while workers and a number of politicians lashed out at unfair foreign competitors. Later, more-considered hypotheses emerged. Product life cycle theories suggested that mature regions were victims of mature products, which had spent out their profit-generating potential (Abernathy and Utterback 1978; Markusen 1985). Another theory focused on the notion of institutional rigidities and lock-in (Olson 1982). Still others focused on the organization of production, and in particular, the predominance of bureaucratic mass production combined with the need for more flexible ways of generating and producing innovative new products (Piore and Sabel 1984).

Dire predictions were leveled as the problem of deindustrialization and the human suffering associated with it worsened.[6] Yet in the 1980s

Table 2.1 Selected Ohio and Pennsylvania metropolitan areas by employment growth, 1992–2000

Metropolitan area	Employment growth	Wage growth	Job creation	Job destruction	Employment (thousands)
Toledo, OH	0.55	0.40	7.6	7.0	259
Akron, OH	0.51	0.23	4.9	7.3	264
Allentown, PA	0.34	0.24	5.3	6.9	227
Scranton, PA	0.34	0.26	7.2	7.0	231
Youngstown, OH	0.24	0.16	6.8	7.2	207

Source: Faberman (2002).

and 1990s, it became clear that most predictions had been too pessimistic, and in particular, that considerable variation had emerged within the region. What had been seen as one large declining agglomeration has been revealed to be a loosely federated collection of localities that are diverging in their ability to adjust to the new globally competitive environment. As a number of recent studies have shown[7] (and as indicated in Table 2.1), some regions have experienced high rates of job creation, often accompanied by almost equally high rates of job destruction, while others have seen stagnation on both measures.[8] The fact of this divergence has led, at a minimum, to a reassessment of the notion that old industrial regions must necessarily wither and die.[9] The divergence has also caused a search for the underlying causes of successful and not-so-successful processes of local economic transformation.

The Divergence of Allentown and Youngstown

In their prescient book on the competitiveness crisis facing the United States in the early 1980s, Barry Bluestone and Bennett Harrison (1982) argued for a "multi-pronged" industrial policy to counter the dehumanizing effects of deindustrialization. In addition to reforming labor and employment law and rebuilding the social safety net, they called for policies that would nurture "sunrise" industries, such as electronics and biomedical technology, while addressing challenges facing "sunset" industries, such as steel and automobiles. Their program for supporting new industry included fostering " 'public-private partnerships' between the companies manufacturing projects in potentially profitable growing markets and the government that 'targets' fi-

Figure 2.1 Manufacturing as a percentage of total employment

nancial and regulatory policy to help those companies grow."[10] To ease sunset industries' transformation, Bluestone and Harrison suggested transforming existing plants and equipment to new uses or, where possible, transforming old facilities that could have remained economically viable if not for a lack of a community-based response to reinvigorate them.

Leaders of both Allentown and Youngstown were intimately aware of the choices that Bluestone and Harrison described. And given the remarkable similarities surrounding the cities' emergence and growth, one might expect that experiencing simultaneous economic crises in the late 1970s and early 1980s would have led them down similar paths. Yet this is not what happened. Allentown has come to embody Bluestone and Harrison's vision of a community that succeeded by striking a high-road strategy of facilitating the growth of sunrise industries and smoothing the transition from sunset ones. Similar efforts in Youngstown have largely been frustrated.

As the data in Figure 2.1 indicate, manufacturing remains more prominent as a percentage of total employment in both cities than in the rest of the United States and actually increased slightly in Youngstown in the mid-1990s. Nevertheless, stark differences are apparent with respect to the *kinds* of manufacturing that take place in the two cities. In

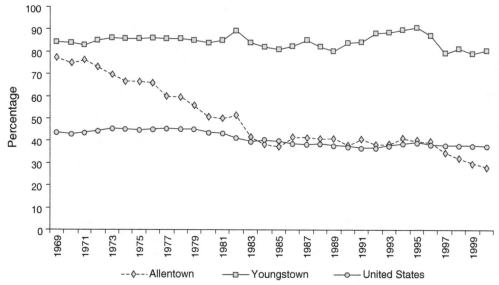

Figure 2.2 Steel, autos, textiles, apparel, and cement as a percentage of manufacturing employment, 1969–2000

Youngstown, steel, auto manufacturing, cement, textiles, and apparel continue to account for about 81 percent of total income derived from manufacturing (Figure 2.2). Allentown, on the other hand, has largely shed its old industrial stock. While these five industry segments composed 77 percent of manufacturing-based income in 1970, today they account for only 28 percent.

Figures 2.3 and 2.4 give an indication of what has taken their place. Figure 2.3 shows that knowledge-intensive growth industries of the 1980 and 1990s, including electronics, instruments, and specialty chemicals, have increased dramatically over this period of time. Allentown has also experienced significant growth in the "high-end" service sector, including finance, insurance, and real estate services. In both cities (as shown in Figure 2.4), these jobs accounted for less than 5 percent of employment in 1970. But today the numbers in Allentown are close to national levels, with one in six workers in the Lehigh Valley employed in the health or education sectors, while employment in these sectors remains stuck at the previous levels in Youngstown. Automobiles, transportation equipment, and some small-scale specialty steelmaking represent the bulk of that city's manufacturing base, and the

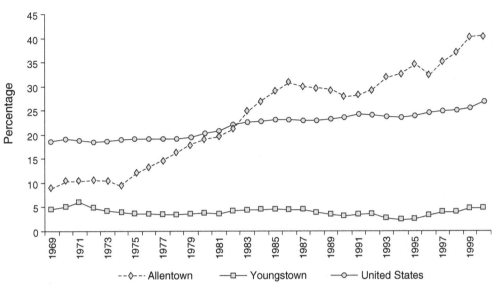

Figure 2.3 Electronics, instruments, and specialty chemicals as a percentage of manufacturing employment, 1969–2000

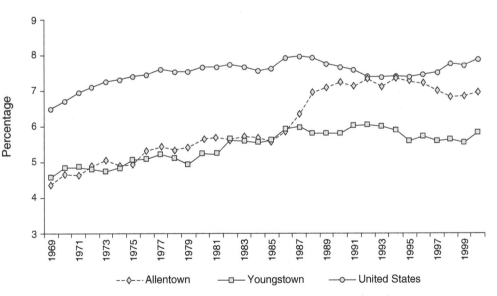

Figure 2.4 Finance, insurance, and real estate as a percentage of total employment

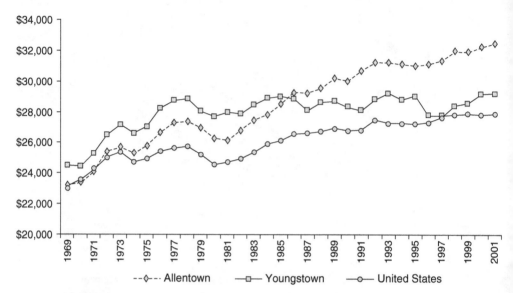

Figure 2.5 Average earnings per worker: 1969–2000 (adjusted for regional CPI, 1984 dollars)

service industries that have emerged in Youngstown are concentrated at the lower end of the skill range. Call centers made significant inroads in Youngstown in recent years. In the 1990s the region became home to a cluster of private and publicly owned prisons.

Finally, the differences in the cities' economic trajectories have had an impact on standards of living. Figure 2.5 shows income growth in the cities since the 1970s. Allentown and Youngstown essentially tracked each other, above the national average, until around 1977. Indeed, until the mid-1980s, wages were on average higher in Youngstown than in Allentown. But by 2000 the cities had diverged significantly; average wages in Youngstown were several thousand dollars below both the national average and the average in Allentown.

The first question one might ask about the two cities is how well do these two cities match up? The beginning point in any such analysis is to establish the cities' comparability at a logical starting point. As will become clear later, the cities' entire histories—reaching back to the eighteenth century—are relevant in this respect, and, indeed, they compare well in the broad sweep of their economic development. However, perhaps a more convenient starting point with respect to the empirical

Table 2.2 Demographic and economic descriptive statistics, 1950

	Allentown	Youngstown	United States
Metropolitan area population	437,824	528,498	
Population of major cities	208,728	218,186	
Median years of schooling	8.9	9.7	8.4
High school graduates	29%	35%	14.1%
Employed in steel	20%	36%	3%
Median income	$3,360	$3,447	$2,570

Sources: U.S. Bureau of the Census, *City and County Data Book* (1952); U.S. Bureau of the Census, *Statistical Abstract of the United States* (1951).

puzzle as it has been stated is 1950. By this time, both cities were at their peak as centers of industrial manufacturing. Table 2.2 provides some basic demographic statistics; the two metropolitan areas were medium sized—around 500,000 residents—and, for the time, fairly urban, with just under half of their residents living in urban areas. Furthermore, as indicated in Table 2.2, the cities shared very similar economic profiles at that point. In both, over 50 percent of workers were employed in manufacturing, and breaking this category down further, it is clear that steel was the most important component of manufacturing employment, accounting for 20 percent of total employment in Allentown and 36 percent in Youngstown.

These data provide a strong starting point for the claim of comparability. However, the question can be pushed even further through rigorous statistical modeling. To do so, I constructed a data set of fifty-nine metropolitan statistical areas in the United States and gathered data on the rate at which average wages increased over a twenty-five-year period. Among these, I included thirty-eight rust-belt metropolitan statistical areas, defined as cities with populations of less than 1 million residents in the eight states bordering the Great Lakes. Independent socioeconomic measures considered in the analysis included the following variables:

- manufacturing as a percentage of total employment in 1975;
- change in manufacturing as a percentage of employment, 1975–2000;
- percent decline in manufacturing, 1977–1983;
- percent decline in manufacturing, 1983–1987;
- percent completing high school, 1975;

- change in percent completing high school, 1975–2000;

- percent African American, 1975;

- percent change African American, 1975;

- number of Fortune 500 company headquarters, 1975; and

- log population, 1975.

The model took the form of a standard linear regression, $y = X\beta + \varepsilon$, with y being the log change in average incomes 1975–2000 (standardized across regions using regional consumer price indexes as a measure of inflation). The vector X contained independent variables. Predicted values from this model ($r^2 = 0.47$) were then plotted against actual outcomes. As shown in Figure 2.6, Allentown and Youngstown emerged as outliers in this analysis; Allentown fell above predicted outcomes and

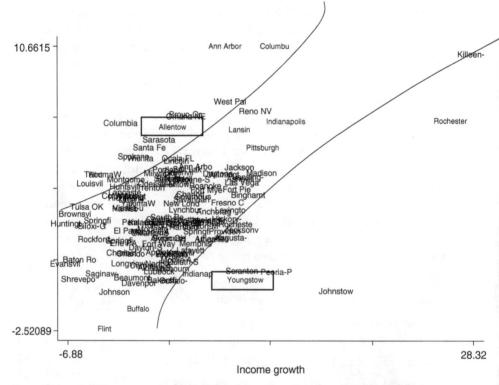

Figure 2.6 Wages growth, 1980–2000. Plot of predicted vs. actual values

Youngstown below. The results provide a strong basis to claim that the cities' baseline comparability, controlling for some obvious potential points of difference, cannot explain their divergence.[11]

The Usual Suspects

The large and contentious conversation that emerged during and after the competitiveness crisis of the late 1970s and early 1980s generated several possible explanations for the observed divergence between the two cities. This section visits several prominent theories of how regional economic change happens and how those theories hold up in relation to the experiences of Allentown and Youngstown.

Industrial Composition and Concentration

One set of explanations concern the structure of local economies in the two areas. Much of the debate surrounding deindustrialization in the 1980s suggested that the problem facing industrial communities was the degree to which economic activities had become concentrated in a limited number of mature industries. Industrial concentration is problematic because it renders communities overly vulnerable to cyclical shocks. In addition, being too focused on one particular industry and its associated customer base may make it difficult to acquire and assimilate new flows of information, which are required for innovation, a key driver of economic growth. Don Sull (2001), for instance, suggests that the overconcentration of tire-related companies in Akron generated blinders as companies become too focused on Detroit automakers as their primary customers, thus missing both the important replacement-tire market and the extent of the threat posed by the radial tire.

Therefore, one way to explain the different outcomes we observe in Allentown and Youngstown is the mix of industries in each city and the degree to which any one industry may have overshadowed others. However, the data (Tables 2.2 and 2.3) indicate that Allentown and Youngstown were not different enough in this respect to determine outcomes. Although steel was more important to Youngstown's economy, it accounted for over 20 percent of employment in both places. Moreover, the industries that made up the rest of Allentown's economy—textiles and concrete manufacturing—were undergoing crises essentially concurrently with steelmaking and were not the kinds of industries that might have provided a base for economic recovery. Industrial diversity, or lack thereof, cannot explain the outcome.

Table 2.3 Industrial composition: Employment, 1950 (in percent)

	Allentown	Youngstown	United States
Agriculture	5	4	17
Mining	1	0	2
Construction	0	5	5
Manufacturing	55	52	18
Transportation	7	7	9
Wholesale	17	18	6
Finance	2	2	16
Services	5	5	11

Sources: County Data Book (1952); *Statistical Abstract of the United States* (1951).

The steel industry in Youngstown was a larger part of the local economy than it was in Allentown. Moreover, it is important to note that Youngstown's steel industry was more integrated, in the sense that a fairly large number of related customers and suppliers had grown up around Youngstown's steel industry, whereas ancillary companies in Allentown were less integrated into relationships with Bethlehem Steel. Undoubtedly, the greater degree of integration in Youngstown contributed to the city's difficulty in adjusting to the economic realities it faced (along with Allentown) in the 1980s. However, that said, it is also the case that this difference alone cannot explain the depth to which the city's economy has declined over time. Again, we can turn to the cities' neighbors for an indication. Akron, for instance, was just as—if not more—concentrated in its core industry of tire and rubber production (as shown in Table 2.4). Akron's score on the most prominent diversification index of the time, developed by Rodgers (1950), shows that its economy was as concentrated as Youngstown's at the time, yet it has had a much smoother postindustrial transition experience. The conclusion to be drawn is that while the degree of industry concentration in Youngstown is not trivial in explaining the city's subsequent experiences, it is not a sufficient explanation in and of itself. On the economic diversity of Allentown, see Slick (1967).

Geographic Proximity

A separate set of explanations for regional economic change focuses on the importance of proximity to customer and supplier markets. For obvious reasons, one would expect the economic performance of one region to be at least somewhat correlated with the performance of nearby

Table 2.4 Industrial diversification index of selected cities in 1950

City	Score	City	Score	City	Score
Trenton	148	Syracuse	416	Davenport	702
Buffalo	243	Allentown	430	Youngstown	709
Columbus	298	Reading	440	Akron	717
Milwaukee	363	Rochester	498	Winston-Salem	728
Grand Rapids	369	Fort Wayne	606	Fall River	742
Toledo	372	Birmingham	615	Peoria	773
Providence	402	South Bend	641	Flint	934

Source: Adapted from Rodgers (1950).

regions. Krugman (1991) showed that transportation costs vary with distance and therefore one can explain clustering effects through simple economies-of-scale arithmetic. Firms that are likely to trade with each other are also likely to show similarities with respect to the cyclicality of outcomes. "Firms," he argues, "have an incentive to concentrate production at a limited number of locations [and] prefer, other things equal, to choose locations with good access to markets; but access to markets will be good precisely where a large number of firms choose to locate."[12] Much of Krugman's analysis concentrates on the agglomeration effects that come with reaching some kind of critical mass (for example, banking in New York, cars in Detroit), which attracts factors of production and drives clustering effects such that two identical regions with identical transportation costs both within and between the regions should generate symmetry with respect to outcomes. However, a slight—possibly random—increase in the concentration of industry in one area will begin to lower transportation costs (either of goods or even of ideas), leading toward a clustering effect within that location. But in both Allentown and Youngstown, the cities are too small to have achieved such a critical mass.

An ancillary to the theory suggests that regions in proximity to large markets (or particularly important resource inputs) will do better than those that are not. Yet the evidence on these effects in Allentown and Youngstown is inconclusive. Both cities are close to major metropolitan areas with strong concentrations of manufacturing and therefore a demand for goods and services that might be produced in peripheral regions. Allentown is located approximately seventy miles from both New York City and Philadelphia; Youngstown is located approximately seventy miles from Pittsburgh and Cleveland in the center of the industrial manufacturing heartland and boasts of being the midpoint between New York and Chicago. In terms of proximity to major markets, the cities are roughly equivalent.

Moreover, the same logic with which we addressed the question of industrial concentration through a comparison to the two cities' neighbors strengthens the point. Allentown has done better on a number of dimensions, including income growth and measures of innovation, than some of its close neighbors, such as Scranton and Reading. Youngstown, on the other hand, has done much worse than its neighbors Toledo and Akron, each of which saw modest improvements over the course of the 1990s.

Human Capital

The emergence of the postindustrial and "knowledge" economy has placed a premium on the availability of a well-educated workforce. It has long been argued that one of the most important assets any economy possesses is the skills and abilities of the men and women who do the work. The classic measure of human capital is education levels. Today it is clear that Allentown and Youngstown have diverged on this particular dimension. Allentown's population is, on average, better educated than is the case in Youngstown; over 17 percent of its population holds bachelor's degrees versus just 12 percent in Youngstown. However, this is largely a *product* of the cities' economic divergence. The more important question is how well educated the citizens were at the outset of the crisis. Data from 1980 made it clear that, if anything, the general population of Youngstown was slightly better educated than that of Allentown, at 10.7 and 9.8 years of schooling on average, respectively. Differences in human capital fall short as an explanation.

Policy Explanations

The last thirty years have been a time of tremendous change and experimentation in the way that economic policies are crafted and implemented in the United States. While the federal government had been the dominant actor setting economic policy since at least the Great Depression, the arrival of the Reagan administration signaled a shift toward decentralization of policymaking, with states and municipalities taking on a much more important role.[13] Thus, another potential source of variation between the cases concerns the kinds of policy structures available to them at the state level.

To answer this question, I examined several industrial policies enacted in the early 1980s, which emerged directly in response to the crisis that was unfolding then in places like Allentown and Youngstown. The states of Pennsylvania and Ohio were both early adopters of the enterprise zone concept. Indeed, Ohio has made enterprise zones a central component of its economic development strategy—there are nearly four hundred of them in the state—and the state's program is fairly generous, providing significant tax breaks with relatively light eligibility requirements when compared with Pennsylvania. For instance, companies that might want to locate in the Youngstown technology incubator pay no local or state taxes, pay no rent for a year, and enjoy free broadband access. Pennsylvania's plan is not as generous. Both states adopted very similar programs coming out of the Job Training Partnership Act of 1982, which initially targeted displaced workers (and then morphed over time). Finally, both states were among the first to pay attention to technology as an economic development strategy. In fact, Ohio essentially copied Pennsylvania's plan, with both states setting up several university-industry partnerships that were (and remain, particularly in Ohio) focused on what is essentially a cluster approach of upgrading geographically embedded groupings of technological abilities. This, of course, says little about the implementation of policies in the two states, let alone the specific regions in question. But the nature of the policies that were in place and available to actors in both places was similar.

Social Capital

A final set of potential explanations—one with important implications for the approach taken in this book—concerns the notion of *social capital*. The concept of social capital has been around at least since Coleman and Bourdieu first introduced the term in the early 1980s,[14] but recently its most forceful proponent has been Robert Putnam, whose book *Bowling Alone* argues that strong civil society is the bedrock on which economic prosperity is built. Putnam relies on a large body of data—much of it longitudinal—that shows a decline in participation in activities such as attendance at club meetings, participation in the Parent-Teacher Association, and voter turnout. Geographic variation in this decline, moreover, is correlated with economic outcomes, at least among U.S. states.[15]

Putnam provides access to much of the data on which his claims are based. But unfortunately, the data at the metropolitan statistical

Table 2.5 Social capital indicators (in percent)

	Allentown	Youngstown
Voter turnout		
1984	74	72
1992	56	59
Attends church regularly	61	58
Identifies as Roman Catholic	49	53
Attends club meetings at least once per month	52	49
Agrees with the statement "Most people can be trusted"	34	41
Bowls at least once per month	29	30

Sources: Voter turnout: U.S. Bureau of the Census (2000); church attendance: American Religion Data Archive (www.thearda.com); all else, DBB Worldwide via www.bowlingalone.com.

area level on Allentown and Youngstown were too sparse to permit a longitudinal analysis. However, combining responses and secondary data culled over several years provides some indication of relative levels of social capital as Putnam defines it (see Table 2.5). The data provide evidence that, once again, Allentown and Youngstown essentially come out even. Indeed, on several measures, Youngstown comes out on top. For instance, over 41 percent of respondents in Youngstown agreed with the statement "most people are honest," compared with 34 percent in Allentown. Overall, it seems apparent that conventional approaches to social capital contribute little to the explanation.

Discussion

Several explanations for the two cities' divergence have been introduced and shown to be lacking. Economic and demographic explanations in particular can be ruled out at this point. However, a lack of adequate data combined with what appear to be inherent contradictions in the prevailing approaches to measuring a community's "stock" of social capital raise questions that I take up later in an attempt to develop an alternative perspective on how social structure might have driven the cities' divergent outcomes.

Each of these potential explanations focuses on the categorical attributes of regions (such as the rust belt) and the inalienable drives of individuals within them that may have led to the regional divergence. Yet what we know from numerous case studies and empirical work is that the locus of economic change is not really at the national, regional, or local level; it is contained within organizations. As was mentioned previously, firms that faced the competitiveness crisis had many options with respect to *how* they reacted to the challenges of the early 1980s. High-road approaches focused on ways of generating innovation and incorporating greater skill and responsibility into work. Low-road approaches followed an inexorable "lean and mean" logic of the race to the bottom.[16] But each of the preceding explanations lacks a way of linking the micro-level explanation for how and why organizations undertake high-road transformations as opposed to low-road ones to the macro context in which they are embedded. What aspects of the environment in which they are embedded leads to one set of outcomes or another?

Toward Linking Micro and Macro: A Methodology

"Network analysis," as Emirbayer and Goodwin (1994) put it, "allows historical sociologists to pinpoint . . . the actual histories we observe." The analysis of network structure requires attention to the quality of the ties, including their frequency, intensity, and—perhaps most important as far as this book is concerned—their multiplexity. In contrast to much of the literature associated with network analysis, which has tended to explain action as deriving solely from the structure networks,[17] the approach taken here attempts to maintain the critical notion that human agency is the primary driver. Networks do not determine human action. Rather, networks are constituted *by* human action. Coleman (1984) argues that parents' human capital contributes little to a child's educational growth if it is not complemented by the parent's social capital; by social capital he means the structure of social relationships in which parents are embedded. Action is shaped by social embeddedness and in turn recursively influences social structure itself. Yet, few researchers have adopted the longitudinal approach that would be necessary to show this process.[18] The approach taken in this book does so by reaching back into the origins of Allentown and Youngstown to examine the evolution of social structure over time and how those evolutions have produced the unique paths we observe in each city's economic development trajectories.

Social structure refers to "regularities in the patterns of relations among concrete entities" (White et al. 1976: 733). A social network is one of many possible sets of relations in a specific context that links actors within a large social structure. The structure of networks is important, mainly because it provides insight into the linkages between individuals and groups. The nature of groups is determined by the ties of their members to one another. At the same time, however, the nature of actors can be seen as being determined by their affiliation to (and identification with) various groups.[19] The structure of relations among actors and the location of an individual actor in the network have important behavioral and perceptual consequences. Controlling for socioeconomic characteristics and other potential explanations, Fernandez and McAdam (1988; McAdam 1988), for instance, have shown how the intersection of relationships among interlocking activist organizations at universities affected the likelihood of students joining the Freedom Summer movement of 1964. Gould (1991) similarly examined militants associated with the Paris Commune of 1871 to show that embeddedness within overlapping neighborhood and military social structures affected the militants' commitment to the cause.

In each of these cases, the questions being asked have to do with influences on action (and specifically collective action) in the face of some overarching threat. McAdam makes no claims as to the outcomes of the Freedom Summer movement itself in relationship to the recruitment patterns of its participants (although he does make claims as to the impact participation had on the members of the movement). Gould's case ends in disaster for the militants associated with the commune. Ganz (2000) examines farm workers organizing in California by comparing the social embeddedness of the leadership teams of two competing groups: the AFL-CIO–backed Agricultural Workers' Organizing Committee and the ultimately successful United Farm Workers. His research suggested that the farm workers' victory was owed mainly to the cross-cutting embeddedness of the movement's leaders; they had ties that were both local and national in scope and thus had greater access to salient information that could be used to formulate more effective strategies.

A similar strategy can be used in attempting to understand why Allentown and Youngstown took such different paths despite surface similarities in histories and circumstances. It is clear that obvious parallels between regions can mask underlying stable differences in local unfoldings.[20] What is distinctive about these two places is not a list of external attributes, but how the social structure of each place shaped the structuration process over time. By examining the configuration of social structures in which various crises and external events played out, we can see how very similar outside forces translated into very different—even opposite—consequences.[21]

The methodological strategy used in answering these questions draws on historical comparison, specifically "the method of similarity."[22] Under ideal conditions, the method of similarity dictates comparing two contexts that are similar with respect to all potential explanations except for (a) the variable one is trying to explain and (b) the proposed explanation for those outcomes.[23] In reality, of course, it is never possible to achieve an exact match; many mitigating circumstances inevitably muddy the water. Comparative approaches, therefore, cannot "prove" a given finding. Nevertheless, when rigorously conducted, the method allows insights to emerge that can be contrasted to plausible alternative explanations, providing compelling evidence in support of the claims being made.

Beyond its obvious policy relevance, the location of these cities within the rust belt offers a number of methodological advantages for comparative analysis. The circumstances that gave rise to what was then known as the American manufacturing belt—the westward expansion of the United States and the Second Industrial Revolution—mean that many communities in the region have common economic, social, and political origins.[24] Moreover, the centralized, oligopolistic structure of the industries that took hold there—centered on steel and automobile production—ensures that various shocks that shook core industries descended upon communities simultaneously. Both in terms of the timing of their development as centers of manufacturing and the nature of the manufacturing that took place within them, with respect to the narrative thrust of their histories and the various crises each faced within those histories, the cities share remarkable similarities.

Data

Three kinds of data are used to compare these two cities. The data in Chapters 4 and 5 come from archival research and a careful reading of primary and secondary historical accounts of the sociopolitical processes surrounding exogenous shocks that struck both regions simultaneously. The case selection provided the guide for this inquiry. Because these two cities shared such similar economies and social histories, it was possible to identify several exogenous events from the historical record that struck the two places simultaneously. Specifically, these were (1) their origins in the years following the American Revolution, (2) the period of industrial consolidation after the Civil War, (3) the successive waves of immigration that began in the 1880s and the social strife that broke out related to it after World War I, (4) labor organization in the 1930s, (5) the consolidation of pricing mechanisms for steel and transportation within the steel industry after World War II, and (6) the steel industry competitiveness crisis that erupted in 1977. For each of these, I gathered important primary and secondary data, showing how each of these exogenous events played out in the chosen communities, with an eye toward the interaction of various categories of social actors: elites, corporate leaders, labor leaders, ethnic leaders, government leaders, and so forth. Wherever possible, more than one historical data source was consulted to corroborate accounts of the historical events. Appendix A provides a synopsis of major historical events in the cities laid out in parallel and chronological order. Appendix B provides a full listing of historical documents consulted. Conflicts among various historical accounts of the same event are noted in textual footnotes.

The comparison of these historical events has two goals. The first is to trace the economic and social development of the regions over time and, in doing so, reveal patterns of differentiation. The second is to reveal differences in the cities' underlying social structures as various simultaneous crises washed over the cities; that is, the way that the crises played out within them reveals axes of identity within the communities and, therefore, of the social structure in which different groups are embedded. To gain objective insight into the nature of the key hypothesized difference—structure of social networks—data were collected on interlocking directorates.

An interlocking directorate occurs when a person affiliated with one organization sits on the board of directors of another organization.[25] Board interlocks have long been a way of examining community networks, stemming from studies of community elite structures,[26] and have been used to examine mechanisms of corporate control,[27] financial institutions' role in corporate governance,[28] and processes of isomorphic diffusion.[29] Interlocking is also recognized as, at least partially, a location-driven phenomenon.[30] As such, corporate board interlocks have been used as a means of capturing social cohesion among community elites[31] and, in the critical literature, as a means of observing capitalist class integration.[32] Interlocks have also been used to analyze the mechanisms by which business and government elites band together to generate economic and population growth, becoming "urban growth machines."[33]

The role of board interlock data presented in this book is to illuminate those elements of social structure that may underlie observed differences between the two regions. The data were gathered in such a way as to provide as much leverage as possible in deciphering questions concerning causality; specifically, data were gathered on relationships that existed *prior* to the outbreak of the crises that are analyzed. However, it is important to be clear that the network data are not sufficient to *prove* causality, which would require finer-grained data collection than is available. Nevertheless, in combination with a deep understanding of the historical processes that unfolded, the network data do help provide important insight into the nature of each city's social structure and thus build the book's overall argument concerning the role that social structure plays in shaping regional economic trajectories.

The final source of data comes from interviews with contemporary actors in the two cities. Between the fall of 2001 and 2006, I conducted interviews with selected informants in each city, in addition to collecting much of the archival data on which earlier parts of the book are based. The procedure for selecting interviewees was rigorous. For each city, a list of potential interviewees was identified, with careful consideration paid to ensuring that the lists were parallel. For each category (labor leaders, university leaders, political leaders, and so forth) efforts were made to identify and interview individuals of roughly similar rank and experience across the two settings (see Appendix A for a full list of interviewees). In addition, the analysis in Chapter 6 relies on a comparison of organizations within the two communities. Again, particular organizations were selected for comparison based first and foremost on their comparability at the outset of the period of analysis.

The qualitative data were analyzed largely by laying out the facts in parallel, constructing separate narrative accounts, and then comparing salient differences (see Appendix B). The results are therefore iterative in the sense that they were informed by a thorough reading of the relevant literatures and comparison to the empirical record. As the research turned more and more toward structural explanations, the network analysis was added as a way of triangulating the findings.

Historical Antecedents:
The Divergence of
Social Structures, 1743–1945

Allentown and Youngstown were established early in America's history as a country under conditions that differed, sociologically, along one very important dimension. The hamlets of the Lehigh Valley were settled in the decades just before the American Revolution, and its settlers were colonists still tied in many ways to their ancestral experiences in Europe. As they forged new communities for themselves, Allentown's settlers clustered into separate ethno-religious enclaves: one for English Yankees, another for German Lutherans, and another for Scots Presbyterians. The villages of the Mahoning Valley were established just after the Revolution. Although they hailed from the same mixture of predominantly Northern European (mostly British and German) settlers, the settlers who arrived in northeastern Ohio at the end of the eighteenth century nevertheless did not separate themselves into co-ethnic communities. Youngstown's earliest settlers mingled ethnically and religiously.

This small difference had a lasting impact on the pattern of social structures of the two valleys and, therefore, on the context in which actions were taken and decisions made well into the twentieth century (and beyond). Subsequent chapters will show the consequences of this divergence for the cities' postindustrial paths. But what makes that story compelling is the fact that the two cities seem—on the surface—to have been subjected to the same economic and demographic forces over the course of their history. Yet, by the crucial period of the 1950s, their underlying social structures differed markedly. This chapter further develops the framework introduced in Chapter 1 to show how a small difference in the regions' eighteenth-century origins produced different patterns of cooperation over the course of three subsequent critical moments: (1) the period of industrial consolidation that followed the technological shift from iron production to steel (1865–1910); (2) the period of eastern European immigration and the social strife that accompanied it (1910–1935); and (3) the intense period of industrial labor organizing activity (1935–1942) that preceded America's involvement in the Second World War. Each of these periods presented the city's leaders with complex problems that required a collective response.

As we will see, existing patterns of social structure constrained who was likely to ally with whom when faced with unfamiliar and complex problems and opportunities. By reaching out to partners in the face of these challenges, actors in each city extended, modified, and reinforced initially minor differences in the social structures of the regions over time. The process of evolution, in other words, was largely path dependent, as the social structure that existed at any given point in time shaped the nature of collective actions, and participation in these collective actions, in turn, shaped the identities of actors from that point forward—a theme to which we will return in order to understand differences in postindustrial organizational adaptation in Chapter 6.

Building on the steps introduced in the first chapter, this chapter shows how and why that divergence occurred. First, as early settlers established a foothold, they began to confront problems too complex for any individual or small, heterogeneous group of individuals to solve. Pragmatically responding to these challenges, individuals drew on the most salient social connections available to them in order to choose whom to cooperate with and on what terms. Cooperation—where successful (and what history records for the most part are the successful efforts)—reinforced the relationships from which it was drawn.

Second, as those social bonds became stronger, feelings of solidarity and identity emerged. In Allentown, the most readily available relationships were among people of one's own ethno-religious identity. With time, the ethnic flavor of these connections dissipated, but solidarity continued to focus on the separate towns within the region. Identities, in other words, were ultimately geographic in nature, with elites focusing on protecting and preserving their particular enclaves of Bethlehem, Allentown, and Easton. This orientation toward place subsequently led community leaders to forge coalitions within each of these towns, often crossing class boundaries to do so. It also led them to invest particularly lavishly in the quality of civil society, largely out of a competition with their neighbors, each trying to outdo the other, for instance, in the quality of their institutions of higher education and health care. In Youngstown, the intermingling of ethnic groups in the early stages of the region's development led to a social structure in which solidarity focused predominantly on socioeconomic class. As the region developed economically, dense connections—both economic and civic—were established among the region's elite, which were used to mobilize efforts to protect, preserve, and further progressively intensify class-based interests.

Settlement and Early Industrialization

The men and women who made their way to America's interior in the eighteenth century were pursuing perhaps the most central and enduring of American values: the desire to begin afresh, freed of the social, religious, political, and economic structures that constrain freedom in order to forge one's own path. The romanticized view is of rugged individualists hewing out a patch of earth to call their own. But the reality, of course, is that the challenges of such an undertaking were far too complex to be a solitary exercise. Settlers organized for self-protection against the elements, to worship and educate their children, and—initially—to divide the labor required to provide basic needs. Eventually burgeoning new technologies in transportation and manufacturing made it possible to pursue goals well beyond mere subsistence. These opportunities required cooperation to finance, engineer, manage, and operate an increasingly complex social and physical infrastructure.

But, given the need to cooperate in the face of complex challenges and opportunities, with whom does one chose to cooperate? And under what rules? Despite the desire to start afresh—free of preexisting social constraints—the fact is that settlers' choices were constrained, first, by the pool of fellow travelers available to them, and, second, by the necessity of a shared language and baseline understanding of how to proceed—an understanding strongly informed by the inherited social structures of their homelands and childhoods.

Settlement of the Lehigh Valley

The borough of Bethlehem was founded in 1743 by members of the Moravian Church, a German religious sect. The basic social unit of Moravian society was the choir. Serving as a family surrogate, Moravian choirs provided members with food, clothing, and communal housing. They carried on economic functions as well, characterized by communal sharing of property, labor, production, and consumption. Moravians believed that all labor belonged to God and organized their society around a communitarian ideal in which all members shared the fruits of the community's labor equally. But by the 1760s, this ethic had begun to erode, and a growing number of the Bethlehem's Moravian residents began to demand a share in that prosperity, not as members of a religious community, but as individuals. Church authorities agreed to abolish the communal General Economy in 1761. However, the businesses and industries given up by the church were not sold but rather leased to private individuals, and all land within the boundaries of the town continued to remain the property of the church.[1]

By then, the other major communities of the Lehigh Valley had been established. Easton was settled in 1750. Located at the confluence of the Delaware and Lehigh rivers, it became an important trading point, populated mainly by Scotch-Irish Presbyterians. Allentown itself was founded twelve years later, in 1762. Named after its founder, the chief justice of Pennsylvania's Supreme Court, William Allen, by the time of the American Revolution Allentown was a small village, mainly populated by Pennsylvania Dutch farmers.[2] As early settlements, both Easton and Allentown were more representative of American communities of the time than the closed and ideologically strict Moravian community. But the settlers of each community nevertheless kept mostly to their own kind, worshiping in separate churches and even trading for goods primarily with their own religious and ethnic countrymen outside the region.

The various ethnic groups of the Lehigh Valley were tolerant of each other, but not friendly. This was a matter of policy for the Moravians, as Bethlehem was closed to nonadherents until the 1840s. Allentown, referred to as "perhaps the most intensely German city in the state," was a bastion of Lutheranism. Easton's original settlers were Scots; the Presbyterian Church was its core institution. Each of the communities built churches and schools reflecting their primary religious traditions. Having established thriving communities, the region soon attracted settlers who sought not so much to found a community as to find their fortunes. The Lehigh Valley's industrialization was sparked by the War of 1812, during which Philadelphia was cut off from its supply of Virginia coal. Hearing of a nearby source of coal accessible by the Lehigh River, two businessmen founded the Lehigh Coal and Navigation Company to export anthracite down the Lehigh to the Delaware River and from there on to Philadelphia. It began operations in 1829, with the town of

Maunch Chunk (today known as Jim Thorpe, Pennsylvania) serving as its service and export center. It soon attracted settlers, mainly Germans from Allentown and then later a group of New Englanders, among whom was Asa Packer. Packer had arrived in the Lehigh Valley from Connecticut to build a new life and make his fortune. He invested his earnings wisely, and moved into coal operating in the 1840s when he invented a novel way of efficiently transporting coal down the steep slopes of the craggy valley, an innovation that quickly made him wealthy. Packer befriended Edward Leisenring, who was president of Lehigh Coal and Navigation Company at the time.[3]

Packer and Leisenring were both friends and competitors; indeed, their competition would set in motion a series of economic patterns that would persist well into the twentieth century. In the 1830s Edward Leisenring brought David Thomas from South Wales to start an iron company. Thomas had learned techniques in Wales that allowed him to set up the first blast furnace in the United States able to make use of the relatively low-quality anthracite coal found throughout much of the eastern United States. The Lehigh Crane Iron Company began opera-tions in 1839, with Thomas as its superintendent and Leisenring a member of the board. Several other iron mills emerged later, with groups of Philadelphians establishing the Allentown Iron Company in 1851 and the Roberts Iron Company in 1862. Thomas left Lehigh Crane in 1858 and started his own company. By 1860 Allentown was home to several small iron mills producing rails, munitions, and other goods. Leisenring and his associates had taken control over much of the re-gion's most prosperous companies.

Asa Packer's successes in the 1840s allowed him to mount a chal-lenge to Leisenring and his group. In 1841 a major flood had broken out on the Lehigh River following a heavy winter that had already dis-rupted the flow of goods on the canal, leading many in the area to call for the construction of a rail line as an alternative means of transporta-tion. In 1851 Asa Packer set out to build the line. He appointed Robert Sayre as the railroad's chief engineer. By 1855 the railroad was opera-tional, and in 1857 a junction was established at South Bethlehem linking it to the Northern Pennsylvania Railroad, thereby giving it a more direct route to Philadelphia. Sayre—who was operationally in charge of the railroad—established its base of operations in South Beth-lehem that same year.[4]

Packer and his associates controlled the Lehigh Valley Railroad, while Leisenring and his group were associated with its rival, the Lehigh Coal and Navigation Company. Leisenring dominated the First National Bank, while Packer controlled the Linderman National Bank. Packer was Yankee Episcopalian and a Democrat (indeed, he was the Democratic candidate for Pennsylvania Governor in 1869). Leisenring was Scotch-Irish, Presbyterian, and Republican. Finally, Leisenring had struck on a very profitable idea with the creation of the Lehigh Crane Iron Company. So Packer and his associates, perhaps inevitably, needed to move into iron making as well. Their chance came in 1854 when a relative of Packer's, Charles Broadhead, purchased a piece of former Moravian grazing lands on the south side of the Lehigh River and adjacent to the Lehigh Valley Railroad's new junction. Broadhead persuaded the owner of a nearby iron mine to locate a blast furnace there in 1857. The firm incorporated as the Bethlehem Iron Company in 1860, and in 1863 it began producing the rolling iron rails for the Lehigh Valley Railroad. By 1866 the Lehigh Valley Railroad carried twice the traffic of Lehigh Coal and Navigation, with the Bethlehem Iron Company among its most important customers.[5]

With their most significant holdings in South Bethlehem, the Packer group eventually quit Maunch Chunk and began settling Fountain Hill, establishing a small community adjacent to the emerging industrial town. From 1858 to 1870, four leading families in Packer's orbit—the Wilburs, Sayres, Lindermans, and Cleavers—resettled in South Bethlehem. They brought with them their Yankee Democratic politics and their Episcopalian faith, making South Bethlehem a fourth ethno-religious pole within the region. Like the ethnically oriented communities around them, Packer's clan spent lavishly on founding schools and churches, the most important of which was Lehigh University, established in 1866. The Episcopal bishop of the Philadelphia diocese was made president of the university's board of trustees, and Packer insisted on giving students free tuition. In 1867 Lutherans and Reformed Germans responded by founding Muhlenberg College in Allentown, the fourth college in a region of about 34,000 residents.[6]

Settlement of the Mahoning Valley

Like others among the original British colonies, the state of Connecticut had large landholdings, which extended well into the interior of the country at the time of the Revolutionary War. Most states gave up claims to such territories after the war. Connecticut did so as well, with the exception of a strip of land between the 41st and 42nd parallels extending 120 miles westward from the Pennsylvania line. The land was known as the Western Reserve of Connecticut, and today it makes up the northeastern part of Ohio. Connecticut had sold a tract of 25,450 acres in the Mahoning Valley to the Connecticut Land Company in 1788, and in 1796 Moses Warren was dispatched from Connecticut to survey the area and establish a settlement. On April 17, 1799, Ephrain Quinby and Richard Storer brought their families from Pennsylvania to settle in the town. A year later Warren, Ohio—named after Moses Warren—was designated the capital of the Western Reserve. Settlers began to arrive, mainly by two routes. Connecticut families whose homes had been damaged during the Revolutionary War were given land in the area; they arrived via Buffalo and the Great Lakes. Other settlers—like Quinby and Storer—hailed from German and Scotch-Irish communities of Pennsylvania. They arrived by the Mahoning River via Pittsburgh.[7]

In 1803 James and Daniel Heaton made an important discovery on their land lining the banks of Yellow Creek, just south of Youngstown in the township of Poland: they found a deposit of iron ore.[8] The town of Youngstown had been settled by John Young six years earlier in 1797. The Heaton brothers built a blast furnace on the site—the first blast furnace west of the Alleghenies. The opening of the Pennsylvania-Ohio Canal in 1839 provided inexpensive transportation between Lake Erie and the Ohio River, leading to the establishment of still more mills. In 1856 the Cleveland and Mahoning Railroad arrived. The canal and the railroad provided cheap transportation for pig iron and iron ore. Producing at lower cost and superior quality brought profits that made it possible to build new facilities. The demand for metal during the Civil War brought more prosperity still, which thirty-five-year-old David Tod—eventually one of Ohio's governors—took advantage of. Having made some money developing several area coal mines, Tod financed the construction of a new furnace, the "Eagle," which began operations in 1846, becoming the largest furnace in the Midwest.[9]

The region's population increased threefold between 1840 and 1860. By 1863, on the eve of the Civil War, Youngstown had seven iron blast furnaces, three rolling mills, a steelworks, and a machine shop. The city's first bank—Wick Brothers and Company—was formed that same year. Advantageously located between Cleveland, Pittsburgh, New York, and Chicago, by 1880 Youngstown had become a major railroad center. It served at the junction of four major trunk lines—the Baltimore and Ohio, the Erie Lackawanna, the New York Central, and the

Pennsylvania—and by the turn of the century, more rail cars passed under Youngstown's Center Street Bridge per day than any other location in the country.

Importantly, and unlike settlement patterns in the Lehigh Valley, Youngstown's elite families were not segregated into ethnically, religiously, or geographically distinct groups. Most of Youngstown's iron and steel elite—62 percent to be precise, according to Ingham (1978)—settled together along Wick Avenue and a few adjoining and intersecting streets. Among them were representatives of the Tod, Wick, Butler, Powers, and Stambaugh families. Nearly two-thirds of them were of English ancestry, while the rest were Scottish, Scotch-Irish, German, and Welsh. Religiously, many of them were Presbyterian. But other denominations were both welcome and strongly represented. Most were evangelical Protestants: Methodists, Baptists, Reformed, and Welsh Congregationalists. Lutherans established a church in Youngstown in 1810. The Episcopalians did not start a parish until 1859.[10]

Industrial Consolidation and the Rise of Steel

As we have just seen, the settlement patterns differed subtly between the two valleys: in Allentown, initial settlement patterns formed around ethnic enclaves, while in Youngstown, early settlers intermingled. Some patterns had already begun to emerge in the regions as a result of these differences. Intercommunity rivalry drove residents of each community to invest lavishly in civic institutions, such that the establishment of Lehigh University in South Bethlehem by Yankee settlers, for instance, led the German Lutherans in Allentown to put out a call to their countrymen in America and in Europe to donate to the university in order to protect the pride of the German people (Swain 1967). Socially, then, the regions had somewhat different beginnings. Over time, these initial differences were extended and reinforced as those early settlers came to confront new challenges. The first of these was the discovery of deposits of coal and coke nearby, discoveries that would set Allentown and Youngstown on parallel economic paths associated with the manufacturing of iron and then eventually steel. As we will see, leaders in the cities responded simultaneously to this challenge in ways that were similar; that is, by forming small companies which then consolidated with the transition from iron to steelmaking. But in doing so, the cities' leaders drew on different social structural tool kits.

Industrialization in the Lehigh Valley

In 1855 Henry Bessemer patented a process that could convert pig iron into steel inexpensively by blowing air through the pig iron to oxidize impurities from the material. The process brought the cost of producing steel—at once a more durable and more easily shaped material—to the same level as producing wrought iron while also allowing larger production volumes, improved labor productivity, and lower costs. However, the Bessemer process also required significant capital investments to purchase the necessary equipment. The introduction of the Bessemer process led to a rapid transformation of the industry. A wave of consolidations ensued as iron mills succumbed to competition or else joined forces to convert existing capital to the new process.[11] The companies that had the capital to do so were those that had become military suppliers during the Civil War. Among them was the Bethlehem Iron Company, which had a Bessemer furnace operational by 1873. Its early adoption of the technology came at the urging of its largest customer, the Lehigh Valley Railroad, which had early on—more quickly than its rivals, certainly—recognized the superiority of steel over iron rails. That same year Bethlehem Iron joined the Bessemer Rail Association, a group of eleven firms that agreed to share the use of patents and not to infringe on one another's sales territories. For years Bethlehem's only product line was the steel rails sold to the Lehigh Valley Railroad and other affiliated lines.[12]

Another drawback of the Bessemer process, however, was that it required a higher quality of coal than was locally available. Increasingly, the iron and steel companies were forced to procure their raw materials from higher-quality coalfields in Cuba and the northeast coast of South America, shipping them up the coast to transfer points in Baltimore and Philadelphia and from there on rail to Bethlehem. To justify the added costs of production, the directors of Bethlehem Iron decided to shift away from rails—which it could sell at only ten or twenty dollars per ton—to the higher-value-added structural forms. Bethlehem's directors would only agree to the change in strategy with a customer already in hand. They found that customer in 1887 when the U.S. Navy awarded the company a $4 million contract to produce armor plate and gun forgings. In 1891 it secured a second $4 million contract for large caliber guns from the U.S. Army.[13]

The company was profitable—if conservatively so—throughout the 1890s. Yet its investors felt that it could certainly be more profitable.

They hired Frederick Taylor in 1898 to consult on what could be done. His studies—the basis of much of his subsequent work on scientific management—suggested ways in which the company could eliminate 250 out of 400 jobs associated with the handling of raw materials alone. But Bethlehem's directors rejected Taylor's recommendations. If they were going to grow, it would be by adding capacity and product lines not by "depopulating South Bethlehem" as Taylor recalled after his departure.[14] But to do so, they needed capital. Shares of a holding company—for the first time called the Bethlehem *Steel* Company— were floated, raising $15 million in 1898, and the funds were reinvested into expanding capacity. Two year later the directors sold a controlling interest in the company to Charles M. Schwab. Schwab bought the company outright in 1903. Schwab was then president of U.S. Steel Corporation, which had itself just recently been sold by Andrew Carnegie to J. P. Morgan, but he soon found himself on the outs with the company's directors. After a disastrous attempt to use his stake in the company as leverage in creating a great shipbuilding company, Schwab turned his attention to transforming Bethlehem Steel into a viable competitor to his former employer, U.S. Steel.[15]

For years prior to the sale, Bethlehem Steel's directors had not taken as active an interest in the company as they had in their various other affairs, which included, for many of them, running the Lehigh Valley Railroad. Instead, they devoted their time to building Bethlehem's civic infrastructure. In 1862 the leading families of Fountain Hill had established the Church of the Nativity, an Episcopalian church that was the center of the elite's social life. In 1870 the same group established St. Luke's Hospital, in part to attend to the growing number of men being hurt or injured in the increasingly dangerous process of making steel. Their biggest legacy, of course, was the 1865 establishment of Lehigh University which, by the time of the proposed sale of Bethlehem Steel, had run into financial difficulties. Robert Sayre and Elisha Wilber—both major shareholders in the steel company—personally financed operations at the university from 1895 to 1897 and spent much of 1897 traveling between Bethlehem and the state capital in Harrisburg securing funds from the state of Pennsylvania for the university.[16]

In turning their attention to civic matters, the Sayres and Packers were not alone. Indeed, there is evidence that community elites in Allentown, Bethlehem, and Easton came to see themselves as engaged in a rivalry with each other. Presbyterians in Easton established Lafayette

College in 1826, and the Moravians established Moravian College in 1858. In both cases, university leaders appealed for funds nationally from their respective religious communities based on the desire to keep pace with the fund-raising activities of the wealthier Episcopalians— who originally settled in Maunch Chunk, then later in South Bethlehem—who backed Lehigh University.[17] The division between the Leisenring-connected elites of Allentown and the Packer-connected elites of Bethlehem was further strengthened and extended through this period of industrialization.

Industrialization in the Mahoning Valley

Youngstown's conversion to the steel industry began later than in the Lehigh Valley. Iron furnaces had proliferated in the nineteenth century, but by the time of the Civil War the quick pace of growth had generated intense competition, which began to drive costs down to unacceptably low levels. Two options were apparent to the small local producers of the Mahoning Valley: either reduce costs further or move upmarket into steel production. Reducing transportation costs was one way of accomplishing the first option. By 1879 over 80 percent of the iron ore used in the six largest furnaces in the Mahoning Valley was coming from the upper Great Lakes via barge and rail (Rodgers 1950). Other large-scale producers at the time were either large enough or closely connected enough to negotiate favorable rail prices (as was the case with Bethlehem Steel and the Lehigh Valley Railroad). But the myriad independent producers in the Mahoning Valley had the benefit of neither. In 1891 they formed the Mahoning and Shenango Valleys Iron Manufacturers Association with the aim of negotiating lower rail rates. But the railroads rejected the proposal, so several local mill owners, led by Henry Wick and Joseph Butler, decided to join forces to build a steel plant using the Bessemer process. City officials offered them $25,000 and an exclusion from taxation to ensure that the new furnace would be built in their city and not a neighboring town. Their Ohio Steel Company began operation in 1895. But they quickly sold the plant to National Steel Company—one of several steel concerns controlled by J. P. Morgan—in 1899.[18]

Drawing in part on the windfall generated by the sale of Ohio Steel, several local investors, led by Myron C. and George D. Wick, created the Republic Iron and Steel Company in 1899. The core of the company's steelmaking capabilities came from the consolidation of three Mahoning Valley iron mills that were converted to steel production, the most important of which was the Brown-Bonnel furnace, located in Warren, the largest blast furnace in the region at the time. Republic grew quickly by consolidating twenty other iron mills scattered throughout the South and Midwest.[19]

In just four years, eleven of the twenty-one small, independent companies had been consolidated into the large, integrated firms and were controlled outside of Youngstown. Among the local companies affected by the change was the largest scrap firm in the Mahoning Valley, owned by William Wilkoff. His chief customers had been the various local mills; the consolidation of the industry made it unlikely that they would continue as clients. In 1901 he was approached by Henry Wick, one of the original founders of the Ohio Steel Company, and by his friend James Campbell. Both had been associated with Republic the year before. But, unhappy as employees, they were interested in starting another firm—one that they were determined to keep locally controlled. The three decided to form a corporation to manufacture steel pipe and sheets. The original stockholders were almost all members of the Youngstown community, individuals who had done well in the wave of consolidations but were nevertheless concerned with the sudden loss of local control over the economic fate of their region. The majority of them were also neighbors living near Wick Avenue. They took on significant risk to invest in the Youngstown Iron Sheet and Tube Company, a startup concern wading into an industry that had just produced U.S. Steel Corporation—the largest company in the world at the time, with a capitalization of over $1 billion. The Youngstown startup nevertheless grew quickly. By 1904 the company had dropped the *iron* from its name and was known simply as the Youngstown Sheet and Tube Corporation. By 1910—just nine years after it was founded—the company was capitalized at $100 million, making it the fifth-largest producer of steel in the United States.[20]

Tremendous wealth was generated in the Mahoning Valley. But rather than investing in universities and churches as was the case among the Lehigh Valley's elite, Youngstown's industrialists reinvested their windfalls, creating new companies, including Republic Steel, Youngstown Sheet and Tube, and a slew of related companies, such as General Fireproofing, that consumed much of the steel being produced there in the region. A series of banks were founded around this time as well.

All of these companies were established and controlled by the small circle of Wick Avenue families that had originally settled there a generation earlier. Moreover, these core industrialist families largely retained control over their ventures, rather than giving them over to a new professional managerial class as had been the case in the Lehigh Valley. The few cultural outlets that resulted from the infusion of wealth catered to the tastes of this group, including the Butler Museum of American Art—among the first museums in the United States to concentrate on modern art—and Mill Creek Park, a lush urban park with golf courses and tennis courts located adjacent to the Wick Avenue neighborhood.[21]

The initial settlement patterns therefore laid the groundwork for the patterns of economic development in the two valleys. In Allentown companies were founded within ethnic enclaves that paralleled and competed with each other. Technological change—in the form of the discovery and diffusion of steelmaking techniques—touched off consolidation and the emergence of industrial organizations. Elite families who had founded the region's major companies withdrew from day-to-day operations of these companies and shifted their energies instead into social and civic activities and, in particular, into founding universities and hospitals in support of the ethnically focused communities with which they strongly identified. A managerial class associated with running businesses emerged in Allentown that was separate from the owners of companies, who focused on civic activities. Steelmaking and the consolidation of iron mills into integrated companies happened in Youngstown at precisely the same time. But the initial settlement patterns led to a very different outcome. Rather than give up control, elite families acted in concert to protect their interests by ensuring that companies they founded remained under their direct control. Dense ownership networks emerged, linking various business interests of companies in the region. These same families then established civic and social institutions that further reinforced these ties.

Immigration and Social Strife

By the end of the nineteenth century, then, the cities had taken on very similar patterns of economic development. But the social and economic organization of that development diverged as early settlement patterns, which focused around communities in Allentown and around economic interests in Youngstown, were reinforced as the cities industrialized. This set the stage for the next major challenge to confront the cities. Economic prosperity brought a huge expansion of the cities' factories, requiring massive numbers of workers. Initially these were provided by migration from rural areas surrounding the cities. But this labor supply was quickly tapped, and companies turned instead to immigrant workers from eastern and southern Europe. These new groups posed dual challenges. The first and most immediate was practical: they needed to be housed, and the infrastructure of the cities needed to expand to accommodate them. But these groups also differed from early settlers with respect to religion and temperament. Predominantly Catholic, their arrival sparked alarm among the Protestant northern Europeans who had dominated the cities' histories to that point.

Immigration to the Lehigh Valley

The ethnocentrism that prevailed in the Lehigh Valley was not restricted to the elite; it included workers as well. The five major ethnic groups—German, Irish, Welsh, English, and Scottish—worked side by side in the nearby coalfields, and each group sought to preserve its identity by establishing its own churches and social organizations. Prevailing social norms reinforced the ethnic divisions, with the English, Welsh, and Scottish receiving the highest-paying jobs. The Irish were regarded as undesirable, while language isolated the Germans, so both earned lower wages. Anthracite mining was among the most dangerous occupations in the world. Wages were already low, and mine operators routinely depressed them further by forcing workers to shop in company stores that charged excessive prices, and rent tended to be exorbitant. The Pennsylvania legislature generated some hope, however, when it passed legislation legalizing the eight-hour day in 1868. Miners demanded the shorter day without a comparable reduction in wages. When operators refused the demand, the miners walked off their jobs. Strikers carrying signs reading "Eight Hours" marched through the Lehigh Valley shutting down operations—among the first mass industrial actions in American history. They did not achieve their demand—owing in part to distrust among the various ethnic groups—and settled instead for a 10 percent increase in wages. But the partial success of the effort encouraged the mine workers to establish an inclusive labor organization—the Workingman's Benevolent Association—a precursor to the Knights of Labor.[22]

In 1873 some seven hundred workers were employed by Bethlehem Steel. By 1885 the number was three thousand, and between 1905 and 1920, Bethlehem Steel's labor force doubled every five years. By 1920 the company employed twenty thousand workers in the Lehigh Valley alone. The valley's population growth was driven mainly by foreign workers drawn to work in the mills. Before 1880 the largest portion of immigrants came from Ireland. In 1861 of 947 South Bethlehem residents, 387 were Irish Catholic. In 1870 of 1,106 of immigrants living in the borough, 672 were from Ireland. In 1880 the Irish totaled 1,658 of 4,925.[23]

But beginning in 1880, most immigrants began to come from southern and eastern Europe. By 1920 several so-called new immigrant groups had colonized South Bethlehem. Austrians formed a Catholic Parish in 1886. In 1891 the Slovak Roman Catholic parish of Saints Cyril and Methodios was organized. A Hungarian Reformed church was established in 1906. Two Greek Orthodox churches were started in 1914, and a Russian Orthodox congregation in 1915. These groups had their own mutual benefit societies: the Emerald Beneficial Association and Ancient Order of Hibernians (Irish), Franz Joseph Society (Austrian), St. Stanislaus Society (Poles), and the Brotherhood of St. Nicholas and the Italian Mutual Benefit Society (Italians). Although large metropolitan areas saw the emergence of ethnic ghettos, in South Bethlehem the chronic housing shortage and the town's limited size prevented the creation of ethnic residential districts. Instead, the "foreign section" of South Bethlehem served as one very large ghetto, where a variety of ethnic groups rubbed elbows. Although accounts also make it clear they didn't mingle, there was little hostility among the various ethnic communities. They simply lived near each other. As one commentator put it, "psychologically, there were many South Bethlehems; the boundaries of one did not necessarily coincide with those of another."[24]

While the various Catholic ethnic communities of South Bethlehem got along with each other, considerable tension emerged between them and the Germans, Welsh, Scots, and Yankee "old" immigrants—particularly as the new immigrants began moving up within the ranks of local industry into more lucrative jobs. The Fountain Hill elite took notice of the growing hostility and attempted to take action, creating the Workingman's Club in South Bethlehem with the goal of providing "facilities for social intercourse, instruction and rational recreation at very small cost." The club lasted only a few years, however, as new immigrant workers and old immigrant groups alike already had their own ethnicity-oriented mutual aid societies and clubs. Later, as was also the case in Youngstown, their efforts were coordinated through the YMCA.[25]

The more salient arena in which tension between the old and new immigrants played out was with respect to labor organizing. The Amalgamated Association of Iron, Steel, and Tin Workers formed in 1876 and was soon affiliated to the American Federation of Labor. Founded during the transition of the industry from the small-scale production of iron to the more "rationalized" processes of steel production, the union represented the interests of skilled workers such as machinists, molders, and riggers: jobs primarily held by "old" northern European Protestants. In 1910, however, a strike occurred in Bethlehem that turned out to be consequential both for the future of class relations in the city and the American labor movement more broadly. Among the legacies of Frederick Taylor's brief time at Bethlehem Steel was a bonus system designed to derive higher productivity from workers though the use of incentives. The plan, which was retained and expanded after Charles Schwab took over the company, provided a bonus of 20 percent if a worker's quota was met and 50 percent it if was exceeded. Over time, however, the company had both increased the quota and kept a line on workers' wages. To achieve even the baseline, workers had to work overtime, which was paid at the regular rate. Workers who refused the overtime were threatened with dismissal.

In January 1910 Bethlehem Steel followed through on this threat and dismissed a skilled mechanic in one of its mills for refusing to work overtime. A committee of his fellow workers approached the company's management several days later to demand his reinstatement. They too were fired. Eight hundred workers then walked off the job in protest. In addition to the reinstatement of their fellow workers, the strikers demanded that the company pay time and a half for overtime work. Since the conflict had begun among skilled workers, the company could have stopped the action by appeasing the demand for higher pay. But the company refused to negotiate on principle. The company's refusal meant that the strikers needed to recruit allies from within the plant and were therefore obliged to extend their overtime pay demands to all ranks throughout the mill. Within days immigrant workers throughout the company had joined the strike. On February 26 the company brought in state constabulary troops. Up until that point, the strike had been remarkably free of violence. But troopers—expecting violence—immediately lashed out at a peaceful crowd that had gathered outside Bethlehem Steel's headquarters. One bystander was shot and killed. Others were trampled by officers on horseback.[26]

Winning public support was vital for both the strikers and the company. Sustaining the strike required middle-class merchants and landlords to extend credit. The use of facilities and the behavior of the police toward strikers were also vital. Up until the troopers' violence, the community had largely remained neutral. However, the events of February 26 drove the community to the strikers' side. Workers were allowed to use the municipal hall for meetings, and a group of local businessmen eventually joined a letter-writing campaign to have several of the companies' most important contracts revoked in protest of the strike. The community's shifting sympathies—particularly, the letter-writing campaign—incensed Schwab. He threatened to pull the company out of Bethlehem altogether if he did not receive the community's support. Following this threat, a commercial league of local businessmen was convened and began to agitate for the end of the conflict. With the withdrawal of middle-class support, the strike quickly collapsed, resulting in what was apparently a total victory for the company. The strike had nevertheless had a lasting impact of forging bonds across the skilled/-unskilled new immigrant/old immigrant divide.

The strike of 1910 had boiled over simmering divides among the ethnic groups, the emerging Protestant middle class, and the industrialist elite. Drawing on the Progressive movement's ethic of government reform, a movement emerged to reform municipal government in ways that might help to heal these divisions, with the intention of bridging the divisions that had emerged in the community. In part, the divide was geographic. While lower-skilled ethnic workers lived just outside the gates of the factory, with some of the elite in the hills behind them, much of the middle class lived in Bethlehem, across the river. In 1911 a committee was convened to create a new bridge linking South Bethlehem and Bethlehem. Schwab lent his support to the effort, as did a large number of middle-class business owners. But to get the bridge built, the committee determined that an additional $200,000 was needed. The "hill-to-hill" bridge campaign raised the money by organizing in the neighborhoods, collecting small donations—no amount was too small—from working- and middle-class members of the community. The effort was a huge success, bringing in $450,000.[27]

The success of the bridge campaign became the basis of a new campaign to unite the two cities into one municipality. The effort was conceived, largely, by leaders of the steel company, who were keen to ensure that future industrial actions such as the one that occurred in 1910 would not again find municipal leaders as ready allies. To achieve the change, however, the company needed to overcome middle-class hostility to taking on the ethnic working-class neighborhoods of South Bethlehem. In cooperation with the Bethlehem chapter of the Red Cross, Bethlehem

Steel's leaders decided to revive the organizing tactics and structure of the hill-to-hill campaign. Rallies were held in both Bethlehem and South Bethlehem. Company executives—who rarely addressed unskilled workers—were dispatched to South Bethlehem to generate support. Middle-class workers were approached through the Red Cross, in events designed to appeal to their patriotism in the face of the country's impending entry into World War I. In July 1917 the boroughs voted overwhelmingly to consolidate and the new municipality took on a commission form of government in which power was held mainly by the bureaucratic heads of various city departments under a weak mayor. The mayor, however, was Bethlehem Steel's vice president, Archibald Johnson, and the city's department heads were each appointed and approved by the company.[28]

Immigration to the Mahoning Valley

In the 1850s the coal mines and the iron industry had attracted large numbers of Welsh to the Mahoning Valley, as well as Germans from Pennsylvania. Significant numbers of Irish came to work on the canal and in the nearby mines. A few Catholics had been among the original settlers in Youngstown, but the area remained a missionary outpost of Cleveland's Catholic Diocese until after the Irish immigrations of the 1840s and 1850s. St. Columbia's was built in 1853. Then the same wave of new immigration that hit the Lehigh Valley in 1880 flooded the Mahoning Valley as well. By 1890 there were four more Catholic parishes. The Orthodox Church became organized in the World War I period. The Greek St. John's Parish and Russian Holy Nativity of Christ church were both founded in 1916. Rumanian, Bulgarian, Ukrainian, Carpathian, and Serbian Orthodox parishes followed. Youngstown's population soared from about 45,000 in 1900 to 80,000 in 1910 and 132,000 by 1920. Two-thirds of the population was either foreign born or the children of foreign-born parents.[29]

Unlike the Lehigh Valley, where the ethnic groups overlapped within a few large working-class communities, new immigrants in the Mahoning Valley settled in ethnic enclaves. Brier Hill on the north side and Smokey Hollow on the east became Italian neighborhoods. Our Lady of Mt. Carmel, the center of the Italian Catholic community in Youngstown, was established on Brier Hill in 1910. East Youngstown—an independent municipality next door to the city of Youngstown—became an eastern European enclave including a majority of Slovaks and Ruthenians; the census of 1920 shows that 96 percent of the town's 11,000 residents were either eastern or southern European immigrants or their children. These communities were generally located near the river and close to the five large steel mills that had been constructed by then. Skilled northern European workers had moved farther inland to neighborhoods north and up the surrounding hills.

The segregation was by design. To meet rising demand for housing, the city's steel elite had founded the Buckeye Land Company, which built and sold homes in neighborhoods close to the mills. In doing so, however, they divided the housing into separate sections for English-speaking, foreign-born, and African American neighborhoods. The companies also sponsored athletic activities, parks, and playgrounds for family outings. Mill Creek became a haven for English-speaking workers and the families of the elite industrialists; Isadora Park on the city's south side of the city was primarily Italian and eastern European.[30]

As in the Lehigh Valley, ethnic tensions rose quickly between old and new immigrant groups. In January 1916 workers struck Youngstown Sheet and Tube's factory in East Youngstown to demand higher wages. In response, the company brought in fifteen hundred African Americans from the South to man the mills and break the strike. But the action provoked violence. Rioting broke out, and the central business district of the neighborhood was burned to the ground. Eighty-one men were arrested in connection with the fires. Only seven of them were American, with the remainder being southern and eastern European immigrants. Ultimately, the strike was broken, with workers achieving only a minimal increase in pay. The local elite's actions in response resembled those in Lehigh Valley. At the urging of the city's chamber of commerce, the YMCA—an organization founded initially to assimilate Scotch, Welsh, and German farmers who were immigrating to the city in the mid-1800s—increasingly took on the task of "Americanizing" the immigrant communities.[31]

Despite these efforts, another strike broke out in 1919, the first national steel strike in American history. In August of 1918, a conference of twenty-four trade unions had met in Chicago to establish the National Committee for Organizing Iron and Steel Workers. Throughout 1918 and 1919, the committee had organized workers in many of the steel towns that had emerged since 1900: Johnstown, Bethlehem, Chicago, Cleveland, Wheeling, Buffalo, and Pittsburgh. In Youngstown organizers from the American Federation of Labor had been working since the 1916 strike to organize the ethnic neighborhoods where steelworkers lived. In September of 1919, the committee approached U.S. Steel to demand recognition. When it was refused, the union called a national strike of a quarter million workers. Workers in the Lehigh Valley sat out the strike of 1919, in part because the company's control over the town denied workers the support of the middle class. But in Mahoning Valley, the mills were completely shut down by the action.[32]

Protestant activism through the YMCA and the civic reform spirit of the Progressive Era had sought to impose "traditional" values and moral order within the Mahoning Valley. But by 1920, following the strikes and riots, it was felt that these efforts had failed. After persuading reformers of its honorable intentions, the Ku Klux Klan entered the scene and began assuming a prominent role in community affairs. Working in close association with Protestant church leaders and with the support of many of the old-line elite, Klan-backed "law-and-order" candidates scored electoral victories in 1923, winning mayoral races in Youngstown, Warren, Girard, Struthers, and Niles. Once in power, the Klan increased arrests for liquor violations, restricted "alien" access to licenses, and passed legislation requiring the Bible to be read in schools. But the Klan's policies provoked even more violence in the Mahoning Valley. In 1924 clashes between Catholics and Protestants erupted in Niles in response. By 1925 the Mahoning Valley's flirtation with the Klan had been discredited, and Klan-backed candidates were turned out of office. Nevertheless, the episode caused the ethnic communities of the valley—both English speaking and non–English speaking—to pull inward even further than they had been previously.

The expansion of industrial manufacturing in Allentown and Youngstown brought with it the introduction of new immigrants, whose arrival was seen as a threat to social stability in both places. But the reaction to that threat differed markedly between the two regions. In Allentown the northern European saw the new groups as a threat primarily to their *communities,* and the nature of their response reflected that perception. Community elites mobilized through the civic institutions in response to this perceived threat. Doing so had several effects. First, it established a pattern for civic associations in the Lehigh Valley as bridging platforms. Initially, the bridge was to the cities' middle-class merchants to mount a response in the face of social strife. This coalition faced down social conflict by denying new immigrants support during the strike of 1910. The coalition between elite and middle classes within each of the Allentown region's various cities and

towns also influenced settlement patterns among the immigrants themselves. Different ethnic groups settled in proximity to each other within
just a few densely populated working-class enclaves spread throughout
the Lehigh Valley. Social solidarity came to rest on class-based neighborhoods within the different cities of the valley.

The patterns—both in terms of immigrant settlement and cross-class
coalitions—differed markedly in Youngstown, where the arrival of new
immigrants was perceived less as a threat to the community than as a
threat to class interests of the region's tight core of elites. The connections
among founding families forged through their economic, civic, and
neighborhood ties led elites in Youngstown to circle the wagons against
the new arrivals. The strategy that emerged to deal with the threat was
essentially divide and conquer. By controlling settlement patterns through
their control over real estate, the founding families fragmented the city's
new immigrant working class into separate ethnic enclaves, a strategy
later reinforced by the law-and-order and obviously racially and ethnically divisive approach favored by the Ku Klux Klan. Ethnic differences
among early northern European settlers subsided as salient sources of
identity; class interests were forefront in the minds and actions of various
groups in the Mahoning Valley as the region entered the next phase of its
economic and social development: the arrival of industrial unions.

Industrial Union Organizing

Social strife at the turn of the twentieth century largely revolved around
the arrival of new immigrant groups. Labor unrest was part of the mixture, including the small-scale eruptions of labor-management conflict
of which the 1910, 1916, and 1919 strikes in Bethlehem and
Youngstown were part. But by the 1930s, these conflicts had coalesced
into a new and powerful social movement: the rise of industrial unions.
The Congress of Industrial Organizations (CIO) rose directly out of the
kinds of cross-skill, cross-ethnicity organizing that had occurred in the
Lehigh and Mahoning valleys. In 1933 President Franklin Roosevelt
had secured passage of the National Labor Relations Act, guaranteeing
the right of workers to form and join unions. In 1935 the CIO had organized the Steel Workers Organizing Committee. Following CIO victories at General Motors in Flint and among Akron's rubber companies
in the early months of 1937, the Steel Workers Organizing Committee
(SWOC) approached U.S. Steel for recognition. To the surprise of
many, U.S. Steel almost immediately agreed to recognize the union.

One hundred forty smaller companies followed suit. However, four so-called Little Steel companies—including Youngstown Sheet and Tube, Republic Steel, and Bethlehem Steel[33]—refused, touching off a seminal moment in American labor history, which began with the famous "Little Steel Strike" of 1937 and culminated, eventually, in a victory for labor in 1942. The road there passed through both the Mahoning and Lehigh valleys.[34] The Little Steel strike was one of the seminal moments in the national battle over industrial unions, putting Allentown and Youngstown at the center of a national firestorm. The challenge to local elites posed by the labor movement was acute. But as we will see, the differences in the social structures of the regions led them down very different paths in response.

Industrial Organizing in the Mahoning Valley

On May 26, 1937, SWOC President Philip Murray traveled to Youngstown—which by then was headquarters of two of the Little Steel companies, since Republic had moved its headquarters from New Jersey to Youngstown in 1930. After being refused meetings with Sheet and Tube President Frank Purnell and Republic Chairman Tom Girdler, Murray called a general strike. Twenty-four thousand workers walked off the job in Youngstown and Warren. Ninety thousand workers from Buffalo to Chicago joined them. As had been the case in earlier conflicts, the sympathies of the cities' middle classes became a focal point for both sides in the conflict. Steelmakers adopted what had become known as the Mohawk Valley Formula, following the model of factories in upstate New York in the face of a strike in 1936. The formula relied heavily on manipulating public opinion through newspapers and radio, recruiting "loyal" employees, and establishing citizens' committees.[35]

Republic and Youngstown Sheet and Tube supplied their plants with guns, ammunition, tear gas, and billy clubs in anticipation of violence. In Warren the mills continued partial operations with a contingent of workers who had refused to join the strike. Skirmishes broke out between pickets, police, company guards, and strikebreakers. Unable to move supplies into the factory, Republic Steel officials dropped supplies into the plant from airplanes as strikers sniped at the low-flying planes with rifles. Then, on June 19, a battle ensued between union pickets, their supporters, and company guards at Youngstown Sheet and Tube. Two strikers were killed, and twenty-three others were wounded in the conflict.[36]

Both sides had actively sought the support of the community. Initially, sentiments within the community lay with the workers. But with the eruption of violence, support wavered. In an editorial published a month after the strike had begun, the Democratic-leaning *Vindicator* newspaper switched sides, calling for strikers to allow free passage into the region's factories. During the first week of the strike, SWOC leaders raised relief funds and promises of credit from many area merchants. In response, the companies, harkening back to the Klan years, helped to organize law-and-order committees in Youngstown. In Warren the group was known as the "John Q. Public League." The groups placed ads in the regions' newspapers. Initially, public opinion remained neutral. The region's largest newspaper, the *Vindicator,* supported the strikers' demands for recognition and wage increases. Much of the Protestant clergy stayed on the sidelines.[37]

The companies increased pressure on the mayor and city council, showing a large number of petitions for returning to work signed by employees. On June 22 Sheet and Tube announced it was reopening its mills. Striking workers massed at the mill gates while city police, deputies, and guards prepared to assist the entrance of employees who wanted to return to work. Fearing more bloodshed, Ohio Governor Davey called out Ohio National Guard troops to keep order. However, under Ohio law the guardsmen had to follow orders from local law enforcement officials, not the governor. Under pressure from company officials to end the strike, soldiers in Youngstown soon were harassing SWOC members and sympathizers. Union officials called for a citywide sympathy walkout on June 23, but only two thousand supporters joined the effort. On June 25 troops stood guard at area mills. As the trickle of workers into the plant grew, it was clear the strike had lost support.[38]

Industrial Organizing in the Lehigh Valley

The SWOC had initially called the strike against three of the eight Little Steel companies—Sheet and Tube, Republic and Inland Steel— companies where it thought it had the best chance of victory. However, workers spontaneously walked out at Bethlehem Steel's plant in Johnstown, Pennsylvania, three weeks into the action and later still at the company's facilities in Lackawanna, outside of Buffalo, bringing Bethlehem Steel into the conflict. However, despite the wildcat strikes in its other locations, the strike never reached Bethlehem itself, where the company's control over local politics was extremely strong.

Ironically, though, it was Bethlehem Steel that eventually led to the organization of the Little Steel companies. Following their defeat in 1937, the SWOC leaders resumed their efforts to organize the industry.

They concentrated this time on Bethlehem Steel. In the Lehigh Valley, a man named John Ramsay ultimately came to lead the organizing effort. A devout Presbyterian, husband to the daughter of a Moravian missionary, Republican, and founder of a local Boy Scout troop, Ramsay's was hardly the background of a typical labor activist. But spurred by the suffering he witnessed emerging all around him in the hardest years of the Great Depression, Ramsay and a young Presbyterian minister, Paul Cotton, had formed a work group, called the Unemployed Citizens League, in 1931 to help address the needs of growing ranks of unemployed men in the city. Ramsay and Cotton enjoyed high standing in the community.[39]

Ramsay hailed from the native-English-speaking segment of the population and ministered at the First Presbyterian Church, where Bethlehem Steel Chairman Eugene Grace worshiped. His wife was the daughter of Moravians of high standing in Bethlehem. Cotton, on the other hand, attended the elite Episcopal Church of the Nativity on Fountain Hill. Despite their standing, the two soon confronted the intransigence of local businessmen to the league's efforts and, prompted by the passage of the National Industrial Recovery Act—an anti-Depression initiative of the Roosevelt administration that included some rudimentary protections for labor—they began considering labor organizing as a possible solution.[40]

Although workers at the Bethlehem plant had not joined the 1937 strike, there was nevertheless a significant contingent of SWOC organizers in the city. Ramsay and Cotton approached the union and became involved in the organizing effort. But almost immediately they began to disagree with the national organizers' tactics. The SWOC's organizers hailed from the United Mine Workers union and brought with them a top-down organizing approach. Their strategy was to organize workers into ethnic blocks to rival the political power of the company. Ramsay crafted an alternative strategy, designed primarily to unite the fragmented ethnic groups. Building on his religious convictions and his belief in the power of conversion, he and a band of volunteers (who became known as Ramsay's Boys) took a page from the hill-to-hill and consolidation campaigns and spread throughout the plant's various ethnic communities. The campaign took on the trappings of a religious revival, with radio broadcasts featuring prayers from Catholic and Protestant religious leaders. Rather than giving formal speeches, Ramsay approached local ethnic clubs mainly by mixing into funerals and weddings, converting workers one by one to the union.

Ramsay's bottom-up approach gained momentum in 1939. In March the SWOC organized a march in support of building more low-cost housing in South Bethlehem. Ramsay built on his ties to the religious community to convince the local ministerial association to endorse several union proposals, including the housing drive. The local put on a steady stream of social activities, which attracted workers from each of the various ethnic groups. In response to claims from company officials that the union was Communist dominated, the local organized the Labor Non-Partisan Club, the board of which included representatives from each of eleven ethnic clubs in the city.[41]

Meanwhile, the SWOC's organizing campaign had been ongoing in other parts of the company as well. It finally came to a head in 1941, when the first election took place in Lackawanna. The company had organized a group of local clergy there, who once again portrayed the union as Communist dominated. The union asked Ramsay to travel from Bethlehem to assist. He arranged meetings with Protestant, Catholic, Jewish, and African American religious leaders and secured their support. Having won over these key community leaders, the union easily succeeded in the election, its first major victory in the battle to organize Little Steel. Bethlehem's other plants soon followed. By the outset of the Second World War, the entire steel industry had been organized as a result of the triumph at Bethlehem. After bitterly fighting the union, Republic and Youngstown Sheet and Tube followed suit in 1942 on the eve of the Second World War, waiving the formality of a vote.[42]

Again, we see that differences in patterns of union organizing in the 1930s built on—and reinforced—social structural patterns that had emerged a century earlier: in Youngstown the elite families who controlled the cities' major companies circled the wagons and hunkered down for an extended battle. A long-standing debate about the Little Steel Strike focuses on the degree to which elites were able to co-opt middle classes to shape the outcome of the strike. James Baughman (1978) and Michael Speer (1969) reach diametrically opposed conclusions regarding the agency of managers in lobbying for middle-class sympathies through law-and-order committees. Speer argues for the more widely held view (first advanced by Senator La Follette's Senate investigation) that company managers actively encouraged, bankrolled, and dominated local news coverage and police actions. Baughman, on the other hand, drawing on a reading of the community power literature of the 1970s, argues that it is too simplistic a view to claim that owners and managers overcame otherwise pro-union middle-class sympathies through domination tactics. Rather, he argues, middle-class sympathies in Youngstown initially rested with the strikers, but as the strike wore on and violence ensued, attitudes shifted. This was only minimally spurred by the formation of law-and-order committees. Rather, Baughman claims, the shift was simple economics: middle-class business owners saw their own profits being threatened and eventually turned against the strike. Because Bethlehem Steel's plants in Bethlehem did *not* ultimately participate in the strike (even though its plants in Johnstown and Buffalo did), it is possible to use the kind of network data presented later in this book to evaluate these claims more specifically.

But the comparison with how the strike played out in Allentown suggests another possibility: there, the ties between elite and middle classes were based on preexisting and long-established patterns of social and civic interaction, forged to some degree by shared religious institutions, but more important, through a civic infrastructure exemplified by the hill-to-hill campaign. There was no need to co-opt the middle class because connections among the middle class and the elites were already well established and served as mobilizing platforms when crises erupted. In Youngstown class interests predominated, with the boundaries dividing elite, middle, and working classes clearly defined and rarely intruded on. Civic and social infrastructure reinforced—rather than ameliorated—class-based divisions. The elites were eventually able to secure the support of the middle class, not through forging common cause, but rather through the same divide-and-conquer tactics with which they approached workers.

The Lehigh and Mahoning Valleys in Comparative Perspective

Initial differences in the settlement pattern of the Lehigh and Mahoning valleys shaped the evolution of the cities' social structures over time. Each new challenge faced by the city called for a collective response of some kind. Existing patterns of social relationships shaped the specific way that different types of actors in each city responded. Table 3.1 provides a succinct comparison of the events presented in this chapter. It highlights the findings with respect to the social structural differences revealed in the regions' differing reactions to simultaneously experienced events and shows the impact these reactions had on social structure moving forward.

By the eve of the Second World War, what initially may have seemed to be a subtle difference between the two communities—patterns of

Table 3.1 Summary comparison of phases of development and exogenous shocks, 1740–1946

Event	Youngstown		Allentown	
	Social Structure	Reaction to Shocks	Social Structure	Reaction to Shocks
Settlement and early industrialization (c. 1740–1865)	Migration from Connecticut and Pennsylvania marked by social structure despite mixed ethnic makeup.	High degrees of cooperation across localities and among ethnic groups.	Ethnically and religiously distinct settlement patterns into various small communities.	Despite ethnic differences, friendly competition across communities.
Industrial consolidation (c. 1865–1900)	Emergence of a tight group of elites clustered around Wick Avenue who maintain significant control over local firms.	Community activities focus on elites' interests (parks, museums, capital investments, banks).	Elite founders pass off control of major companies to professional managers and investors.	Elites focus energy on building edifying institutions (churches, colleges) in response to friendly intracommunity competition.
Immigration (c. 1900–1930)	Tight core of elites manipulate settlement patterns to create ethnically homogeneous neighborhoods among "new immigrants."	Initial attempts to bridge elite-immigrant and intra-immigrant tensions are abandoned following riots. Elites embrace "law-and-order" separatism of the Ku Klux Klan.	New immigrants are concentrated into multi-ethnic working-class neighborhoods within the various communities of the Lehigh Valley.	Corporate and founding elites create bridge and alliances among new immigrants and middle-class "old" immigrants.

Labor organizing (c. 1930–1946)	Elites enforce control of middle class through threats of reprisal during labor conflicts in the 1930s.	Violence erupts during Little Steel Strike of 1937 with six pickets killed. Workers lose battle	Corporate leaders maintain control by maintaining presence within both working- and middle-class parts of the community.	Strike misses Bethlehem, but organizers use ties forged during the "hill-to-hill" campaign to win bottom-up victory leading to organization of the industry.

original settlement marked by ethnic fragmentation in the Lehigh Valley and relative homogeneity in Youngstown—led to dramatic differences in the social and economic structure of Allentown and Youngstown. These differences shaped the trajectories of each region's social development. In both, waves of industrialization driven by the arrival of railroads and later steelmaking processes generated significant commercial opportunities and produced extremely successful companies in both places. But the intersection between those companies and the cities they inhabited differed. In the Lehigh Valley, interethnic competition among the original old-line ethnic communities led the elite families of the region to reinvest the profits reaped from the sale of those concerns into building the civic infrastructure of the region's cities. In the Mahoning Valley, such rivalries did not exist, and funds were mainly reinvested into building up wealth among the city's core elite.

Beyond the impact on the economic infrastructure, the differences became particularly important with the arrival of new immigrant groups following 1880. In both cities, initial reactions to the influx of non-English-speaking Catholics centered on a social engineering approach designed to "Americanize" and assimilate the newcomers. But when those efforts failed, the communities' responses diverged. In Youngstown the old-guard elite circled their wagons and joined with the broader region's middle class in backing the heavy-handed approach of the Ku Klux Klan. In the Lehigh Valley the response fell less along class lines than on the community itself, with industrial families and corporate elite enlisting ethnic and "native" workers in collective actions centered on improving the various cities. This reinforced already strong municipal identities among the Lehigh Valley's various cities—Bethlehem, Allentown, and Easton—while simultaneously ensuring the companies themselves had strict control over municipal affairs designed, in large part, to quell labor-organizing efforts.

In neither case, however, were these actions enough to ward off labor-organizing efforts indefinitely, beginning with the Little Steel Strike of 1937. The Mahoning Valley became the center of the strike. The elite once again secured support from the region's middle class, resulting in a protracted and extremely violent battle. The approach that emerged in the Lehigh Valley, on the other hand, once again focused on the community organizing as the union turned the company's community-organizing tactics on itself to eventually achieve a union victory.

Thus, on the eve of the Second World War, the social structure in Youngstown had evolved in such a way that a tight core of northern

European elites had emerged, who regained tight control over their region's economic affairs. This group had emerged from the crucible of industrialization processes as a dense whole, banding together to ensure their autonomy in the context of a rapidly industrializing and nationalizing economy. However, this cohesion led to the development of a highly insular industrial structure in which a core group of elites were intertwined with each other's economic affairs, with strong ownership networks among steel-producing companies, steel-consuming companies, and ancillary organizations. As the industry matured, this group retained control. They did not, in other words, hand off control to a class of managers and executives as was the case in Allentown and the Lehigh Valley. This consolidation allowed them to move into the period of population explosions and immigration with a great deal of control, which they took advantage of by separating the various ethnic groups into separate communities, the better to ensure social peace. As crises inevitably erupted, though, the community's social structure was revealed to be highly fragmented. Crisis only strengthened this phenomenon. Elites essentially circled the wagons in the face of social strife and labor unrest. By the 1930s, with the eruption of industrial unionism, the battle lines were drawn among these groups.

The structure that was in place by World War II in Allentown was almost precisely the opposite. Initially, various ethno-religious communities had settled the region slowly over several decades in the mid- to late seventeenth century. Eventually, two major groups emerged with competing economic interests. As industrialization began to take place, these groups passed economic control on to a group of professional managers, who began to assume very prominent places within the city's economic and social structures. However, the elites left a very important legacy: a thick civic infrastructure toward which they had dedicated significant resources out of competitive zeal with their neighbors. This civic infrastructure was used in highly sophisticated ways as social strife erupted in the early twentieth century, first as a means of consolidating managerial and elite control over government and middle-class sympathies, and then, in an ironic turn of events, by the labor organizers. In the end, the use of the social structure in this way had led to a more variegated social structure. But it was a social structure that provided bridges among important constituencies within the region.

The history suggests important lessons for *how* social structures evolved over this period of time. Geography and happenstance associated with differences in settlement patterns led to the decentralized manner in which the two valleys were settled, both at their founding and then during the period of intense immigration. However, agency also played an extremely important role. The clearest example of this is in the way Charles Schwab approached the social tensions that emerged surrounding immigration. Using both his and his company's considerable social capital, Schwab constructed a social movement around the bridge-to-bridge effort to forge ties between and among working- and middle-class neighborhoods. This had the effect of building strong bridges across divisions in that community, which he then skillfully parlayed into political and social control over local affairs. Interestingly—and unintendedly—it was this social structure that labor activists in the city could also use—again, in highly sophisticated ways—to achieve the bottom-up organizing victory that ultimately led to organizing the entire steel industry on the eve of the war.

But in recognizing the smart ways social structure was used in Allentown, we must also acknowledge the relatively foolhardy ways it was used in Youngstown. Elites in the city were clearly in a strong position to exert tremendous influence over the shape the community took as it grew around the turn of the century. But when push came to shove, the choice was not to reach out and build ties, but instead to use divide-and-conquer tactics first and then circle the wagons when trouble erupted. Ultimately, this left the community with a false sense of strength, centered, as it was, on an extremely cohesive core but rife with internal divisions, which would turn out ultimately to undermine the community the city's founders went to such lengths to protect.

CHAPTER FOUR

Two Critical Choices:
Invoking Social Structure in Crises

The previous chapter examined how the cities' particular social structures emerged and evolved from their origins in the eighteenth century until World War II. By the 1950s the cities had developed very similar economies, which were embedded in very different social structural foundations. The chapter also examined how, in using the social capital they had at their disposal, actors in the two cities shaped and reinforced existing patterns of social structure based around community ties in Allentown and class ties in Youngstown. This chapter examines how those different structures played out in the context of two external crises that would have important and direct consequences for the cities' postindustrial pathways. The first of these concerned the depletion of local reserves of raw materials, the discovery of cheaper plentiful supplies of those materials elsewhere, and the emergence of more sophisticated modes of transportation, which shifted the geography of the steel industry away from inland cities like Allentown and Youngstown and toward cities located on large bodies of water. In responding to this common threat, leaders in the two regions drew on different social resources, thus generating very different responses. These differences became doubly important with the collapse and withdrawal of steel companies in each region in the 1970s. This chapter analyzes the response that emerged to each of these crises in turn. But in doing so, it also introduces a new source of data: network analyses examining the economic and civic connections of elites in the two cities.

Addressing the Future: Reinforce Basic Industry or Diversify in the 1950s

By the 1950s nearly a century of exploitation had depleted much of both regions' coal reserves, while the innovation of the electric arc furnace made it possible to manufacture high-quality steel using even cheaper, lower-quality varieties of coal. These developments led steelmakers in both regions to shift away from locally sourced coal and toward fields in Minnesota and the northeast coast of South America. The historical record shows that civic leaders in both communities were concerned with these developments and commissioned consultants' reports during this time. In Youngstown reports were requested in 1941, 1947, and 1955 by the New Industries Committee of the Greater Youngstown Area Foundation, a group whose membership included several prominent members of the city's economic elite. Similar reports were commissioned separately by the Bethlehem and Allentown chambers of commerce in 1951 and 1953, respectively.

These reports supplied leaders in both communities with remarkably similar information about the challenges they faced and suggested remarkably similar interventions in response. An academic paper on Youngstown's economy published in 1952 is illustrative of their conclusions. Noting that Youngstown's production costs were approximately 55 percent higher than in Cleveland, seventy miles to the northwest, and 19 percent more than in Pittsburgh, the report offered the following:

> In large measure, the future of [Youngstown and its surrounding area] may be determined by forces beyond their own control because local operations are only a small part of the total capacity of the major companies operating in this area. On the other hand, local interests have it within their own power to initiate actions which may be the deciding factors in the continued industrial development of the region. There are at least three possible solutions for the problems faced . . . The first is to increase the size of the local market by the encouragement of steel fabrication in the Valley. The second is industrial diversification. This could be accomplished by encouraging the development of a variety of new industries in the region to take advantage of its latent possibilities. Finally, the third solution and one which is largely beyond the control of the Valley itself is a reduction in steel production costs (Rodgers 1950).

In 1955, a Pace Associates report commissioned by a group of business leaders in Youngstown, for instance, noted the lack of industrial space suitable for light manufacturing in the region and suggested the regional airport and an area near Youngstown State University as possible locations (Blucher 1955; see also Rodgers 1950).

The cities' diversification efforts were accelerated by a pair of labor strikes that simultaneously struck in both Allentown and Youngstown—and other steel towns nationwide—in 1956 and 1959. With the country coming out of a recession in 1956, the steel industry had recorded record profits. Bargaining between the industry and the unions, nevertheless, quickly bogged down. For the first time, all of the industry's major employers—including Bethlehem, Republic, and Youngstown Sheet and Tube—sat down together to reach a joint agreement. Although prepared to give substantial wage increases, the companies wanted wages locked in for a five-year period. The union refused and a three-week strike ensued. The settlement was favorable to the workers. Reached under pressure from the administration of President Eisenhower, who was facing reelection that fall, it called for a three-year contract, pay increases, and a twice-yearly cost-of-living raise, which brought the total increase in pay to approximately 30 percent over the life of the agreement. Smaller companies—including Bethlehem, Sheet and Tube, and Republic—were frustrated by the outcome. Faced with increased labor costs, the companies felt compelled to pass the costs on to consumers. Increasingly, however, those consumers were turning to cheaper foreign-produced steel as an alternative.[1]

The massive steel industry strikes of 1956 and 1959 catalyzed local action in response to concerns about the viability of the steel industry that had been raised in the prior consulting reports. In Youngstown, despite the mounting and apparent need for change, diversification-oriented elements of the consultants' reports went unheeded.[2] Instead, with the backing of the region's banks, steel companies, and labor unions, Youngstown's congressional delegation—led by the city's long-time U.S. congressman, Michael Kirwan—sought federal funding to build a canal linking Lake Erie to the Ohio River Valley through Youngstown. The proposal came up for approval in the U.S. Congress in 1961 and received initial support. But it was ultimately quashed by the intervention of railroad interests, which feared competition, as well as by politicians in bordering states, who questioned the benefits of the massively expensive proposal.[3]

In Allentown the strike catalyzed a very different set of actions on the part of the community's leadership. The first was a decision on the part of Bethlehem Steel to construct a new research facility on South Mountain overlooking both the main steel plant and Lehigh University. This facility, the Homer Research Labs, was the first of what would become a large contingent of corporate research and development laboratories located in the city. The stated goal of the company in doing so was to shift into higher-value-added production. The second, and perhaps the action with a more lasting impact, was the creation of the Lehigh Valley Industrial Park, then a new concept in economic development. A small group of investors eyed a large parcel of land near the Allentown-Bethlehem-Easton Airport and came up with a plan to develop it into an office park that could attract small- to medium-sized companies. In pitching the park to the Bethlehem Chamber of Commerce, one of its investors, Frank Marcon, made the link to economic diversification explicit, stating that it was "imperative that we go out for the greater diversification of our industry" (Stainbrook and Beste 2002).

The Competitiveness Crisis

The steel industry crisis that had been predicted since at least the 1950s finally arrived in the fall of 1977.[4] Consistent with the patterns that had already been established, the nature of these responses differed dramatically. In Youngstown it was characterized by extreme fragmentation, infighting, and ultimately inaction. In Allentown a relatively unified coalition emerged and was able to take a number of key actions.

The first and most notable response to the crisis to emerge in Youngstown came from a group known as the Ecumenical Coalition. Shortly after the first mill closure announcement in 1977, workers and community activists gathered at a local union hall to express their rage as well as their fears. A resolution was drafted under the title "Save the Mahoning Valley," which called for reforms to environmental and trade policies that workers pinned as the cause of the shutdown. The statement garnered over one hundred thousand signatures from area residents in just three days. Buses were hired to carry a large contingent of steelworkers from the area to deliver the statement to policymakers in Washington. At a meeting early on in this process, a member of the Youngstown Board of Education stood up and posed the question, "Why don't we all put up five thousand bucks and buy the damn place?" Led by the Roman Catholic bishop of Youngstown, James Malone, and his Episcopalian counterpart, John Burt, the Ecumenical Coalition took up the suggestion and soon hired a staff to develop and lead just such an effort. They found Staunton Lynd, an attorney, former Yale professor, and activist, who had led training for the Mississippi

Freedom Summer before becoming a prominent and vocal opponent of the Vietnam War. Lynd contacted Gar Alperovitz, a Washington, D.C.–based economist and an advocate of community ownership as a response to economic dislocation. Together they crafted a plan based on the idea of turning the mills into community property by creating bank accounts into which community members could deposit funds that would convert into stock once the new company was under way. The funds, however, could not cover the entire cost of purchasing and modernizing the plants. The coalition therefore also sought federal funds and loan guarantees of up to $500 million.[5]

The coalition's plan, however, failed to catch on among local politicians. In 1978 two additional groups emerged to advance competing proposals. One was led jointly by Youngstown Mayor J. Phillip Richley and Congressman Charles J. Carney. Their organization—the Mahoning Valley Economic Development Corporation—had an agenda of creating a national center for steel-technology development as well as potentially building a new steelmaking facility designed to support the city's remaining steel-production facilities. A third—already existing—agency, the Western Reserve Economic Development Agency, also contributed a plan, which called for federal funds to help modernize remaining facilities. Finally, in 1980 yet a fourth group emerged to represent the interests of several of Youngstown's affluent southern suburbs. This group sought state funds to create a new office and industrial park out of the brownfield site of one of the region's largest former steel-mill sites. As the economic crisis in Youngstown worsened over the next several years, these various proposals—and their backers—battled for attention and funds at the state and federal level. Strikingly absent from the deliberations, however, were the leaders of region's remaining major employers. In the end, with the exception of the construction of a light industrial park at one of the closed steel mills, none of the four proposals was ever fully or effectively implemented.[6]

The crisis and the community's response played out very differently in Allentown. Early on a group of the city's most important economic leaders—mainly the CEOs of its remaining major companies and banks—gathered to address the crisis facing the region. As the crisis worsened in Allentown, this group of leaders began crafting a response. Building on ties to labor and local government, two proposals rose to the top. The first involved an extension of a major highway—Interstate 78—that ran through the city. Improving existing portions of the road, along with the construction of a new bypass route through the city, promised to ease transportation to New York City and its suburbs in northern New Jersey. Walter Dealtrey, the owner of a local chain of tire outlets and a member of various corporate and civic boards in the area, led an effort to push legislation that would ensure the construction took place.

The second proposal concerned a new initiative then being developed by the state of Pennsylvania known as the Ben Franklin Technology Partnership, which was meant to generate endogenous growth through partnerships between industry and research universities. Local business leaders, including Dealtrey, spoke with Walter Plosila, the state's secretary of commerce at the time in the early 1980s. Plosila was a vocal advocate of endogenous growth, an approach that contrasted with the more popular strategy of creating investment incentives designed to attract large employers, which Plosila, among others, derided as "smokestack chasing." The idea was to create public-private partnerships that would build on the state's higher education infrastructure to support existing companies seeking to engage older technologies as well as to generate new ones. Initially, the Ben Franklin program's creators planned on establishing three centers, one in Philadelphia, another in Pittsburgh, and a third covering the rest of the state to be located at State College near Pennsylvania State University. The local group in Allentown, however, succeeded in advocating for a fourth, located near Lehigh University. In addition to creating links between university researchers and the business community, this plan called for a private venture-capital fund, which would be run in conjunction with the Ben Franklin center. The fund drew investments from several of the community's companies and several wealthy individuals.

Interorganizational Networks: 1950 and 1975

To establish what differences, if any, exist between the cities' networks, I use a set of network analytic techniques. As the preceding narrative makes clear, the cities shared remarkable parallels in terms of the timing and magnitude of their economic, social, and political development. However, despite the surface similarities between these two places, important differences existed with respect to the social and economic networks in which people and organizations were embedded. This section presents data from two specific years: 1950 and 1975. The section that follows builds on the findings developed here to analyze their effect on the regions' outcomes.

The list of actors considered for inclusion in the networks includes the officers and directors of all major companies, banks, and utilities, as well as the officers of major universities and civic and cultural organizations and religious and government officials.[7] Ties between these actors are derived from two-mode affiliation data gathered on membership as officers and/or directors of all organizations considered to be in the boundaries of the cities' networks. A tie is recorded between any two organizations when individuals affiliated with them serve together as officers or directors of the same organizations.

Ties are classified as either *economic* or *civic* depending on the organizations involved. The definition of economic organizations versus civic ones follows criteria first used by Laumann, Marsden, and Galaskiewicz (1977).[8] Economic organizations are those for which maximizing either shareholders' or members' profits are primary goals. Civic organizations are those for which the primary goal is to improve the community in some way. These criteria contain considerable ambiguities. In particular, the categorization of several organizations was unclear, either because their goals are indefinite or because their emphasis has shifted over time. Utilities, banks, and unions could be considered both profit maximizing and community oriented. Hospitals' and universities' goals, on the other hand, have arguably changed over time with the onset of managed care and the potential for profit derived from sponsored research in universities. The criteria in these cases rested on a judgment about likely intentions of those who would agree to serve on the boards of directors of such organizations. I included the banks, utilities, and unions in the economic category, since board members are more likely to sit on those boards for instrumental purposes having to do with either their own or their organizations' interests. I included hospitals and universities in the civic category, since members of their boards of directors are more likely than not to view participation on those boards as primarily civic in nature.

Two additional dimensions were taken into consideration with respect to defining the boundaries of the network: time and geography (Laumann, Marsden, and Prensky 1992). Data were gathered at two moments in time: 1950 and 1975.[9] These years were chosen because they occur just *prior* to the decisions that faced regional leaders in the 1950s concerning the future of steel in each area and then in the 1970s and early 1980s as the industry was collapsing. Therefore, they offer some leverage with respect to the direction of causality. In terms of geography, the boundaries of the network were limited to organizations

Table 4.1 Organization descriptive statistics (standard deviations), 1950

	Allentown	Youngstown
No. of economic organizations	37	39
Average age	54 (30.3)	41 (20.9)
Employees	5,789 (18,824)	5,635 (13,809)
Stockholders	7,782 (21,313)	5,691 (14,490)
Income	$58,128,721 ($229,508,180)	$49,141,948 ($133,255,344)
Assets	$66,660,345 ($202,947,043)	$40,836,463 ($88,762,391)
Insiders	39% (0.16)	40% (0.21)
Family	9% (0.15)	11% (0.19)
No. of officers	7 (3.1)	8 (4.2)
No. of directors	9 (2.9)	10 (3.7)

falling within the metropolitan statistical areas of Allentown-Bethlehem-Easton, Pennsylvania, and Youngstown-Warren, Ohio.

1950

Table 4.1 presents data describing characteristics of the economic organizations included in the analysis of the two communities in 1950. In 1950 Youngstown had thirty-nine organizations that met the criteria for inclusion, while Allentown had thirty-seven. The data at first blush appear somewhat lopsided with respect to the sizes of organizations. This is primarily due to the fact that Bethlehem Steel at this time (and indeed, subsequently) was about twice the size of the comparable companies in Youngstown—Youngstown Sheet and Tube and Republic Steel. However, combining these two organizations' assets would yield a company of similar size to Bethlehem Steel. Indeed, including all of the steel-making manufacturers in Youngstown would yield a steel industry that was somewhat larger than Allentown's. Thus for all intents and purposes, the cities' roster of organizations—and therefore the universe on which this network is based—can be considered roughly equivalent.

Figures 4.1 and 4.2 present a graphical representation of the board interlocks among economic organizations in the two cities in 1950. Organizations are represented by dots next to the name of the organization. A line appears when at least one individual from an organization appears on the board of directors or as an officer in another organization. For example, if the CEO of Mahoning National Bank sits on the board of

Figure 4.1 Economic interlocks: Allentown, 1950

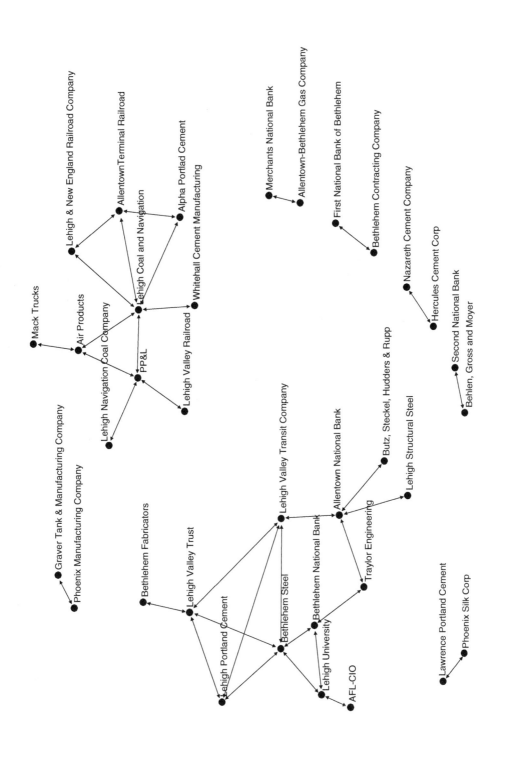

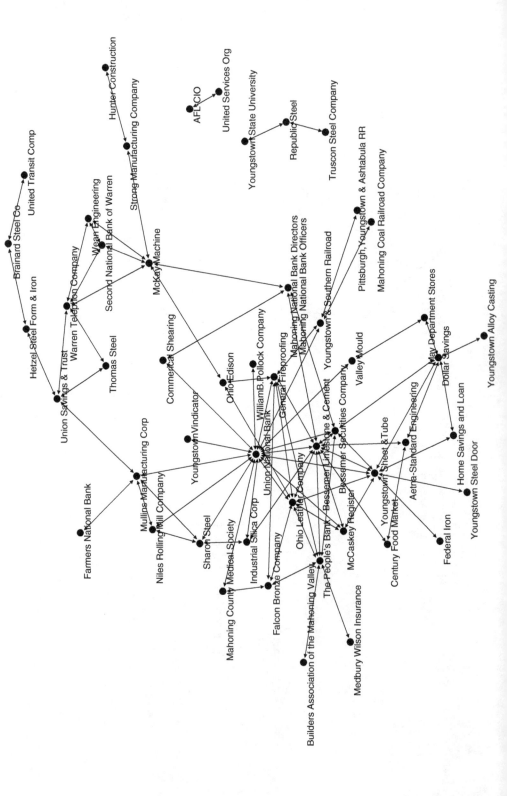

Hunter Construction

United Transit Comp

Brainard Steel Co

AFL-CIO

United Services Org

Youngstown State University

Republic Steel

Truscon Steel Company

Strong Manufacturing Company

Hetzel Steel Form & Iron

Wean Engineering

Second National Bank of Warren

Warren Telephone Company

McKay Machine

Mahoning National Bank Directors
Mahoning National Bank Officers

Pittsburgh, Youngstown & Ashtabula RR

Mahoning Coal Railroad Company

Union Savings & Trust

Thomas Steel

Commercial Shearing

Ohio Edison

William B. Pollock Company

General Fireproofing

Youngstown & Southern Railroad

Valley Mould

May Department Stores

Dollar Savings

Youngstown Alloy Casting

Mullins Manufacturing Corp

Youngstown Vindicator

Union National Bank

Bessemer Limestone & Cement

Bessemer Securities Company

Youngstown Sheet & Tube

Aetna-Standard Engineering

Home Savings and Loan

Farmers National Bank

Niles Rolling Mill Company

Sharon Steel

Industrial Silica Corp

Mahoning County Medical Society

Ohio Leather Company

McCaskey Register

Century Food Market

Federal Iron

Youngstown Steel Door

Falcon Bronze Company

The People's Bank

Builders Association of the Mahoning Valley

Medbury Wilson Insurance

Table 4.2 Economic organizations: Normalized eigenvector centrality

Allentown		Youngstown	
Merchants National Bank	0.316	Union National Bank	0.200
Allentown National Bank	0.310	Bessemer Securities Co.	0.199
Bethlehem Steel	0.270	Youngstown & Southern Railroad	0.196
Heilman Boiler Works	0.267	Mahoning National Bank	0.189
Allentown-Bethlehem Gas	0.261	Youngstown Steel Car	0.189
Bethlehem National Bank	0.258	Youngstown Welding and Eng.	0.188
Penn. Power & Light	0.236	Dollar Savings	0.185
Lehigh Valley Transit Co.	0.220	Mullins Manufacturing	0.180
Lehigh Valley Trust	0.215	Niles Rolling Mill Co.	0.180
Traylor Engineering	0.215	Youngstown Steel Door	0.178
Lehigh Coal and Navigation	0.214	Commercial Shearing	0.176
Air Products & Chemicals	0.208	Youngstown Sheet & Tube	0.176
Lehigh Portland Cement	0.200	Home Savings and Loan	0.175

Youngstown Sheet and Tube, this appears as a tie between the two organizations. Several differences are immediately apparent. Youngstown's graph (Figure 4.2) is dominated by a densely connected group of organizations. In Allentown (Figure 4.1), on the other hand, two distinct groups are evident. As Table 4.2 shows, the most central actor in Youngstown's network in 1950 was Union National Bank, which had a total of sixteen direct interlocks with other economic organizations in the city. In Allentown the most central organization in the network on the left side of the graph is Bethlehem Steel, with five interlocks. The central organization in the network on the right of the graph is Lehigh Coal and Navigation, the company founded in 1824 to build and administer the canal that ran alongside the Lehigh River, which led to the region's initial economic development. It has six interlocks in the network.

To establish the role of civic ties, data were gathered on the membership of boards of directors and officers of civic and community organizations. Particular civic organizations were chosen for inclusion in such a way as to be as comprehensive as possible while at the same time offering comparability across the two cities; these are listed in Table 4.3. Figures 4.3 and 4.4 show the networks among organizations with the civic ties included. Again, important differences are apparent. Perusing the Figure 4.4, it seems evident that civic ties increase the density of the network in Youngstown. Indeed, it is difficult from the graph to clearly

Figure 4.2 Economic interlocks: Youngstown, 1950

Table 4.3 Civic organizations, 1950

Allentown	Youngstown
Allentown Art Museum	American Assn. of University Women
Allentown Chamber of Commerce	American Legion
Allentown Hospital	Boy Scouts
Allentown Old Home Week Cmte.	Butler Institute
Allentown Redevelopment Auth.	Chamber of Commerce
Bethlehem Chamber of Commerce	Christ Mission
Bethlehem DAR	Fresh Air Camp
Bethlehem Library	Goodwill Industries
Bethlehem Municipal Band	Greater Youngstown Area
Foundation	Junior League
Bethlehem Recreation Cmsn.	Mahoning Valley Industrial Council
Boys Club	Red Cross
Cedar Crest College	Rotary
Citizens' Urban Renewal	Trumbull Library
Community Chest	United Way
Girls Clubs of Bethlehem	Youngstown Metro. Area Dev. Corp.
Historic Bethlehem	Youngstown Area Heart Assn.
Lehigh County Historical Society	Youngstown Hospital Bd.
Muhlenberg College	Youngstown Hospital Women's Bd.
Northampton County Bar	Youngstown Sesquicentennial
Weisenberg Church	

discern any structure at all beyond the tight clump of ties existing in the center. A very different picture emerges from Allentown's graph, Figure 4.3. First, adding civic ties unites the disconnected parts of the network that existed when only economic ties were included. Second, the network structure itself is quite orderly. Indeed, it seems apparent from the figure that civic organizations are linking otherwise disconnected economic elements of the network.

The data in Table 4.4 provide a statistically significant test of multiplexity in the two networks. The test is a modification of a procedure developed by Borgatti and Feld (1994) to measure the strength of ties. The test has three steps. First, a proximity matrix **A** is created in which a tie of 1 is recorded between any organizations that share members (the number of ties between organizations is ignored for this analysis). Second, the matrix is transposed (**A'**) and then postmultiplied by **A**. The data contained in the cells of the resulting matrix **AA'** are a count of the number of times that each pair of rows in A has a 1 in the same column, indicating that the

Figure 4.3 Allentown: Economic and civic ties, 1950

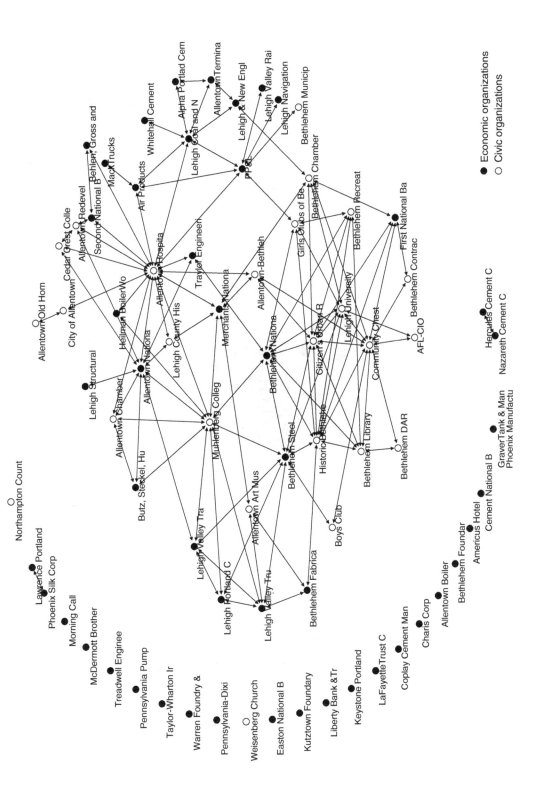

Economic organizations ●
Civic organizations ○

Northampton Count
Lawrence Portland
Phoenix Silk Corp
Morning Call
McDermott Brother
Treadwell Enginee
Pennsylvania Pump
Taylor-Wharton Ir
Warren Foundry &
Pennsylvania-Dixi
Weisenberg Church
Easton National B
Kutztown Foundary
Liberty Bank &Tr
Keystone Portland
LaFayette Trust C
Coplay Cement Man
Charis Corp
Allentown Boiler
Bethlehem Foundar
Americus Hotel
Cement National B
GraverTank & Man
Phoenix Manufactu
Nazareth Cement C
Hercules Cement C
First National Ba
Bethlehem Contrac
AFL-CIO
Bethlehem DAR
Bethlehem Library
Community Chest
Lehigh University
Citizens Utility R
Historic Bethlehe
Bethlehem Nationa
Boys Club
Bethlehem Fabrica
Bethlehem Steel
Lehigh Valley Tru
Lehigh Portland C
Lehigh Valley Tra
Allentown Art Mus
Muhlenberg Colleg
Bethlehem Recreat
Girls Clubs of Be
Bethlehem Chamber
Allentown-Bethleh
Merchants Nationa
Traylor Engineeri
Allentown Nationa
Butz, Steckel, Hu
Lehigh County His
Allentown Chamber
Lehigh Structural
Heilman Boiler Wo
Allentown Hospita
City of Allentown
Allentown Old Hom
Cedar Crest Colle
Allentown Redevel
Second National B
Allentown, Behlen, Gross and
Mack Trucks
Air Products
Whitehall Cement
Alpha Portlad Cem
Allentown Termina
Lehigh Coal and N
Lehigh & New Engl
Lehigh Valley Rai
Lehigh Navigation
Bethlehem Municip
PP&L

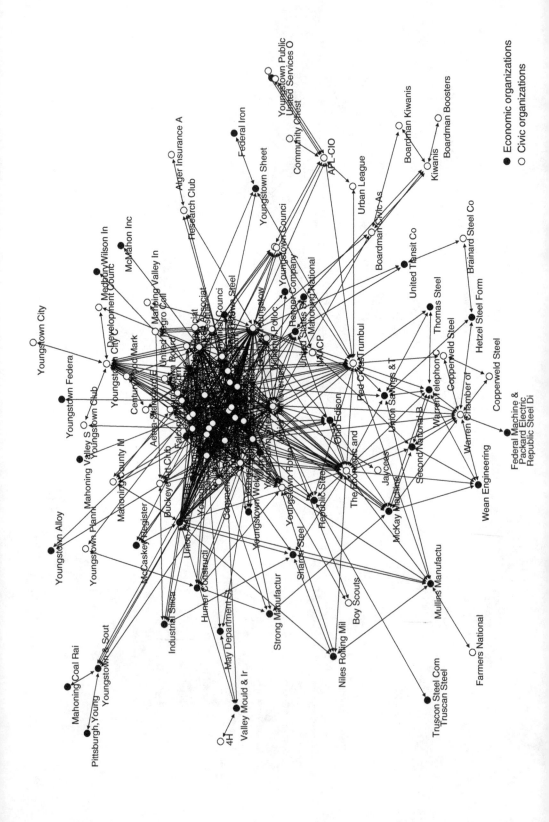

Economic organizations ●
Civic organizations ○

Youngstown Public
United Services
Community Chest
APL-CIO
Urban League
Boardman Kiwanis
Boardman Boosters
Kiwanis
Federal Iron
Youngstown Sheet
Atger Insurance A
Research Club
Youngstown Counci
Boardman Civic As
United Transit Co
Brainard Steel Co
Hetzel Steel Form
Thomas Steel
Copperweld Steel
Copperweld Steel
McMahon Inc
Medbury
Wilson In
Development Count
Valley In
Manning
Youngstown City
Steel
Youngstown City
Mahoning Valley S
Youngstown Club
Mahoning County M
Mahoning Plann
Youngstown Federa
Youngstown Alloy
Youngstown Sout
Mahoning Coal Rai
Pittsburgh, Young
Negro Coll
Research Club
Board
Social
Counci
United
Mark
Century
Aetna-Stan
Falcon
Buckeye rt Club
McCaskey Register
Union
Youngstown Weld
Youngstown Rb
Sharon Steel
Republic Stee
Ohio Edison
Pollock
Renner Company
Mahoning National
ied States Ste
NAACP
Red Cross
Trumbul
Union Savings & T
Warren Telephon C
Warren Chamber of
Second National B
Jaycees
McKay Machine
The and
Warren Chamber of
Wean Engineering
Federal Machine &
Packard Electric
Republic Steel Di
Farmers National
Huner Constructi
Industrial Silica
May Department St
Valley Mould & Ir
4H
Strong Manufactur
Boy Scouts
Niles Rolling Mil
Mullins Manufactu
Truscon Steel Com
Truscan Steel

Table 4.4 Multiplexity, 1950

	Strength of economic ties	Strength of civic ties	Economic and civic combined	n	Observations
Allentown	0.886	0.880	0.447	54	2,862
Youngstown	0.783	0.805	0.763	56	3,162

two actors are connected to the same third party. Finally, the quadratic assignment procedure technique is used to compute the Pearson correlation between **A** and **AA'** while at the same time assessing the significance of the correlation.[10] The correlation is a statistically significant measure of the mean strength of ties within the network. This procedure was conducted on the data in three different ways, as indicated in the table. The data in the first column show the strength of economic ties only. The second column presents a measure of ties derived from joint membership in civic organizations; that is, a tie in **A** is recorded wherever two economic organizations send individuals to sit on the board of the same civic organization. Thus a 1 appears in the cell in **A**, which indicates a tie between Mack Truck and Bethlehem Steel if both organizations each have a representative on the United Way Board of Directors. Finally, the data in the last column present the strength of interorganizational ties when both economic and civic ties are included in the same matrix.

The results show that in Youngstown ties are extremely strong—above 0.75—for all three measures. In Allentown, on the other hand, the ties are equally strong for both economic and civic networks—again, around 0.8—but the strength of ties is cut in half when the two networks are combined. These results represent an important finding. In Allentown the civic ties among elites in 1950 connected actors who were *not* otherwise connected economically. In Youngstown, on the other hand, civic ties amplified contacts among actors who were already well connected. This suggests that civic organizations in the two cities played very different roles in terms of how social capital was organized and used. Specifically, perusing the complete network structure for Allentown in Figure 4.3 suggests that civic organizations may have played a role in providing a bridge between otherwise disconnected organizations in the community. Further evidence of this is presented in Figure 4.5. The graph shows the eigenvector centrality scores—which provide an indication of the degree

Figure 4.4 Youngstown: Economic and civic ties, 1950

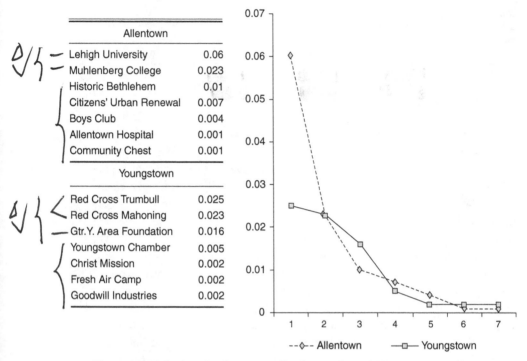

Allentown	
Lehigh University	0.06
Muhlenberg College	0.023
Historic Bethlehem	0.01
Citizens' Urban Renewal	0.007
Boys Club	0.004
Allentown Hospital	0.001
Community Chest	0.001
Youngstown	
Red Cross Trumbull	0.025
Red Cross Mahoning	0.023
Gtr.Y. Area Foundation	0.016
Youngstown Chamber	0.005
Christ Mission	0.002
Fresh Air Camp	0.002
Goodwill Industries	0.002

Figure 4.5 Civic organizations normalized centrality, 1950

to which organizations act as brokers between other organizations while simultaneously "controlling" for the centrality of those organizations' ties—of the top six civic organizations in each city. The raw centrality scores were transformed to add to 1.0. The graph indicates that, in Allentown, a few civic organizations—particularly the city's two largest colleges—occupied very central positions within the network compared with the parallel group of civic organizations in Youngstown—the region's two Red Cross chapters as well as the CEO-dominated Greater Youngstown Foundation—which were largely undifferentiated from each other in terms of their bridging roles.

1975

Table 4.5 presents data describing characteristics of the economic organizations in the two communities in 1975. Youngstown had twenty-seven organizations that met the criteria for inclusion while Allentown had twenty-nine. Again, mitigating for the differences between Bethlehem Steel and the larger but more fragmented steel industry in Youngstown, the net-

Table 4.5 Organizations descriptive statistics (standard deviations), 1975

	Youngstown	Allentown
No. of organizations	27	29
Average age	53 (28.9)	82 (38.2)
Employees	4,624 (8,672)	7,612 (25,284)
Stockholders	13,222 (29,773.9)	16,177 (42,184.1)
Income	$266,490,700	$428,859,577
	($476,114,809)	($1,225,921,381)
Assets	$360,944,296	$458,602,696
	($586,611,174)	($982,824,681)
Insiders	38% (0.23)	28% (0.19)
Family	13% (0.21)	7% (0.14)
No. of officers	10 (4.8)	12 (7.0)
No. of directors	11 (5.3)	12 (6.7)

works are roughly equivalent. Figures 4.6 and 4.7 show the graphical representations of the board interlocks among economic organizations in 1975. Although it is less dense than in 1950, Youngstown's network (Figure 4.7) remains well connected, with several apparent overlapping ties. Allentown's economic network (Figure 4.6) has become more connected, with Pennsylvania Power and Light (the local power utility) serving to connect the two previously disconnected groups of companies.

Turning next to the networks with civic ties included, the data in Figures 4.8 and 4.9 indicate a relatively similar pattern to the one that existed in 1950. Once again, Youngstown's network is densely connected, with numerous civic and economic organizations occupying a tight core at its center (civic organizations included in the analysis are listed in Table 4.6). Allentown's network retains the relatively orderly structure. Table 4.7 shows the normalized centrality scores for the most central economic actors in each of the networks.

Data from the multiplexity test (Table 4.8) prove out these observations. Again, while the ties are relatively strong in both cities when economic and civic ties are considered separately, the strength of ties declines when the two kinds of relationships are considered together in Allentown but remain high in Youngstown. Finally, considering the brokerage scores of the top six civic organizations in each city (Figure 4.10) again shows important differences. In Allentown, a handful of organizations—specifically Muhlenberg College as well as the local chapter of the Boy Scouts—have much higher scores than other organizations, while in Youngstown none of that city's most central civic

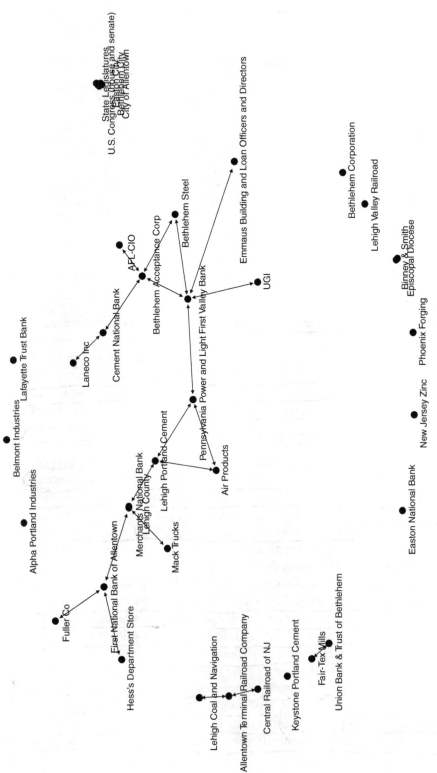

Figure 4.6 Allentown: Economic organization interlocks, 1975

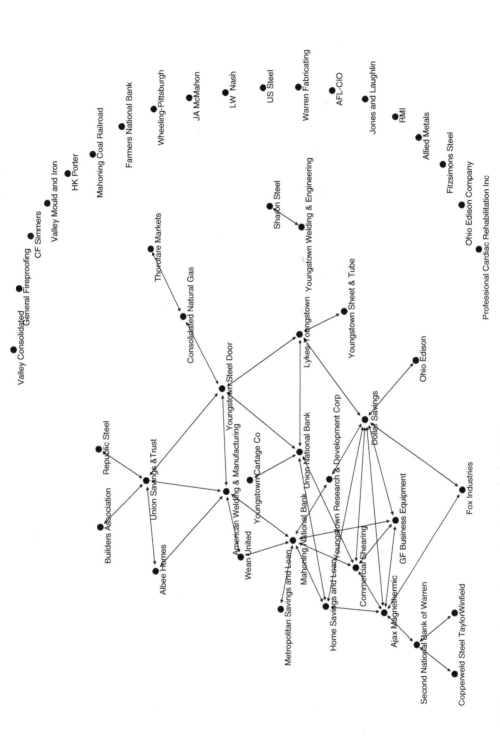

Figure 4.7 Youngstown: Economic organization interlocks, 1975

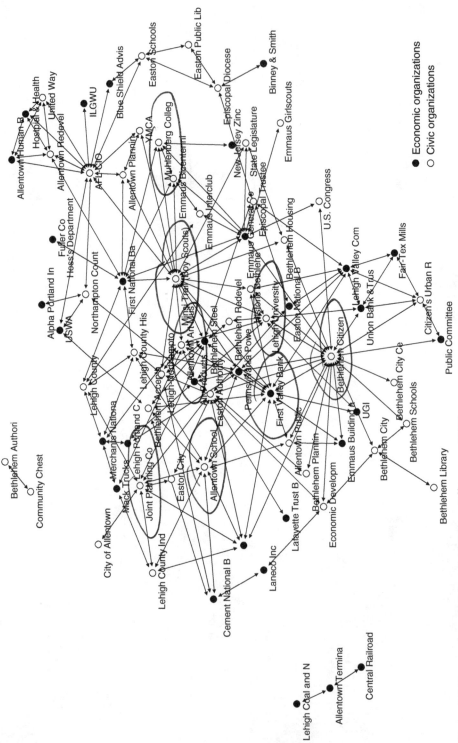

Figure 4.8 Economic and civic organizations: Allentown, 1975

Economic organizations ●
Civic organizations ○

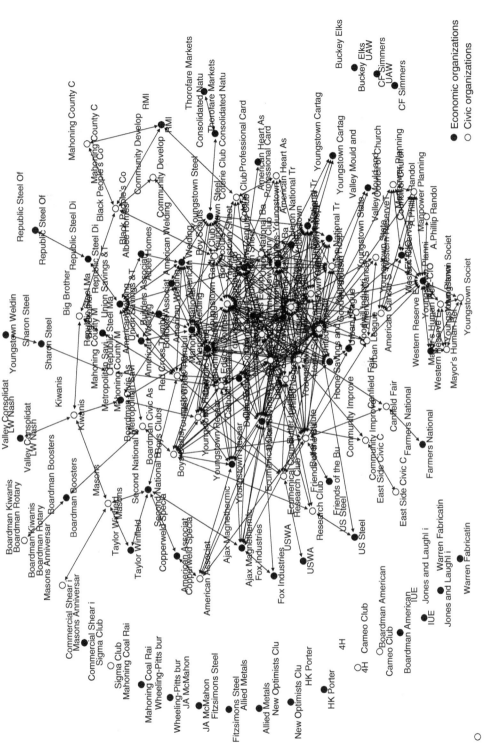

Figure 4.9 Economic and civic organizations: Youngstown, 1975

Legend:
- ● Economic organizations
- ○ Civic organizations

Table 4.6 Civic organizations, 1975

Allentown		Youngstown	
Allentown Art Museum	Economic Development Program Committee	4H	Mahoning County Medical Society
Allentown Human Relations Committee	Emmaus Bicentennial Committee	A. Philip Randolph Institute	Manpower Planning Council
Allentown Planning Commission	Emmaus General Committee	American Association of University Women	Masons
Allentown Public Library	Emmaus Girl Scouts	American Cancer Society	Masons Anniversary Committee
Allentown Redevelopment Authority	Emmaus Interclub Coordinating Committee	American Heart Association	Mayor's Human Relations Committee
Allentown School Board	Episcopal Trustees	Big Brothers	Red Cross
AAUW	Historic Bethlehem	Black People's Convention	Research Club
Bethlehem Authority	Hospital & Health Council of the Greater Lehigh Valley	Boy Scouts	Rotary
Bethlehem Citizens Committee	Joint Planning Commission Lehigh-Northampton	Boys Clubs	United Appeal
Bethlehem City Center Authority	Lehigh County Historical Society	Butler Institute	United Negro College Fund
Bethlehem DAR	Lehigh County Industrial Development Authority	Canfield Fair	United Way Campaign Committee
Bethlehem Housing Authority	Lehigh University	Catholic Charities	Urban League
Bethlehem Library	Lehigh Valley Committee	Chamber of Commerce	Western Reserve Economic Development Agency
Bethlehem Planning Commission	Lehigh-Northampton Airport Authority	Community Corporation	Western Reserve Transit Authority

Bethlehem Redevelopment Authority	Lehigh-Northampton Transportation Authority	Community Development Council	Youngstown Club
Bethlehem Schools	Muhlenberg College	Community Improvement Corporation	Youngstown Garden Club
Blue Shield Advisory Board	Northampton County Bar Association	Coterie Club	Youngstown Hospital
Boy Scouts	Northampton County Hospital Authority	Council of Churches	Youngstown Hospital Association
Citizens' Urban Renewal Enterprise	Northampton County Republican Committee	East Side Civic Club	Youngstown Hospital Women's Board
Community Chest	Public Committee for the Humanities	Ecumenical Council	Youngstown Planning and Administration Committee
Easton Authority	United Way	Goodwill Industries	Youngstown Society for the Blind
Easton Public Library	Women's Club of Bethlehem	Kiwanis	Youngstown State University
Easton Schools	YMCA	Mahoning Citizens Action Coalition	

Table 4.7 Normalized eigenvector centrality of economic organizations, 1975

Allentown		Youngstown	
First Valley Bank	0.456	Dollar Savings	0.319
Penn. Power and Light	0.361	Mahoning National Bank	0.312
Bethlehem Steel	0.331	Commercial Shearing	0.300
Merchants National Bank	0.245	GF Business Equipment	0.292
First National Bank of Allentown	0.220	Union National Bank	0.286
Air Products	0.206	Home Savings and Loan	0.278
Union Bank & Trust of Bethlehem	0.190	Ajax Magnethermic	0.238
Bethlehem Acceptance Corp.	0.189	Youngstown R&D Corp	0.211
AFL-CIO	0.173	Lykes-Youngstown	0.211
Emmaus Building and Loan	0.169	Ohio Edison	0.206
Lehigh County	0.168	Youngstown Steel Door	0.200
Mack Trucks	0.166	AFL-CIO	0.195
State Legislatures	0.163	Youngstown Sheet & Tube	0.187

organizations—the Youngstown Garden Club, the Butler Art Institute, and the Youngstown Chamber of Commerce—stand out.

Discussion

The political processes that emerged around two key historical moments differed dramatically; the responses in Allentown coalesced around a relatively unified set of community-oriented actions, and Youngstown's balkanized along the narrow interests of powerful elites. Thus, despite having access to the same information and ideas, the implementation of those ideas into policy and strategic action was very different.

Examining social networks among elites in the two regions paints a vivid picture that both supports the main argument of the previous chapter concerning the community orientation of social structure in Allentown and the class-based cohesion in Youngstown. But the data allow us to look much more closely at the details of these ties, revealing the importance of multiplexity. Significant differences existed with respect to configuration of multiplex economic and civic ties in the two cities. In Youngstown the networks among economic organizations in the 1950s and 1970s are densely connected; in particular, the multiplex economic and civic ties' overlap indicates that actors' civic relationships brought together people who were already well connected. In Allentown, although economic ties were deeply fragmented along commu-

Table 4.8 Multiplexity, 1975

	Strength of economic ties	Strength of civic ties	Economic and civic combined	n	Observations
Allentown	0.871	0.532	0.301	54	2,862
Youngstown	0.771	0.724	0.619	56	3,162

nity lines, a few civic associational ties had emerged by the 1950s that served as a bridge that cut across the community-based divisions. In Youngstown no one organization or set of organizations emerges as particularly prominent. In Allentown, on the other hand, a few civic organizations emerged at various points as places where socially important actors gathered.

The key question to be answered here is how these few bridging civic institutions emerged in Allentown. The answer lies first in the separation of ownership and control reaching well back into the early history of Allentown's industrialization discussed in the previous chapter. Economic and civic institutions were clearly connected in the city, but they were populated and controlled by different populations: managers came to control economic life as elites focused on their civic obligations. The two networks existed on largely separate planes. But eventually, elite families receded from direct involvement in civic life as well. This drew managers into the civic sphere more directly. The most important of these was Charles Schwab as head of Bethlehem Steel. His approach, however, was to rationalize his involvement, concentrating it on one key organization: the Boy Scouts. As we saw earlier in the previous chapter's discussion of John Ramsay and the organizing of the steel industry, the Boy Scouts themselves were a cross-class-based organization, and his involvement in that particular group was in keeping with the general approach that had emerged in Allentown of forging cross-class ties to ensure stability and control within localized communities. But Schwab was no ordinary citizen; he was arguably the most important—highest status—individual in the region, and his decision to concentrate his civic involvement in one place had an unintended consequence: the Boy Scout board became *the* board one needed to be on if one wanted to accomplish goals in the Lehigh Valley because involvement on that board provided access to Schwab. The Boy Scouts and the ideology they espoused were attractive and complementary to the goal; but more important was the role the Boy Scout board came to play in

Allentown	
Muhlenberg College	0.297
Boy Scouts	0.138
Lehigh County	0.103
Historical Society	0.018
Allentown Planning	0.017
Bethlehem Citizen's	0.01
Youngstown	
Youngstown Garden Club	0.021
Butler Institute	0.016
Chamber of Commerce	0.015
United Appeal	0.009
United Way	0.008
Youngstown Hospital	0.008

Figure 4.10 Civic organizations normalized centrality, 1975

serving as a bridge across ethnic, class, and indeed, geographic divisions within the valley. As a result, it became a vital meeting point and mobilizing platform when crisis eventually ensued. In some ways, organizations such as the Boy Scouts and the Bethlehem Citizens' Association resemble the position the Medici assumed in Florence as described by Padgett and Ansell (1993): they were members of both of the "camps" or network cliques in the community, but were not necessarily *of* either camp in particular. Yet the role these civic organizations played in connecting these groups was not self-interested in the way the Medici's seem to have been; indeed, their role seems largely to have emerged as an unintended consequence.

Deliberately or not, the role these few civic organizations played in Allentown was vital in shaping the city's postindustrial trajectory. Serving on the boards of organizations like the Boy Scouts and local universities in Allentown provided local economic actors who did not have intersecting economic interests a forum in which to develop, enact, and reproduce community-oriented identities and values. The Boy

Scouts organization's role as the key mobilizing structure around which the response to the crisis of the 1970s was mounted is suggested by the fact that the majority of the staff for both of the most powerful organizations to have emerged from this period of uncertainty—the Lehigh Valley Partnership (whose members are CEOs of major area companies) and the eventually independent Lehigh Valley Industrial Park—were recruited primarily from among the ranks of Boy Scout staff.

In Youngstown, on the other hand, the data show the most prominent civic organization to be the Youngstown Garden Club. This organization was populated mainly by the wives of the business elite in Youngstown. Perusing the list of names associated with the Garden Club and other prominent civic organizations in Youngstown, it becomes clear that a number of names are repeated: Wick, Campbell, Tod, and Stambaugh. These families founded the original steel mills in the late 1850s. They had settled in a small neighborhood near the center of Youngstown and then turned their attention to founding and running the city's prominent banks (most importantly, Union National Bank) and elite cultural institutions, such as the Butler Art Institute (located near the corner of Wick and Campbell streets).

By the 1970s Youngstown's dense economic and social core was populated by the third and fourth generations of the city's original elite; relatively little "turnover" had occurred. Yet it is also clear that by this time those ties had grown increasingly brittle. Families maintained their names and faces in the community through such memberships, but their time and effort were spent outside of it. The implication is that, although the network indicates a strong and highly dense network, in fact the ties were quite brittle. When ultimately those ties were tested during the crisis of the 1970s, the dense core played no significant role in formulating a response and, indeed, was largely destroyed by it. Instead, the response was left to the disjointed groups who had been cut off from each other by the divide-and-conquer approach that the elite had taken to social control in earlier eras. These elements of the network, however, lacked the history of interaction—particularly through the forum of civic associational ties—that existed in Allentown. By the time the crisis hit, it was too late to establish those ties. The fragmented response that emerged was a reflection of the underlying weakness of the community's social networks.

CHAPTER FIVE

How Allentown Got Its Groove Back: Rebuilding Social Infrastructure in the Wake of Economic Crisis

The manufacturing crisis was a fundamental crisis in the sense that it upended not only the daily lives and livelihoods of millions of blue-collar workers and their families but—perhaps more fundamentally—the very identities of those workers on the job and in their communities. And it did not stop there: organizational and indeed community identities were upended as well. The collapse of the industrial *system* meant that the roles and expectations associated with categories such as "suppliers," "local government," "local bank," "local university," and a whole range of other socially constructed categories, which made sense in a world dominated by industrial manufacturing, were suddenly and often violently called into question as each struggled to adjust to a new world. More than two decades on, those struggles have largely unfolded, and the results have come into focus. Companies that have survived have done so by finding new ways to compete, which can be reinterpreted as finding new ways to define themselves in a global economy. Similarly, communities—and the constellation of organizations of which they are composed—have adjusted. Some have found a new role to play in the global economy. Others have not.

The two processes of organizational change and community change are, I argue, intimately linked. The collapse of the industrial order within manufacturing communities undermined the institutional order within which organizations came to define themselves. And, as we saw in the last chapter, it also created a dramatic leadership vacuum. Industrialists and bankers had occupied the center of social and economic networks in these cities. But as the structure of industry and locally based banking transformed, those sources of leadership dried up—in some cases overnight. Those who remained were left to rebuild local infrastructures.

The environment in which that rebuilding effort took shape was largely predetermined by existing patterns of interaction among elites in these cities. The previous two chapters have shown that the social structures of Allentown and Youngstown differed in important ways and that those differences shaped the kinds of collective actions that emerged in the face of parallel challenges. It has been argued that, although these two cities' economies had been incorporated into the same overarching set of economic structures associated with the American steel industry, important underlying differences in the configuration of local networks emerged in the wake of the industry's decline to shape the way each city responded to the challenges it faced. This chapter argues that a certain set of network structures made it possible for Allentown to successfully reconfigure itself and arrive at a new, stable social arrangement, which has been vital to the region's postindustrial success. Conversely, Youngstown's problems over the last few decades have stemmed from the inability of actors in that community to arrive at new ways of relating to each other, a failure that has increasingly driven organizational leaders to turn away from the community. What this suggests is that the availability of a largely independent civic network provided grounds on which actors in the Lehigh Valley could engage in collective action. This action produced meaningful organizational change and provided an environment in which entrepreneurship flourished in the aftermath of the collapse of steelmaking as the central economic activity of the region. As that crisis unfolded, it undermined established patterns of organizational identity. Organizations sought out allies and interlocutors with whom to make sense of the acute uncertainty. In doing so, they built on their preexisting social ties within the community. Organizational strategies and identities inevitably evolved in the aftermath of the crisis. But in Allentown organizational transformations became part and parcel of the transformation of the broader social structure of the Valley, producing a virtuous circle. Organizational change in Youngstown and the Mahoning Valley, on the other hand, suffered because of the lack of constructive dialogue within the region. As organizations and groups within the community evolved, they did so in ways that were increasingly disconnected from the community in which they resided.

This ultimately led to the divergence of the regions' postindustrial economic outcomes we observed in Chapter 2.

This chapter is organized as follows. The next section presents an introductory anecdote focusing on the emergence and growth of two entrepreneurial companies and how their growth has been received in each community. The following section shows how interorganizational networks in the two cities have evolved and establishes that Allentown today benefits from greater participation from the leaders of large companies than is the case in Youngstown. The importance of this is made apparent in the discussion of the three drivers of economic change: (1) the transformation of large companies, (2) the infrastructure (or lack thereof) supporting the formation of entrepreneurial companies, and (3) the attraction and retention of outside investment into the regions.

An Anecdote

Ask people in the Lehigh Valley for an example of a successful company started since the crisis of the early 1980s, and it is likely they will mention IQE. In 1986 Tom Hierl was an engineer living in Somerville, New Jersey, working at a major telecommunications company. He and a colleague had an idea about how to produce molecular beam epitaxy—specialized wafers used to make sophisticated optical semiconductors. His employer liked the idea but felt that the market potential for the product was too small. Hierl approached Ben Franklin Technology Partners with a business plan. His new company was provided with space in an incubator facility located on the campus of Bethlehem Steel's research and development laboratories, situated on the hill above Lehigh University. The company leaders were also introduced to Mid-Atlantic Partners, a venture-capital firm backed by local financiers, as well as to a local bank that helped with securing a loan, and finally to a researcher at the university who was pursuing research in a related area of technology.[1] By 1993 IQE had outgrown the incubator and moved into a new building located on the site of Bethlehem Steel's massive abandoned mills. In 1998 the company merged with a competitor based in Cardiff, Wales. The combined companies soon went public with annual revenues of $36 million.

The same year IQE was founded, Terry Buss, a professor of urban planning at Youngstown State University, traveled to Australia to speak about Youngstown's experiences during the steel closings. There he met Donald Mitchell, who headed a company located in Corby, England, that produced sophisticated semiconductors for use in extreme environments, such as military combat and space exploration. Like Allentown and Youngstown, Corby was a steel-producing city that had fallen on hard times. Buss soon traveled to Corby and was impressed with what he saw: a high-tech company flourishing in the British rust belt. He asked Mitchell to consider starting another new company in Youngstown. To Buss, attracting the company would help change the approach local leaders had been taking in their efforts to stimulate the local economy by demonstrating that Youngstown could build a new indigenous economic base that incorporated high-technology firms. After several trips to the United States and meetings with local banks, potential financiers, and government officials, Mitchell and Buss secured over $2 million in state and federal loans for a new venture to be located just outside Youngstown.[2] The new company, Sovereign Circuits, was finally established in 1987 and achieved profitability in 1992. It had annual revenues of over $56 million when it was acquired in 2006.

IQE and Sovereign Circuits are in related markets, and both have achieved comparable levels of commercial success. Where they differ is in the networks they have been able to tap into to succeed and the ripple effects their own growth has had within their communities. IQE has reached a stage of maturity where its leaders are *expected* to take part in a growing network of mentors and venture financiers that support local entrepreneurship efforts in Allentown. One finds Tom Hierl's name on several boards of directors associated with those networks, including the scientific advisory board of the Ben Franklin Partnership. On the other hand, Sovereign Circuits—despite having reached a similar level of success and despite the very public circumstances of its origins—has largely shunned involvement in economic development efforts of the Youngstown area. It is not alone; stung by years of frustration with such efforts, several successful companies in Youngstown report a fear that getting too involved in economic development might invite unwelcome demands on their time and resources. These companies' leaders see little benefit to the bottom line from taking an active part in Youngstown's future.

These differences have contributed directly to Allentown's economic turnaround since the 1980s. Between 1990 and 2002, thirty-seven high-tech startups in and around Allentown received $1.8 billion in venture-capital investment;[3] more than twenty companies won competitive Small Business Innovation Research (SBIR) awards,[4] and the number of new companies in growing industries grew at an annual rate of over 0.4 percent.[5] In Youngstown over that same period less than $125 million in early-stage venture-capital funding was secured,[6] companies received only three SBIR awards, and the number of high-tech firms grew only 0.1 percent annually. The efforts of Terry Buss and others in Youngstown to spur the growth of new firms have largely been met with disappointment. The entrepreneurial networks in which Tom Hierl is now expected to take part, on the other hand, represent a significant and growing part of Allentown's economy. High-tech entrepreneurship has been integrated into the local economy so completely it is thought of simply as one of the pillars on which Allentown's economy is based.

The Evolution of Interorganizational and Leadership Networks: 1950–2000

The fact that Allentown and the greater Lehigh Valley have become home to a set of these entrepreneurial networks is surprising given its industrial history—at least according to those who hold that such networks can only emerge from a clean slate in which there is no prior legacy of large-scale industrial manufacturing (as was the case in Silicon Valley; see Scott 1988 and Saxenian 1996). Just as surprising, perhaps, is who populates the upper echelons of those networks: corporate CEOs of large bureaucratic companies, that is, men and women who have had bigger issues to deal with in recent decades than attending to the economic development of what might have otherwise been a decaying rust-belt backwater. Companies like Air Products and Chemicals and Pennsylvania Power and Light (PP&L)—formerly the local electric utility, which has become a major global player in energy markets—have made transforming themselves to compete effectively in the face of a rapidly changing global market a high priority. Yet as the data presented in this section show, the leaders of these and other major companies in the Lehigh Valley are, nevertheless, remarkably integrated into the region's social infrastructure.

Youngstown's experiences on this score provide a stark contrast to Allentown as indicated by an interview with Betty Jo Licata, dean of the Youngstown State University's School of Business.

> There was an article in the paper recently asking, "Where are all the local leaders?" It's really sad. I don't think it's true that we don't have local leaders. There just hasn't been a mechanism to bring those separate enti-

ties together. I can't tell you why. But, for instance, we tried to give an award out to a local company that had done well—an example. That sort of thing. We called ten companies that had been nominated, and five of them asked us to take their names off the list. They didn't want to be identified. They didn't want people knocking on their doors.

If the direct participation of corporate CEOs in the affairs of Allentown is notable, Dean Licata's comment suggests the equally startling about-face that has occurred in Youngstown over the last twenty-five years. The city had long been dominated by a core group of economic elites, whose relationships and ties to the community were dense to the point of being stifling. But by the turn of the twenty-first century, those networks had been almost completely decimated. Indeed, Allentown and Youngstown seem to have swapped places in terms of the ways in which key economic actors are connected to each other. Whereas Allentown's networks had historically been loose and somewhat disconnected, today a dense core has emerged that has been instrumental in shaping the city's postindustrial transformation.[7] On the other hand, the patterns of network formation in Youngstown are missing a key component; while there remains a fairly dense core of civic leaders in Youngstown, the region's most important company leaders have kept their distance from it. Civic and governmental leaders (who populate the network's core) are doing their best to turn the region's economic prospects around, but their efforts have been hampered by the disaffection of the region's most powerful economic actors.

This statement can be shown empirically. As we saw in the previous chapter, the networks linking organizations and actors in Allentown and Youngstown were highly articulated in the 1950s, with fairly dense economic networks prevailing in both cities. Since then, the relationships among organizations have changed dramatically. While in the past, many—if not most—major companies had numerous board interlocks to other local companies and banks, economically based ties such as these are now rare. Indeed, as indicated in Table 5.1, ties associated with companies in general have declined as a percentage of total interorganizational ties—in Allentown; they have gone from accounting for over 60 percent of all interorganizational ties in 1950 to less than 20 percent today. The most dramatic declines have come, of course, from the decimation of the cities' steel industries. In Youngstown, ties associated with steel companies have gone from 12 percent of all interorganizational relationships to less than 5 percent. In Allentown, Bethlehem Steel's decline has been even more striking. Bethlehem Steel and a handful of

Table 5.1 Organizational network density

	Year	Allentown	Youngstown
Economic organizations	1950	0.0489	0.0509
	2000	0.0059	0.0065
Economic via civic	1950	0.1055	0.3362
	2000	0.0442	0.0433

other small steel producers accounted for a remarkable 20 percent of all interorganizational relationships in 1950. Today they account for less than 1 percent.

What has taken the place of large companies at the center of the cities' networks? Important differences emerge between Allentown and Youngstown. In Youngstown the most prominent category of actors today among interorganizational networks is banks. Several area banks and financial institutions remain located in the city—standing in many ways as the last legacy of the city's industrial past. But remarkably, despite their prominence, when one analyzes the banks' pattern of interorganizational relationships, the bulk of their ties are neither to companies in the region nor to civic organizations; their ties are concentrated among other banks. In Allentown banks account for a smaller proportion of the city's current leadership network—just 7 percent of interorganizational ties—but those ties are spread out among a wider array of local actors, including local firms, chambers of commerce and business associations, educational institutions, and civic organizations.

But perhaps the best indication of the differences in the cities' networks is the data contained in Tables 5.2 through 5.5, which show the names and affiliations of the twenty most prominent individuals within each city's networks in the 1950s and again in 2000. As one might expect, in the 1950s these people in the networks are associated with many of the cities' prominent manufacturing interests and banks, accounting for fully nineteen of the twenty most central in Allentown. In 2000, though, the cities diverge. Only six of the most prominent individuals in Youngstown's current network are associated with large employers and, of these, two are retired. In Allentown, on the other hand, ten of the twenty are affiliated with major employers, and all but one is the CEO of the organization. Several key government leaders are also clearly well integrated in Allentown's current network, including the

Table 5.2 Youngstown, most prominent individuals (betweenness centrality), 1950

Name	Score	Title, organization	Organization description
Ford, J. W.	6.974	Director, Youngstown Sheet and Tube	Manufacturing, steel
Henderson, C. P.	4.920	Mayor, Youngstown	Government
Pollock, W. B., II	4.647	Owner, William B. Pollock Company	Manufacturing, railroad cars
Roemer, H. A.	4.533	President, Mullins Manufacturing	Manufacturing, munitions
Bender, W.	4.450	President, General Fireproofing	Manufacturing, office equipment
Cox, J. W.	4.394	President, Daniels Motor Freight	Transportation
Graf, J. H.	4.294	Officer, Republic Steel Corporation	Manufacturing, steel
Thompson, G. V.	3.512	President, May Department Store	Retail store
Beeghly, L. A.	3.404	Founder, Standard Slag Company	Manufacturing, cement
Ullman, C. W.	3.211	President, Dollar Savings Bank	Bank
Jones, Howard	2.981	Several charities	Philanthropist
Sampson, W. J., Jr.	2.949	Director, Union Savings and Trust	Bank
Kennedy, P. H.	2.887	Youngstown Sheet and Tube	Manufacturing, steel
Wean, R. J.	2.498	President, Wean Engineering	Manufacturing, equipment
Holmquist, C. W.	2.486	Copperweld Steel Company	Manufacturing, steel
Strouss, C. J.	2.464	Several charities	Philanthropist
Fowler, J. D.	2.399	Several charities	Philanthropist
Robinson, C. L.	2.357	Several charities	Philanthropist
Ramage, W. H.	2.241	Union National Bank	Bank
Maag, W. F.	2.219	Publisher, *The Vindicator*	Newspaper

Table 5.3 Allentown, most prominent individuals (betweenness centrality), 1950

Name	Score	Title, organization	Organization description
Oakes, C. E.	17.497	President, PP&L	Utility
Young, R. A.	6.572	President, Lehigh Portland Cement	Manufacturing, cement
Neuweiler, L. P.	6.337	President, Merchants National Bank	Bank
Clauss, O. N.	5.631	Vice President, Merchants National Bank	Bank
Trexler, C. H.	5.195	President, Heilman Boiler Works	Manufacturing, containers
White, R. V.	4.975	Officer, Lehigh Coal & Navigation	Transportation company
Bender, J. P.	4.862	Vice President, Bethlehem Steel	Manufacturing, steel
Laros, R. K.	4.798	Founder, RK Laros Mills	Manufacturing, textile
Knowles, J. C.	3.741	Vice President, PP&L	Utility
Schmidt, V. R.	3.599	Director, Allentown National Bank	Bank
Miller, R. D.	3.416	Officer, Merchants National Bank	Bank
Cort, S. J.	3.363	Vice President, Bethlehem Steel	Manufacturing, steel
Brillhart, D. H.	3.243	Director, PP&L	Utility
Dodge, H. W.	3.005	Officer, Mack Trucks	Manufacturing, trucks
Kline, C.	2.930	Officer, Allentown National Bank	Bank
Johnstone, W. H.	2.587	Officer, Bethlehem Steel	Manufacturing, steel
Congdon, W. H.	2.535	President, Lehigh University	Education, university
Roberts, W. J., Sr.	2.451	President, Traylor Engineering	Manufacturing, equipment
Albert, H. L.	2.449	President, Lehigh & New England RR	Transportation
Fosdick, A. H.	2.371	Plant Manager, Bethlehem Steel	Manufacturing, steel

Table 5.4 Youngstown, most prominent individuals (betweenness centrality), 2000

Name	Score	Title, organization	Organization description
Wilson, M.	4.644	Director, Home Builders Association	Civic organization, business
Siffrin, R., III	4.575	General Vicar, Catholic Diocese	Civic organization, religious
Maass, H.	3.802	Manager (retired), General Motors	Manufacturer, cars
Baun, S.	3.532	Women's Chair, Home Builders Assn.	Civic organization, business
Cagigas, D.	3.532	President, United Way	Civic organization
Bunn, W.	3.339	Chairman, Andrews Trust	Civic organization, charity
Faulkner, R.	3.152	Vice President, Chamber of Commerce	Civic organization, business
Bresnahan, W.	3.137	Commercial Shearing	Manufacturer, equipment
Johnson, C.	3.051	Principal (retired), Warren Schools	Education, secondary
Lewis, S. R.	2.748	First Place Financial	Bank
Cushwa, C. B., III	2.673	Commercial Shearing	Manufacturer, equipment
Anderson, D.	2.555	CIO (retired), Delphi-Packard	Manufacturer, electronics
Mast, D.	2.374	Second Bancorp	Bank
Atwater, T.	2.136	Provost, Youngstown State University	Education, university
English, B.	2.074	Superintendent, Warren Schools	Education, secondary
Kaback, N.	1.959	Partner, Cohen & Co.	Business service, accountant
French, D.	1.948	Mahoning Valley Econ. Dev. Council	Economic development org.
McNair, M. M.	1.850	Urban League	Civic organization
Fitzwilliams, T.	1.803	Boy Scouts	Civic organization
Humphries, T. M.	1.791	First Place Financial	Bank

Table 5.5 Allentown, most prominent individuals (betweenness centrality), 2000

Name	Score	Title, organization	Organization description
Hecht, W. F.	5.827	President, PP&L	Utility
Dowd, J. M.	5.147	Northampton County	Government
Wagner, H. A.	4.728	Chairman, Agere (and former CEO, Air Products)	Manufacturer, electronics
Gigou, M.	3.884	CEO, Mack Trucks	Manufacturer, trucks
Fainor, S. V.	3.245	President, First Colony Group	Bank
Cunningham, D.	3.171	Mayor, Bethlehem	Government
Snyder, D.	3.098	President, Lehigh County Comm. College	Education, community college
Williams, J.	2.570	President, LV American Lung Assn.	Civic organization, health
Butz, L. A.	2.284	CEO, Alvin Butz Inc.	Construction
Ervin, J.	2.206	County Executive, Lehigh County	Government
McMakin, J.	2.047	President, Air Products	Manufacturer, industrial gases
Daday, R.	2.038	Embassy Bank	Bank
Balog, I.	1.912	Partner, Parente, Randolph & Assoc.	Business service, accountant
Gadomski, R. E.	1.767	Exec. VP, Air Products	Manufacturer, industrial gases
Gates, E.	1.748	Embassy Bank	Bank
McHale, P.	1.742	U.S. Congressman	Government
Butz, G.	1.665	President, Alvin Butz Inc.	Construction
Iannelli, T. A.	1.630	President, Chamber of Commerce	Civic organization, business
Dickson, J. T.	1.524	President, Agere	Manufacturer, electronics
Taggart, D.	1.514	Lehigh Valley Econ. Dev. Cmte.	Economic development organization

mayor of Bethlehem and the head of the county in which Allentown it-self is located. In Youngstown none of the region's major politicians are included among the top twenty.

This difference can, in part, be explained by what kinds of organizations have become—or remain—prominent in the two regions. Tables 5.6 and 5.7 show data on the eigenvector centrality of prominent organizations in 1950 and 2000, respectively.[8] In 1950, as we might expect, economic organizations—especially banks and major manufacturers—are prominent in both cities. But the cities diverge by 2000. In Youngstown the organizations at the top of the list in 2000 include a number of cultural and civic organizations. But most are not organizations that have an explicitly economic focus. In contrast, the organizations at the top of the list in Allentown include several industrial corporations that were either created or significantly altered in the 1980s to help turn the region's prospects around in the aftermath of the city's economic crisis. Their centrality scores indicate quantitatively that they enjoy the support and participation of a number of other prominent organizations in the region.

These data are significant because they speak directly to the central argument of this book. For much of American history (certainly though the 1950s), economic and civic interests largely overlapped, and the "growth coalitions" that governed them included (and indeed were led by) key economic leaders of industrial manufacturers and banks. By the turn of the millennium, the world had changed significantly, and in both places the structure and composition of the elite social structure had changed dramatically but with one key difference: in Allentown economic actors remained part of the scene; in Youngstown they did not. We turn now to why that has mattered to the cities' postindustrial economic trajectories.

Three Drivers of Postindustrial Economic Development

As the collapse of America's industrial economy came into focus, commentators and academics coined any number of phrases to capture the nature of the economy that has emerged in its stead. The prevailing narrative about the transformation of the American economy has held that the industrial economy has been replaced by the arrival of the "knowledge economy." Workers have been instructed that succeeding in today's economy requires high levels of education and the ability to adjust in the face of rapidly changing technological and economic demand. Small and

Table 5.6 Most prominent organizations, Allentown and Youngstown, 1950

	Allentown			Youngstown		
Rank	Organization	Score	Description	Organization	Score	Description
1	Allentown Hospital	39.573	Hospital	Greater Youngstown Area Foundation	58.534	Civic organization
2	Muhlenberg College	21.655	Educational, university	Youngstown Chamber of Commerce	52.364	Civic organization, business
3	Community Chest	19.597	Civic organization	Union National Bank	36.635	Bank
4	Allentown Natl. Bank	17.064	Bank	Junior Achievement	35.37	Civic organization
5	PP&L	16.319	Utility	Youngstown Hospital	31.193	Civic organization, health
6	Historic Bethlehem	16.090	Civic organization	Youngstown Hospital	30.578	Hospital
7	Citizen's Urban Renewal	15.338	Civic organization	Economic and Business Foundation	28.594	Civic organization
8	Bethlehem Natl. Bank	15.337	Bank	Youngstown State Univ.	28.419	Education, university
9	Bethlehem Steel	15.257	Manufacturer, steel	Red Cross, Mahoning	27.506	Civic organization
10	Lehigh Coal & Navigation	14.882	Transportation	Youngstown Sheet & Tube	26.476	Manufacturer, steel
11	Lehigh University	12.649	Educational, university	Youngstown Heart Assn.	26.443	Civic organization
12	Merchants Natl. Bank	11.004	Bank	Bessemer Lime. & Cement	25.792	Manufacturer, cement

	Bethlehem			Youngstown		
13	Bethlehem Chamber	10.839	Civic organization, business	Youngstown Sesquicentennial	24.642	Civic organization
14	Girls Clubs of Bethlehem	9.780	Civic organization	Red Cross, Trumbull	23.945	Civic organization
15	Allentown-Beth Gas	9.156	Utility	Youngstown Metro Area Development Corp.	23.89	Civic organization, business
16	Lehigh Valley Trust	9.069	Bank	Christ Mission	23.686	Civic organization, charity
17	Bethlehem Library	8.809	Civic organization	Library Board of Trustees	22.431	Civic organization
18	Lehigh Valley Transit	7.313	Transportation	Citizens' Council	21.638	Civic organization
19	First Natl. Bank	7.258	Bank	Mahoning National Bank	21.494	Bank
20	Air Products	7.229	Manufacturer, gases	Butler Institute	20.328	Civic organization, arts

Table 5.7 Most prominent organizations, Allentown and Youngstown, 2000

	Allentown			Youngstown		
Rank	Organization	Score	Description	Organization	Score	Description
1	Minsi Trails (Boy Scouts)	4.8	Civic organization	Youngstown-Warren Chamber	5.933	Civic organization, business
2	Lehigh Valley Partnership	4.755	Civic organization, business	Youngstown Incubator	4.36	Civic organization, business
3	Minsi Trails Advisory Board	4.433	Civic organization	Butler Institute	3.729	Civic organization, arts
4	Musikfest	2.678	Civic organization, arts	First Place Financial Directors	3.32	Bank
5	Lehigh Valley Planning	2.676	Government	Trumbull Red Cross	2.562	Civic organization
6	DeSales University	2.373	Education, university	Youngstown United Way	2.323	Civic organization
7	Ben Franklin Partnership	2.195	Civic organization, business	Western Reserve Council (Boy Scouts)	2.067	Civic organization
8	Lehigh Valley Chamber of Commerce	2.093	Civic organization, business	Kent State, Trumbull	1.98	Education, university
9	Lehigh Valley Comm. Foundation	1.966	Civic organization	Eastgate Economic Dev.	1.934	Government
10	Air Products & Chemicals	1.775	Manufacturer, gases	Second Bankcorp	1.563	Bank

11	Northampton Comm. College	1.631	Education, university	Kent State, Trumbull Emeriti	1.52	Education, university
12	Lehigh Valley Economic Development	1.607	Government	MV Economic Development	1.512	Government
13	Bethlehem, City of	1.273	Government	Health Valley Alliance	1.48	Hospital
14	Northampton County	1.25	Government	Youngstown Symphony	1.324	Civic organization, arts
15	Mack Trucks	1.242	Manufacturer, trucks	Youngstown Area Heart Assn.	1.095	Civic organization
16	Keystone Bank	0.733	Bank	Kent State Trumbull Advisory	0.978	Education, university
17	Allentown Art Museum	0.719	Civic organization, arts	Com. Foundation of the MV	0.97	Civic organization
18	Allentown Symphony	0.701	Civic organization, arts	United Way Com. Investment	0.917	Civic organization
19	Good Shepherd Hospital	0.651	Hospital	Fine Arts Council of Trumbull	0.886	Civic organization, arts
20	TeenWorks	0.633	Civic organization	Commercial Shearing	0.854	Manufacturer, equipment

medium-sized companies have also heard, time and again, that the key to surviving in the global economy is to upgrade their capabilities. It is no longer possible simply to provide needed goods and services; companies must have the capacity to innovate and the ability to branch into new markets at home and around the globe. Old, hierarchical ways of organizing workers into companies and companies into industries have been washed away in favor of the second-most prominent descriptor of postindustrial America: the "network economy." Workers no longer expect to proceed up career ladders inside companies; rather they move from company to company, project to project, over time acquiring skills and relationships. Companies are no longer embedded simply in customer-supplier relationships, but rather within business ecosystems in which collaborators may also be competitors as well as customers and "complementors."

Many workers and companies have suffered in the last thirty years for failing to heed these warnings and have suffered under the weight of globalization. But it is also a remarkable—and underappreciated—fact that the American economy (and the rust-belt's economy in particular) has made the transition from industrial modes of production and into the knowledge and network economy with notable success. Companies that have survived to this point in history bear little resemblance to their counterparts a quarter century ago. They are leaner, more efficient, and more innovative. And the production systems in which they are embedded are vastly more challenging, demanding, and complicated.[9] The workforce has shifted as well. In 1960 only 36 percent of the most skilled workers employed in manufacturing—foremen and craftsmen—had high school degrees, and just 8 percent had some college. Today 64 percent of the workers in the lowest-skills manufacturing-related occupations have at least a high school diploma, and 24 percent have at least some postsecondary education.[10]

What these data—and my own observation of the transformation of rust-belt economies—suggest is the reason some manufacturing-based communities have successfully adjusted to a postindustrial world is not a matter of whether their workers and organizations have made the necessary changes. Economic adjustment has occurred everywhere. The question is rather whether workers—and perhaps more important, the companies they work for—have adjusted in ways that build up the community or tear it down.

To gain further insight into that question, the remainder of this chapter focuses on the organizational side of the question. Three primary drivers of economic change in rust-belt regions can be identified: first, the transformation of companies that were born during these cities' industrial era, but have had to learn to compete in the global-knowledge-network economy; second, the crop of new, entrepreneurial companies that have emerged endogenously within communities since that transition began; and finally, companies that have sought to invest in the rust belt. Comparing similar companies in each category offers insights into how the differences in the evolution of local leadership networks discussed in the first part of this chapter have shaped these drivers and their impact on local economic development.

The Transformation of Existing Firms

In 1946 scientists at AT&T's Bell Laboratories in Murray Hill, New Jersey, invented the transistor. Two years later a sites committee of another of AT&T's subsidiaries, Western Electric, looked for a place to put the promising invention into production. They chose Allentown from a field of ninety locations. Located sixty miles west of Bell Labs, Allentown had good proximity, but what won over the selection committee was the abundance of disciplined female assembly workers who had recently lost work following the closure of several of the city's silk and hosiery mills after the war. Building transistors was done by hand and required nimble fingers and patience; the powers that be at Western Electric concluded that Allentown would provide them with an abundant supply of appropriately skilled labor. The plant was built in 1948 to make electronic tubes. But in 1951 the facility was retooled to become the first transistor manufacturing facility in the world.[11]

Over the course of the next thirty years, Western Electric's Allentown plant and its sister plant in Reading, Pennsylvania, garnered reputations for being particularly adept at taking on new innovations quickly and effectively. The reason, according to an extensive study of the facility's history by Stuart W. Leslie, can be traced back to the philosophy of Bell Labs President Mervin Kelley.[12] Kelley felt that the key to introducing new cutting-edge products was to locate production and research engineers on site and to integrate them into the workings of the shop floor. To encourage contact between engineers and production workers, the company set up classes—taught by production engineers—that provided workers with a sophisticated understanding of the processes on which they were working. Moreover, the company maintained a policy of manufacturing the sophisticated machines and tools in house, building up from scratch. The policy was not efficient—indeed, competitors quickly gained cost advantage over AT&T both by copying and improving on processes developed at the facility, then by outsourcing much of the production. Nevertheless, as new innovations were introduced—silicon was first introduced into making transistors in Allentown in 1955, satellite communications components in 1960, photonic components in the 1970s—close contact between scientists, production engineers, and production workers allowed the plant to reconfigure production lines at pace with rapidly evolving technology. This flexibility, it is worth noting, could only have been achieved with the buy-in and support of the plant's union, Local 717 of the International Brotherhood of Electrical Workers, which had organized the plant in 1949.

The pace of change quickened in the 1970s. In 1971 AT&T ranked among the top five semiconductor manufacturers in the United States, with Allentown as headquarters of AT&T's microelectronics business. Its entire production line was destined for only one customer: Ma Bell. The company gradually lost market share as production of integrated circuits shifted to Silicon Valley and Japanese firms, which had developed specialized infrastructures (both physical and knowledge based) to support this industry.[13] Layoffs at the Allentown facility in the late 1970s and early 1980s only added to the economic troubles of the Lehigh Valley. By the time of AT&T's divesture of Lucent Technologies (which took possession of the Allentown facilities at that point), the Allentown labs employed just 639 workers from a high of nearly 4,000 in 1951.

In 1988, however, Lucent completed a new facility—the Solid State Technology Center (SSTC)—in the Allentown suburb of Breiningsville, which was given the task of designing and building the company's long-haul photonics business. Envisioned as an advanced development laboratory, the SSTC quickly grew into a full-fledged manufacturing facility with 2,300 workers, about half of them in research and engineering, the other half in manufacturing and production. The telecommunications boom of the mid-1990s led to explosive growth. By 1999 the microelectronics group of the SSTC had $3 billion in revenues and began construction of both a new headquarters and an expansion of its production facilities. This led to another divestiture in 2001, this time spinning the microelectronics group into a separate company with its headquarters in Allentown. Shares of the new company, called Agere Systems, went on the block just as the telecommunications bubble was bursting. Even so, the sale raised a "disappointing" initial public offering of $3.6 billion (among the largest IPOs of that difficult year). Interestingly, however, even as the company began to shrink in the face of broad declines in the telecommunications sector, the company shrank *into* Allentown, closing facilities in New Jersey and moving that production to the Lehigh Valley.[14] By then, a billboard had been placed on Route 22—the main thoroughfare of the Lehigh Valley—that read "Move Over Silicon Valley. Here Comes Lehigh Valley."

The series of transformations that resulted in Western Electric's Allentown Works eventually becoming Agere Systems shares several parallels with the transformation of Youngstown's most advanced electronics manufacturer: Packard Electric. Founded in 1890 in Warren, Ohio, by William and James Packard as the sister company to the Packard Automobile Company, Packard Electric was eventually acquired by General Motors in 1932. As with Western Electric in Allentown, its entire production of cable wire harnesses was directed toward just one customer: GM. Also like Western Electric, its main product went through several generations of technological change, gaining in sophistication and complexity over time. However, unlike Allentown, where each generation of new technologies built on the ingrained capabilities of the workforce and the flexibility of the production system, at Packard Electric the introduction of new technologies has resulted at each step in more and more of the work moving out of the region.

Labor relations at Packard Electric were famously contentious. Collective bargaining agreements in the 1950s stipulated that no more than twenty-two workers could speak to one another at the same time, and lunch time was limited to twenty minutes, with two tables and chairs provided.[15] Yet employment grew quickly as General Motors cars began requiring more and more electronics. By 1960 the division employed 13,500 workers, and between 1962 and 1973, 1,000 workers joined the rolls each year. As has been documented by a number of researchers, including Arturo A. Lara Rivero, who conducted an extensive examination,[16] the core product of the Packard Electric division evolved significantly over the decades. Initially concerned simply with providing power to the dashboard, ignition, and lighting systems of vehicles, by the 1970s the sophistication of electrical systems in automobiles had grown exponentially. In particular, information processing was being integrated into the systems beginning with computer-controlled fuel injection systems replacing carburetors and automatic transmission systems overtaking manual shifting, requiring further integration of microelectronics. The number of electrical wire harnesses in each GM vehicle had increased from three to twelve as a result.

The innovations driving this evolution came from Packard Electric's research facilities, which are located near the firm's headquarters in Warren. However, unlike Western Electric in Allentown, research and production were not integrated at Packard. Nick Border, former president of Packard Electric's largest union, the International Union of Electrical Workers (IUE) Local 717, put it this way:

> Our job was to make a quality product with as few rejects as possible. . . . We have never been close to [production engineers] and never had a desire to. I can't tell you what's coming out of there. Upper management would share it with us and we'd pass it around and we'd say great . . . fit that into any car in any assembly in the world. High speed presses: that's the way we would share stuff. But we never worked with the engineers closely. They would come out on the floor, and they might try something and see if it would work or not. They were close-jawed. Because of competitors. We've had people leave management and open a small shop. Those are competitors. If we knew something and it hadn't been patented, I could go and get ten thousand dollars for it.

In addition to the lack of interaction between production and engineering workers, Packard Electric also represented a major bottleneck in the company's supply chain as the sole supplier of GM's electrical systems. Strikes in the late 1960s and early 1970s proved that workers at Packard were aware of the bargaining power that position provided them. In part to counter this, General Motors announced in 1973 its intention to open a new production facility to be located in Alabama, a nonunion "right- to-work" state. Another blow to the local workforce came in 1978 with the announcement that a major new facility was to be built in Ciudad Juárez, Mexico, just across the U.S. border at El Paso, Texas. Packard's presence in Mexico increased steadily after that. Of the twenty-two plants built by Packard Electric between 1978 and 1994, twelve were located south of the border. Today it is the largest foreign employer in Mexico, employing nearly forty-five thousand workers in the country in 2003.

Divisions between production workers and engineers grew wider, particularly as the bargaining position of the union grew weaker over time. A low point came in 1984 when workers at Packard accepted a two-tier wage system in which incoming workers were paid on a separate pay scale, with a substantially lower rate of pay than veterans, in exchange for lifetime job guarantees for current employees. However, a possibly more telling contrast between the divergent evolutionary paths of Packard and Western Electric came in 1995 with the announcement that

Packard—by then part of GM's Delphi Division—would build a new technical center for research and development. Rather than construct the showcase facility nearby, as was the case in Allentown, Delphi management decided to locate it in Ciudad Juárez, Mexico, making it the first foreign-owned and -operated research and development facility in that country. The company's expressed purpose in doing so was to *better integrate engineering and production* processes in the company, a goal it felt it could not achieve at its existing research and development facilities in Ohio. In 1999 Delphi spun off of General Motors, and since then Packard Electric has moved aggressively into higher-technology areas of expertise. However, despite maintaining its headquarters in Warren, its manufacturing presence has continued to diminish.

Similarly contrasting stories could be told for other large companies in the two regions. Air Products and Chemicals and Pennsylvania Power and Light are both large companies headquartered in the Lehigh Valley that successfully transformed their operations in the 1980s and 1990s. Like Agere, they have largely done so without undermining the viability of the community in which they reside. Even the one major exception— Mack Trucks—seems to have proved the rule. Along with Bethlehem Steel, Mack Trucks had been a cornerstone of the local economy since the Mack brothers moved their company from Brooklyn, New York, to Allentown in 1901. But by the 1980s, it was in trouble and entered into a period of heightened tension with its unions and disaffection with the community following its sale first to Renault and then Volvo. In 1987 it announced it was moving its operations in the Lehigh Valley to South Carolina. A major battle with the United Auto Workers ensued; the union mounted and won a rigorous challenge to organize the plant. Production was eventually cut back in South Carolina and moved back into Allentown, where the company remained headquartered.

In Youngstown the region's other remaining major manufacturers— including the General Motors fabrication and assembly divisions at Lordstown—have shared a similarly rocky history of labor relations. Most recently the Lordstown facility has been able to improve its productivity markedly and was rewarded with an announcement in 2002 that the facility would be retooled to produce a new line of GM cars. However, these successes have been predicated on threats to relocate (both grounded in reality and also beyond the control of local plant leadership). The bottom line: although large manufacturers have been transforming themselves to compete on a global stage over this period of time, in Allentown they have done so in ways that have not necessarily undermined the community and, in some cases, even helped build it up. The same cannot be said for the ways in which major companies in Youngstown have transformed.

Entrepreneurship

As we saw in the example of Sovereign Circuits and IQE, entrepreneurial companies have been a factor in the changing economic climate of both cities. A few numbers were provided earlier that give some indication of relative magnitudes between the two places. A more detailed look suggests some significant differences. For instance, data on the number of companies that either received an SBIR/STTR award,[17] venture-equity-related venture-capital funding or both in the last twenty-five years suggests some (predictable) trends. First, there are more of them in Allentown (forty-one companies) than Youngstown (sixteen). Moreover, looking over the products and services these companies provide, it is also clear that many of Allentown's startups are in the areas of electronics and biomedicine, which have experienced high growth rates in recent years, while almost none of the startups in Youngstown fall into these categories (with the exception of Sovereign Circuits). Finally, a significant number of Allentown's startups have benefited from locally headquartered financiers, whereas almost none—again, the exception is Sovereign Circuits—in Youngstown have.

Orasure Inc., like IQE, is another prominent entrepreneurial company in the Lehigh Valley. Founded just a year prior to IQE in 1987 (in fact, the two companies shared space at Ben Franklin's new company incubator until they eventually became neighbors in the Bethlehem Technology Center created from one of Bethlehem Steel's former mills), Orasure's first product was a balm that soothed sunburns. But over time it opportunistically pursued a wide range of commercial opportunities before finally finding success with a diagnostic kit used to test drug abuse orally. This gave way to an oral HIV test, which was later approved by the U.S. Food and Drug Administration for wide use, along with a major contract from the U.S. government.

Mike Gausling, one of Orasure's founders and the chairman of its board of directors, came to Allentown with his partners from St. Louis. They were attracted to the Lehigh Valley after one of Gausling's colleagues noticed an advertisement in the Lehigh University alumni magazine announcing the establishment of the Ben Franklin Partnership's center. The three made the move to the Lehigh Valley to take advantage of the very favorable conditions for leasing space in the incubator and the promise of a significant amount of help and assistance from the center. Orasure became an enthusiastic participant. Indeed, Mark Lang, Ben Franklin's director at the time, reported that he "loved to send students to Orasure . . . at Orasure, they were part of the whole team." Gausling, for his part, embraced the philosophy of the program and has since become an active part of the region's economic development efforts. He described his company's success as partly due to a group of men and women he referred to as "rainmakers"—a group of local businessmen, some affiliated with the Ben Franklin program— who acted as mentors and facilitators. Gausling suggested that there was something of a hierarchy to local entrepreneurship networks, with the first tier being occupied by the people who were initially responsible for putting together the Lehigh Valley Industrial Parks in the 1960s, who remain active in local affairs. "Walter Dealtrey is a legend around here for creating all of this. He should take a lot of credit. He has played a real leadership role."[18] In the second tier, Gausling identified several local business leaders who had done well in business and are now poised to play central roles in local entrepreneurship networks. Those leaders include Scott Fainor, the president of a small local bank in the region. Gausling conceded that his personal goal was to one day become a rainmaker himself. He takes pride in the role his company is playing in the region as an example of its postindustrial success.

As the examples of IQE and Orasure suggest, the Ben Franklin Partnership has played a pivotal role in developing the region's entrepreneurial infrastructure. Ironically, the Ben Franklin program was initially intended to help develop networks among existing—"old economy"— companies, mainly the region's dying textile and metals manufacturing industries. Building on the concept of "flexible specialization,"[19] the goal was to help these companies build networks among firms that would make them more productive and, potentially, more innovative. Quickly though, the program's goals shifted toward technology-based entrepreneurship, particularly as its relationship with Lehigh University became better articulated. The incubator has graduated forty companies since 1983, which (according to data collected by Ben Franklin) create more than 2,400 jobs annually and a total of $560 million in revenues as of 2008.

Mark Lang—who led the local Ben Franklin affiliate—described his role:

> We set the tone. Like an ombudsman. Helped the companies to under-
> stand; not like consultants but also, not totally hands off. Help them [en-
> trepreneurs and university professors] understand each other and don't let
> them get disconnected . . . Overall, my job was to bridge and provide
> leadership. What kept us alive was that companies talked to legislators
> and informally—genuinely—said that Ben Franklin was the key.

When Ben Franklin was founded, local leaders established a sister organization, which is known today as the Mid-Atlantic Venture Partners. A locally headquartered venture-capital firm, the concern's early
investors included many of Allentown's most prominent high-net-worth
individuals as well as several of the region's most prominent companies,
including PP&L, Air Products and Chemicals, and Bethlehem Steel.
The scope of Mid-Atlantic's investment activity was initially limited to
companies in northeast Pennsylvania. Several local firms that have become successful were among its early investments. But the group
quickly brought in experienced venture investors who pushed to expand beyond those local boundaries, arguing that the fund's health and
ability to fulfill its mission depended on finding a more stable deal flow
than could be found by remaining strictly local. By 1985 it had taken
the $11 million raised by local financiers and turned it into $100 million, the best return of any venture-capitalist group that year.

Ben Franklin—in cooperation with Lehigh University, Mid-Atlantic
Partners, and other local organizations that took on the task of formulating a more deliberate approach to generating entrepreneurship in
the early 1980s—has been widely touted as a success story and de-
servedly so. But it is both interesting and important to note that much
of the most recent entrepreneurial activity in the Lehigh Valley has had
very little to do with this infrastructure until recently. In the late 1990s
with the telecommunications boom in full swing, Kal Shastri, a scien-
tist at Lucent's Solid State Technology Center, started AANetcom Inc.
The company, which makes high-speed semiconductors, was quickly
sold to a California-based firm for $1.3 billion. Its success spurred a
wave of other startups populated by former Lucent scientists, including
Cenix, T-Networks, and Akrion. For the most part, these companies
have operated outside of the entrepreneurial infrastructure that had
emerged in the Lehigh Valley, finding most of their funding and customer base elsewhere. This is not to say, however, that the companies

are disconnected. Rather, since they all emerged out of Lucent or Agere, the leaders of these companies all generally know each other and are in regular contact about the general issues associated with technology-based startups.

As Aaron Fischer, the CEO of optoelectronics startup T-Networks, put it:

> There is a community of entrepreneurs. They came out of Agere and so that's the source of a network. They interact, talk about how things are going. It's a benefit of this area that there are eight or nine startups. A couple could end up customers. It's a smaller pond, but there's value in that.

The availability of these local networks has helped to secure these companies' presence in the Lehigh Valley. Rather than set up shop in more prominent centers of technology-based activity, such as Silicon Valley or the Route 128 area around Boston, these companies have, for the most part, brought both investment and know-how *into* the Lehigh Valley. Very recently the telecommunications sector's precipitous decline since 2001 has encouraged these companies to reach out and tap into the preexisting local entrepreneurial infrastructure as they have been forced to abruptly shift gears, moving away from the highest possible performance and toward cost efficiency. In attempting to make this shift, local microelectronics startups have begun to rely more on the resources available at Lehigh University and Ben Franklin. In 2003 a new center was established at Lehigh dedicated to boosting the competitive standing of local optoelectronics startups.

The most prominent examples of entrepreneurial "success stories" in the Mahoning Valley are a far cry from the uplifting stories that emerge from IQE, Orasure and, latterly, Cenix. There have been many fewer companies in Youngstown with the potential for significant growth over the same period of time. Yet there have been *some.* The most prominent—and the most deeply disappointing—of these was the Phar-Mor Corporation. In 1982 Phar-Mor's founders, Mickey Monus and David Shapira, set out to build a chain of pharmacies that offered deep discounts to customers by buying in bulk and driving hard bargains with suppliers. By 1990 the company had three hundred stores nationwide and reported annual sales of over $3 billion. But perhaps just as important as the company's commercial success was the role that the company and its president came to play in the community. Phar-Mor renovated what had been an abandoned office in a largely deserted area of downtown Youngstown in a deliberate attempt to set itself up as a beacon for the city's postindustrial future. Mickey Monus wanted to follow in the footsteps of his own local role model, real estate developer Edward J. DeBartolo, by investing much of the profits from his company in building sports franchises, including a semiprofessional World Basketball League team in Youngstown, as well as the Colorado Rockies baseball franchise, in which he purchased a partial stake.

Monus was lauded as one of the city's postindustrial heroes. But the acclaim ended abruptly in August of 1992, when it was revealed that Monus had embezzled up to $10 million from Phar-Mor—most of it in order to subsidize his money-losing basketball team—while also overstating the assets of the company by $350 million. In a pattern that was repeated around the country in years to come, Monus was exposed as a fraud, and his company quickly descended into bankruptcy before finally being dismantled in 2003. Like subsequent cases (Adelphia Cable and even Enron come to mind), the ironic cruelty of Phar-Mor was that Monus had gotten into trouble by trying to maintain the overly exalted standing he had achieved within his down-and-out home community. Youngstown residents had in many ways tied the narrative of their city's transformations to the blazing success of his company. Monus apparently felt compelled to meet their inflated expectations to the point of committing egregious acts of fraud.

Phar-Mor may be taken as an extreme example, but its impact within the community is undeniable; it undermined a significant amount of hope that had emerged for an economic turnaround. Beyond Phar-Mor, only two other companies—an aluminum extrusion company called Easco and Sovereign Circuits—have emerged with significant growth potential from the region in the last twenty years, and both of those companies maintain low profiles within the community as a whole.

Yet the dearth of entrepreneurial success stories in the region was not for lack of opportunity. In 1984 Ohio enacted the Thomas Edison program. Based in many respects directly on Pennsylvania's Ben Franklin initiative, Edison directed funds through local universities to encourage ties to local industry with the goal of spurring entrepreneurship. Centers were located in several other of Ohio's smaller cities, including Akron, Toledo, and Dayton. But Youngstown did not receive funds through the program until 1998, when the Youngstown Business Incubator was established. The incubator secured enough financing to renovate an abandoned building in the downtown area and install a highly sophisticated communications infrastructure. Of its nine resident companies, most are software businesses attracted to the area from universities in Cleveland and Pittsburgh by the extremely favorable rental terms and support services offered. Very recently the facility has begun producing results with the spin-off of two successful companies in 2003. But despite the promise of success, the Youngstown Business Incubator has struggled to find friends in the community. In 2002 Youngstown's mayor, whose office is merely blocks from the facility, had not yet set foot in it, and there was no formal relationship with the local partner one might expect to have been its closest ally, Youngstown State University. Jim Coessler, the incubator's president and CEO, expressed frustration:

> It's not the funds, it's the leadership. What we have now are companies that aren't based here. Generally the communities that benefit are the ones where the CEO parks his butt. We just don't. The community isn't behind the incubator, and I am at a loss to know why. We are the one with the least community support.

More recently, the incubator has seen more success, but it has climbed a steeper road to that point than its counterparts in Ohio and certainly when compared to its counterpart in Allentown.

Inward Investment

Clearly, the economic development emphasis in Youngstown has not hinged on indigenous capabilities. Instead it has been directed toward attracting investment from outside. The outcomes of these efforts have not only been disappointing, they have in many ways put the region in a worse position than it began.

Regional governmental leaders came up with a number of innovative ways of attracting investment. Among the difficulties they found themselves confronting was the fact that anyone willing to redevelop land once associated with the city's former steel mills would be saddled with the costs of environmental cleanup. The City of Youngstown began buying polluted land, cleaning it at taxpayer expense, and then offering it for free to willing buyers along with a ten-year tax abatement and a promise to cover the costs of any lingering environmental problems. Yet investors failed to materialize.

Beyond the extensive—and according to many, protracted—efforts to save the region's existing steel infrastructure, early economic development efforts in the region focused on attracting another large employer to the region. In the late 1980s, for instance, Youngstown made a concerted and highly publicized effort to attract the Saturn manufacturing facilities that were eventually located in Spring Hill, Tennessee, by forming a " 'We Want Saturn" committee, which flew the boxer Harry Arroyo (a Youngstown native) to Detroit to help make the region's case.[20] A later scheme focused on attracting a Russian dirigible manufacturing operation to locate near the regional airport. Yet despite these and other efforts—nearly the entire metropolitan area has been designated an enterprise zone, which provides tax breaks and incentives for investment— such efforts have almost universally fallen short. The exception, again, proved the rule in Youngstown. In 1987 Youngstown real estate developer J. J. Cafaro acquired the rights to the Avanti, a fabled luxury coupe automobile originally built by the Studebaker Company in South Bend, Indiana. Setting up a small production line in Youngstown, Cafaro's plan was to build several hundred of the fifty-thousand-dollar vehicles by hand, modifying premade Chevrolet Monte Carlo chassis and using nonunion labor. More than twelve thousand people applied for the 165 openings at the plant. But the venture quickly went sour as it ran into production delays. Cafaro eventually sold his share in the company, and the new owners moved production to Georgia.

Having met so much frustration in their efforts to attract large-scale manufacturing to the city, Youngstown leaders honed their economic development efforts in the 1990s to focus on two areas that were seen as being more realistically within the region's reach. In a strategy that became common among economically depressed regions of the Midwest in the 1990s, the Youngstown area became home to a large number of telemarketing call centers. These centers, in many ways the ugly underbelly of the telecommunications boom, employ large numbers of often marginally skilled workers under highly stressful conditions. Later still, the city struck on the idea of building and attracting prisons as a means of generating employment. By 1999 Youngstown was home to four new prisons and four thousand inmates. This quickly turned against the city's designs when a private $65 million "supermax" prison, built to house inmates shipped in from crowded jails in Washington, D.C., suffered a series of violent clashes, resulting in two deaths and an escape. A court eventually ruled that the facility's great distance from Washington imposed too great a burden on families wishing to visit their relatives, and the facility was mothballed.

If you ask Allentown leaders what has been most responsible for the region's economic turnaround in recent years, they generally do not cite the transformation of large companies or entrepreneurship but rather the success the region has enjoyed in attracting companies to the multiplying industrial parks that now surround the region's urban core. Much of this investment has been in light manufacturing. However, a not-insignificant portion is associated with a concentration of Wall Street financial companies that have located back office operations in the region. One of the most prominent of these is Dun and Bradstreet, which has a data collection and analysis office employing four hundred people located in Bethlehem Steel's former headquarters building.

A great deal of the credit for this is given to the coordination of economic development activities across municipalities. As Romo and Schwartz (1995) showed, most external investment is actually not large-scale manufacturing. Most is generated by smaller companies that move, generally, within the same state in search of better real estate terms. Municipalities—even within the same geographic area—often wage debilitating battles with each other over the rights to attract a potential employer. Such battles have been a drag on economic development efforts in Youngstown and the Mahoning Valley. Indeed, battles over proceeds associated with the development of an industrial park near the city's airport, which was owned and operated by the city of Youngstown but located in Trumbull County closer to Warren, resulted in a quagmire until the mid-1990s, when a deal between the various municipal actors could be reached. As effort was then made to position the Youngstown-Warren Regional Airport as a cargo-handling hub. However, rather than attracting an outside investor into the region, the opening of this industrial park resulted in one of downtown Youngstown's few remaining operations—a Timken roller-bearing manufacturer—to set up shop on the newly developed land; this produced a round of outcries. In Allentown, on the other hand, the precedent was set by the original Lehigh Valley Industrial Park in the 1950s, which was located in such a way as to straddle the regions' two major counties, who agreed to a revenue-sharing settlement. Since then the consolidation of economic development agencies throughout the region into one large organization—the Lehigh Valley Economic Development Corporation—has allowed for coordination in attracting investment across municipalities, which has quelled a good deal of interregional squabbling.

The Puzzle Revisited

Allentown consistently outperforms Youngstown on each of the three drivers of economic change. Large companies in both cities have transformed to become globally competitive, but in Allentown they have largely done so in ways that have built the community rather than tear it down. Entrepreneurial companies have emerged in both places, but in Allentown those companies have brought know-how and investment to the region rather than exploiting the resources and good will of the community solely for personal gain. Finally, both places have attracted outside investment, but Allentown has done so without engaging in a debilitating race to the bottom as local communities compete with each other for investment dollars. The prosperity of Youngstown remains closely tied to the fortunes of a few very large employers, putting the community in a weak bargaining position and keeping the community essentially hostage to the demands of large employers. The former general manager of GM–Lordstown, Maureen Midgley, put it this way: "Whenever I sneeze, ten people put their houses up for sale." Youngstown is so desperate for homegrown success stories that the community has latched onto a few high-profile businessmen but lacks visions for how to convert those business's successes into gains for the community. Internal quarrels within the highly fragmented community—between labor and management, ethnic and racial communities, and cities and suburbs—have served as impediments to developing and implementing an effective strategy for turning the region's economy around.

Again and again, informants in the two cities, when asked what might explain the differences, came around to the notion of leadership. Dean Licata and Jim Coessler were not the only ones in Youngstown to question where all the community's leaders had gone. When Ohio's governor appointed Julie Michaels as his liaison to the region, she found the lack of local leadership so troubling that she set identifying potential leaders and developing ways of cultivating their participation in regional affairs as one of her first priorities. Herman Maas—another former general manager at GM–Lordstown—echoed the sentiment: "We have a lot of great companies, small businessmen too. They play roles in their little circles. But no one is bringing them together. They work in their own little towns. No one looks at the valley." On the other hand, more than one informant in the Lehigh Valley cited a culture of leadership and participation—not just among government and civic leaders, but among CEOs, university presidents, and union leaders—as reasons for that region's successes. As Joe Daddona, who was mayor of Allentown at the height of its economic turmoil, put it:

> We still have strong corporate citizens. What we have is a strong corporate civic community. The corporate community is involved. The Lehigh Valley Chamber of Commerce, the Downtown Authority, the Lehigh Valley Partnership . . . They provide leadership and support for the city. The Liberty

Bells, the Brothers of the Brush, Kiwanis, Sartoma Club . . . these organizations help to fill the gaps. Partnerships were formed to take advantage of government and private investments, to be able to concentrate in those new areas of services and communications which were growing at the time.

It is commonplace to hear that companies have turned their backs on communities with which they had long been identified. Yet it seems that economic leaders remain engaged in the community in Allentown. Given the findings of the earlier chapters about the important role that local leadership networks have played in the regions' histories and the evolution of those networks over time, these comments raise a number of intriguing questions: How have local leadership networks changed in recent decades? What explains the evolution of these networks? Do those changes help us to understand why outcomes in Allentown have been consistently better than in Youngstown in the last twenty-five years?

Organizational Change and the Evolution of Interorganizational Networks

Two salient facts have been established so far in this chapter. First, the cities' economies faced similar challenges in the late twentieth and early twenty-first centuries. However, the performance of organizations in the two communities in the face of those challenges was very different. Second, the cities' networks have evolved over this period of time, with networks in Allentown becoming more cohesive, retaining the participation of some of the region's most economically important individuals, while Youngstown's networks lack the full participation of these kinds of people. Linking these two facts together requires examining the historical processes that drove the evolution of interorganizational networks in the two regions.

We saw in the previous chapter that the structure of social networks in Allentown prior to and during the competitiveness crisis provided forums in which actors in the region could engage each other to formulate a coherent response; the structure of networks in Youngstown provided fewer such opportunities and, ultimately, a highly fragmented response in the face of the crisis. Those differences were of immediate importance because they determined whether and how the communities were able to take advantage of various policy initiatives available to them, such as the Ben Franklin program. But beyond these direct effects, the processes set in motion during that very critical period had crucial—and largely unintended—follow-on effects with respect to the evolution of networks in the two communities. Here we can examine what impact those forums had as the community began to assess its postindustrial possibilities.

The crisis undoubtedly represented a critical moment for actors in both valleys; this was a time that upended taken-for-granted assumptions about how to interact and behave within the community, affecting a wide range of actors from the organizations at the center of the crisis all the way down to Parent-Teacher Associations and hospitals. Perhaps the most important single organizational response to emerge from the steel crisis in Allentown was the Lehigh Valley Partnership. Organized in 1985, the partnership was conceived as a forum for the region's remaining corporate executive officers. Burt Deday, an executive at Pennsylvania Power and Light, was one of the original organizers.

> We first got the notion that Bethlehem Steel was really going to cut back. Mack Truck was looking at a place down south in South Carolina. Textile industry was diminishing, and cement, twelve or thirteen cement plants were also going south. We ended up with three or four. So, also at that point in time, you had very prominent provincialism among communities and businesses. The superhero was Bethlehem Steel, but because of their status, they weren't talking to anyone else. My boss was [PP&L CEO] Bob Campbell, and he and I worked closely together. We said we have to do something. All of the chambers of commerce were wrenching their hands, and what we did was we called the CEOs of the thirty-five major players in the Lehigh Valley at a luncheon meeting and told them what we thought was the dilemma. The trend was factual: steel was no longer going to be the most prominent employer. We invited Bob Pease—head of the Alleghany Conference in Pittsburgh, a nonprofit set up in '43 or '44 by [Pennsylvania] Governor Lawrence and the business community, and it was intended to deal with the problems they saw Pittsburgh facing in the future. They were on high ground in '43/'44, but they had vision there. Set up this organization whose goal was to promote economic development and quality of life, and he came in and talked for half an hour to explain the fact that there were problems that were going to occur at a rapid pace in terms of the area's economic future. The value of doing things on a regional basis—getting together—they were homogeneous in all of the issues and problems they were facing. He convinced the group that regionalism was the way to go because you are competing on a minor scale with the three cities in the two counties. Following the meeting—at that meeting—we agreed we should set up an organization to deal with regional issues, which would focus on quality of life and economic potential and growth in the valley.

The partnership set out with one primary goal in mind: regionalization.

What we did immediately, we began to do research on various things. One of them was economic development. There were twenty-eight or thirty organizations doing economic development. Again, none of them were talking to each other. We identified what they were doing. Brought them together and put together a Lehigh Valley Economic Development Council, an informal group where we had a meeting on a regular basis to begin the communications.

By 1995 the Lehigh Valley Economic Development Council had been transformed into the Lehigh Valley Economic Development Corporation, which consolidated economic development efforts within the region. This notion of regional consolidation then became, in many ways, the driving mission of the Lehigh Valley Partnership. Between 1985 and 1995, the organization used its influence within the community to unite many of the region's most important civic organizations. Historically, there were three Red Crosses, two United Ways, three arts councils, two central labor councils of the AFL-CIO, and numerous local chambers of commerce corresponding either to the three major municipalities of the valley (Allentown, Bethlehem, and Easton) or the two counties (Lehigh and Northampton). By 1995 all of these and several other important elements of the civic infrastructure—including its economic development infrastructure—had been coaxed together, with a strong nudge from the partnership, to form a regional unit.

The partnership was conceived of and remains something of an exclusive club restricted to the CEOs of major companies (and, just recently, the presidents of the region's major universities). In some ways this exclusivity came as a reaction to the exclusivity Bethlehem Steel executives had historically maintained within the community—living in a separate community, Saucon Valley, with their own golf club. However, the partnership has not conducted itself in a disconnected way; it has become instead a lightning rod for actors in the region. Members of the partnership bring considerable social capital, which is able to attract the attention of other kinds of regional actors; solicitation for funds of any kind is forbidden at their meetings.

The partnership has reached out to organizations such as the Community Action Committee (CAC) of the Lehigh Valley, founded in the 1964 as an umbrella organization for community activists. Over time it has become something of a peak organization within the valley, including representatives from the Hispanic community, environmentalists, neighborhood activists, and health-care advocates. As this comment from CAC President Alan Jennings makes clear, the realignment of organizational

relationships in Allentown has brought different kinds of actors—
actors who would not necessarily have been in contact—into a meaningful dialogue, which has in many ways shaped organizational strategies.

> The Lehigh Valley Partnership has been pushing regionalism. The business
> community started with regionalism in order not to deal with fifty little
> fiefdoms. The anti-corporate crowd would say that's all about profits. But
> I don't say that. This plan expresses new ways of thinking. Pushing re-
> gional economic development and human capital. More efficient.
> Thinking from a wider view. It is remarkable. But is it progressive? I de-
> fine progressive as "willing to change in a way that is respectful." I wanted
> to push how critical the urban areas of the region are. In 1996 we pro-
> duced a proposal. . . . What I'm doing is developing programs while
> speaking to policy issues programs are trying to address. Our economic
> development agenda has been oriented to community problem solving . . .
> What I'm prepared to do is embrace market approaches. Recognize the
> value of competition. Rules are stacked against poor neighborhoods. When
> capital followed home buyers to the suburbs, we didn't do enough to de-
> velop indigenous commerce. They got it and they funded our space cam-
> paign which locked in money to cities.

As these and other organizational strategies have been enacted, they
have led directly to important shifts in the identities and identifications
of organizations in the valley; how organizations see themselves and
their place within the community has changed, generally in ways that
have tied organizations more closely to the community. The best example of this is Lehigh University. As we saw in Chapter 3, Lehigh University was founded with a very strong connection to the Episcopalian,
ethnically centered agglomeration that included Bethlehem Steel and
the Lehigh Valley Railroad. This connection was strengthened over
time as the university became a primary conduit of managers and engineers to Bethlehem Steel. However, perhaps because of this tight affiliation, its connections to the rest of the community had been somewhat
limited. Like the steel company itself, it was seen as being in the community, but not really *of* it. That changed, however, when the company's
fortunes began to decline as made clear by the university's current president, Gregory C. Farrington:

> The institution was evolving out of a set of relationships to Bethlehem
> Steel. The university was extraordinarily wealthy as a result of its rela-
> tionship to the company. That relationship influenced it in intellectual and
> other aspects. The chair of its board was on our board and vice versa. But
> it was also estranged from the community. We have become more central

in this community since Bethlehem Steel started to decline. I often say that the day Bethlehem Steel started to withdraw from this community was the day this university was liberated. Fortunately, this community had the foresight. It continues to be well-to-do. It's not a rust-belt community in its outlook. It has stability because it has been engaged over the course of its history by several institutions.

The changes that President Farrington refers to range from the seemingly superficial—for example, the university is currently engaged in an effort to refurbish street lights and otherwise beautify its surrounding neighborhood in South Bethlehem—to the economically substantive, including its integral participation in the Ben Franklin Partnership and the Lee Iacocca Institute for International Competitiveness. Both of these programs are part and parcel of the university's attempts to carve out a new niche for itself as a partner to local businesses as signaled by a pronouncement in the early 1990s that it was moving into the "technology transfer business."

The shifts that have taken place at the Lehigh Valley Partnership, the Community Action Coalition, and Lehigh University are important and, in many ways, remarkable. In each case, the crisis of the early 1980s represented a moment of dire uncertainty, which threatened to tear the community apart. But a dialogue emerged in that critical period of the early 1980s, which over time has allowed organizations in the region to redefine themselves and their place within the community. This process of organizational identity redefinition is, more than anything else, responsible for the pulling together of actors and the deep engagement of key individuals within the Lehigh Valley over the last twenty-five years.

It is this same process that has generated the otherwise mysterious alchemy that has produced consistently better outcomes within each of the various drivers of economic change in the region. As organizations have undergone their individual processes of organizational change, they have done so within the broader context of the transformation of local networks in the community. The two processes—organizational change and network evolution—have evolved in tandem iteratively into the overall transformation of the community. Today Allentown has regained coherence as a community of organizations, albeit on a very different model than the one that existed previously.

The significance of this point is driven home in the counterpoint by drawing out the comparison to the way organizational and institutional change unfolded in the Mahoning Valley. As we saw in the previous chapter, when the competitiveness crisis finally erupted, the immediate effect of the collapse of local economic networks was to bring the civic infrastructure down with it. Lacking either a central leadership group or forums within the civic infrastructure where such leadership could emerge, the community fragmented into several camps, which competed for federal and state redevelopment dollars. It did not take long, however, for a group with considerable social capital in the Mahoning Valley to fill the vacuum: the mob moved in. Youngstown had had a strong Mafia presence since at least the 1920s when speakeasies sprung up in many of the community's ethnic working-class neighborhoods. Indeed, the mob's influence grew stronger as the community elite withdrew. One local story suggests that the town of Halls Corners, near Warren, was incorporated specifically so mobsters could install their own law-enforcement officials and avoid prosecution for a group of gambling halls there. By the 1960s mob influence was rampant among local politicians, so much so that a cover story of the *Saturday Evening Post* described the city as "Crimetown USA" following a number of mob-related assassinations that struck the region.

Mark Shutes, a professor of anthropology at Youngstown State, argues that there were actually two competing social structures governing the Mahoning Valley in the mid-twentieth century. The dominant one was the labor-management infrastructure that emerged following the Little Steel Strike of 1937. Its collapse in the late 1970s and early 1980s paved the way for the alternative, mob-centered social structure to emerge full force in the early 1980s. The theory gained credence in the mid-1990s as the FBI began making headway in fighting the Youngstown mob. What has emerged from prosecution testimony in these cases is that the vacuum of leadership that emerged in the collapse of the steel industry created an opening for mob families from Cleveland and Pittsburgh to move in. Ten men were killed between 1978 and 1981 in mob-related violence as the two crime families competed for territory and for the patronage of local politicians—including the popular county sheriff, James Traficant, who refused to foreclose on unemployed steelworkers' houses and was rewarded by being elected the region's U.S. representative in 1984. As a 2000 report in the *New Republic* put it, "the mob which had once competed with the valley's civil society largely *became* its civil society. As late as 1997, in the small city of Campbell, [Genovese family boss Lenny] Strollo controlled at least 90 percent of the appointments to the police department" (Grann 2000:23; emphasis added).

Terry Buss—one of the drivers behind Sovereign Circuits—reported numerous interactions with local Mafia figures. As the former president of Youngstown State University, Leslie Cochran, stated in an Associated Press article after leaving his post in 1997, "campus trustees and public officials often pestered me for hiring favors. We got calls all the time; 'Could you give special consideration for this; could you give this person an interview?' I got leaned on by senators and congressmen and mayors, prominent people, some people who I didn't even know."[21] Without the ability to engage in constructive dialogue, key actors failed to converge in the immediate aftermath of the steel crisis. The lack of a core provided a vacuum for the Mafia to fill. In this environment, it is hardly surprising that the kinds of dialogue and engagement that unfolded in Allentown did not materialize in Youngstown. Consequently, the community was largely held in abeyance until the mid-1990s, when federal officials gathered the strength and the evidence needed to overtake those elements of the community that had become most corrupt. Soon after, the community started—finally—to rebuild its shattered social infrastructure. A movement emerged in the mid-1990s to oust the deeply ingrained—and largely corrupt—Democratic Party machine (one of the last old-style, neighborhood- and precinct-based party machines in the country), installing a reform slate of candidates in 1995. That same year efforts were set in motion to bring the business and labor communities together in ways that resembled the efforts that were begun in the Lehigh Valley ten years earlier. The region's two major chambers of commerce, for instance, merged to form the Youngstown-Warren Regional Chamber, and a new labor-management committee was convened in order to address the region's concerns. The final blow to the destructive postindustrial patterns that emerged in the aftermath of the crisis was the indictment and conviction in 2003 of Congressman James Traficant on racketeering charges. There is guarded hope in the region that it has turned a corner and can begin to mend its broken social and economic infrastructure.

Discussion

This chapter began by discussing the patterns of organizational change in the Lehigh and Mahoning valleys as contributors to the regions' economic divergence. It then presented evidence of the changes that have taken place with respect to the civic and economic networks. This analysis showed that—consistent with much of the literature on globalization and economic restructuring in mature industrial regions—direct economic ties among organizations have almost completely disappeared in both places. Where they differ is in the ways that the social and civic infrastructure incorporates, or fails to incorporate, key leaders back into the community. In Allentown those leaders are deeply intertwined at the nexus of local relationships; in Youngstown they are not. Finally, this chapter has presented an examination of the processes that underlie the evolution of local leadership networks.

In Allentown a dialogue was started in the immediate aftermath of the steel crisis that incorporated a broad spectrum of local economic and civic actors. These actors were undergoing tremendous—and in many cases, traumatic—organizational changes simultaneously. While the opportunity was certainly there for these organizations to turn their backs on the community as they sorted out their own organizational trajectories, they did not. By participating in the collective process of making sense of the problems facing the Lehigh Valley, these organizations' own identities were tied back into that of the valley. The networks we observe in the 2000 are a reflection of this reconfiguration and restoration of relationships within the community. These relationships, in turn, have contributed to shaping the possibilities for prosperity in the region, giving local actors access to needed resources—social, financial, and otherwise—which they have used to rebuild the economic viability of their community.

In Youngstown the lack of a similar dialogue in the immediate aftermath of the steel crisis generated a vacuum of social engagement, one that was almost immediately filled by the opportunism of the Mafia. In an invidious example of Burt's (1992) idea of filling structural holes, the presence of that particular actor at the center of the community's social and economic networks in the 1980s and 1990s helped to ensure that the actors who were already at an arms length when the crisis erupted remained that way. As they engaged in their own organizational change processes, they did so in ways that drew them further afield from the community and, as a result, their organizational identities have become less and less integrated with others in the community and, therefore, with the community itself.

CHAPTER SIX

Conclusions and Implications

There are some who assert that the problems facing America's industrial heartland in the 1970s and 1980s subsided with the economic boom of the 1990s. The 1990s did see some places successfully shift their economies toward higher-technology manufacturing and service industries.[1] Although the road has been rocky and the journey remains incomplete, American companies have adapted to compete globally, and many of them have done so without abandoning their communities. These kinds of transformations—specifically companies like Pennsylvania Power and Light (PP&L), Air Products and Chemicals, spinoffs from the former Lucent, and even Mack Truck—have been the real savior of Allentown. And, where they have occurred elsewhere, they have been the savior of those parts of the rust belt that have adjusted relatively well to the forces of globalization. But that path is by no means universal. Youngstown is certainly not the only example of a region where companies have transformed in ways that have undermined regional economic and social prosperity. It is not the only city that has gotten lost on its postindustrial path. It is this divergence of trajectories among the cities and towns of the rust belt that has been the puzzle driving this book.

A surplus of studies suggests the role and importance of social capital in explaining this kind of variation. Robert Putnam's work is the most celebrated, suggesting that the decline of social connections—the growing tendency to stay in one's home, interacting only with one's family and one's co-workers rather than participating actively in the organized civic life of communities—is correlated with a decline in economic prosperity in the United States.[2] This work was an important influence on me when I started the research for this book because it is such a powerfully simple concept. But then a realization hit. I grew up in a city—Buffalo, New York—where people do still bowl in leagues. The same could certainly be said for Youngstown. These are places where, driving down the street, it is by no means unusual to hear your name called out as you pass an old familiar street corner. These are places where people not only belonged to bowling leagues and garden clubs; they clung to them. And these are also the kinds of places that have been passed by globalization.

Robert Putnam's argument focuses on social networks as they impact the daily lives of individuals working and living together in communities.[3] But his is not the only major voice contributing to policy debates that draws on the concept of networks and social capital. A large (and growing) body of research has emerged around the networks within and among organizations in cities. Leading lights include Piore and Sabel's[4] work on flexible specialization, that of Annalee Saxenian[5] on regional advantage, Michael Porter's[6] work on clusters, the literature on local innovation systems,[7] and more recently Richard Florida on the creative class.[8] Each—to some extent—argues (or has been interpreted as saying) that the salvation of mature industrial regions lies in abandoning old bureaucratic models of organizing the economy and embracing the power of networks to generate innovation, break free of stale production methods, exploit the full value of existing capabilities, and attract and retain the best qualified, most talented workers.

I don't disagree with them. Like each of these authors, I argue that social networks have the power to shape regional economic outcomes. And I agree that healthy networks among companies and among individuals are vital to ensuring a vibrant local economy. But like many, I have found myself frustrated by working with companies and living in cities that seem to have all the makings of success in the global economy—intelligent and creative people, a strong physical infrastructure, top research institutions, well-heeled and historically successful companies—which nevertheless seem unable to build on all of these strengths to turn the corner to economic prosperity.

But this book's focus has been less on the role that networks play in facilitating economic exchange than on the role networks play in navigating change. The research points more concretely toward unique—and implementable—policy implications for mature industrial regions.

Revisiting Lock-In: Trajectories of Regional Economic Change

The key question facing rust-belt regions is whether (and if so, how) they can successfully reconstruct local civic infrastructures in the aftermath of economic crises. More generally, this raises the question of what makes institutions and the networks in which they are embedded adaptable and therefore resilient in the face of acute crises and significant environmental change.

Chapter 1 outlined a fundamentally evolutionary theory of how that happens. The reconstruction of civic networks happens (to paraphrase Gernot Grabher and David Stark)[9] not *on* the ruins of the industrial era's social infrastructure, but *with* the ruins. The social and civic structure of relationships in a community prior to a crisis is the context in which new patterns of interaction—both economic *and* civic interaction—will emerge. How the civic intersects with the economic shapes the possibilities for recombining talents, identities, roles, and norms toward establishing new patterns better suited to the challenges of a globalized economy.

The key argument is that different *kinds* of social networks shape key decision makers' ability to form coalitions and take collective action during moments of acute crisis. In particular, the structure of ties facilitated cooperation in Allentown while acting as a barrier in Youngstown. Communities can be described as accumulations of relationships among some defined group of people, say in a town or a neighborhood. Those relationships exist in multiple intersecting layers: one layer may, for instance, characterize business relationships; another layer, religious; a third, recreational; and so on. The core argument of this book has to do with how those layers intersect. This is related to a term found among network analysts—multiplexity—which refers to the degree that the relationship between two individuals exists on multiple dimensions. People who work together *and* attend church together *and* play on the same sports team are likely to know each other very, very well. They are likely to have access to the same information, and they are likely to interpret that information in similar ways. And they are likely to have the ability to exert greater amounts of power and influence over each other through social mechanisms like enforcement. Scaling this illustration up to the level of a community, the notion of multiplexity implies a community thick with overlapping ties, which in the extreme would imply a total institution in which the relational dimensions of daily life melt into each other.

But one could imagine a different individual who leads separate lives along these different dimensions; her business life is held separate from religious networks, which are different still from her recreational activities. These different networks give her access to a wider range of information, multiple perspectives from which to interpret that information, and—if she is socially skilled—the ability to leverage her connections across these dimensions to achieve her goals. This is essentially what my colleague Ron Burt refers to as an entrepreneur or what Merton, years earlier, referred to as a cosmopolitan.[10] Scaling up suggests a community in which layers of society do not map directly onto each other, but are rather connected at various points where cosmopolitans meet and interact. The layers are independent, connecting many of the same actors but in different ways.

The latter structure—characterized by intersecting rather than overlapping multiplexity—is more robust in the face of economic change. This is true for three reasons. First, uncertainty calls for interpretation, and interpretation is facilitated by access to different sources of information. A multiplex structure in which actors are connected to each other along separate dimensions allows diverse information sources to be brought to bear on understanding the problem at hand. Second, that structure provides greater opportunities for actors to emerge who can play leadership roles. Drawing on Burt's arguments about entrepreneurship and the value of structural holes, it suggests that organizations that span disparate groups in a community can become places where entrepreneurs can emerge and drive change processes. Finally, the independence of relational dimensions ensures that when crisis erupts in one sphere, other spheres will be relatively protected and can therefore serve as a platform for actors to engage each other. Unpacking how the differences explain the outcomes leads to three fundamental insights. First, the kinds of networks that produce economic prosperity during periods of economic and social stability are very different from the kinds of networks required at moments of social and economic change (let alone crisis). When it comes to change and instability, more is not necessarily better: more important are linkages across salient boundaries of industry, class, and geography. Second, social capital cannot be forged from whole cloth. Once a challenge or crisis ensues, it is too late to forge new ties; existing relational patterns are invoked, and indeed, reinforced.

Together these first two insights may suggest that a region's fate is beyond human control: the winners and losers are determined by the chance likelihood that they have the "right" kinds of networks in place at the right time. Yet the historical and qualitative research presented in this book suggests there is considerable room for policy makers and others to actively shape the structure of ties in communities. Doing so is not simply a matter of gathering more people on boards of directors. Change of this kind requires a long-term perspective involving deliberate, targeted, and sustained attention to building and maintaining a robust social structure. The key implications for policy makers are to develop a concrete understanding of where those linkages do and do *not* exist within their own communities and to develop strategies for forging closer ties across the most strategically important disconnects in their communities.

This leads to the third insight: the kinds of networks that are called for in mature industrial regions are different from the ones that are often discussed in economies like Silicon Valley or in the myriad proposals for creating "clusters." As industries mature, production and knowledge both become much less stuck to place. To survive, companies and the people who populate them need to develop a global perspective extending well beyond their backyards. Economically, their networks must extend well beyond the local region. But as companies engage global business partners, they need not necessarily abandon local ties. For mature industrial regions, ensuring that organizations are engaged by and participate in local decision-making processes is vital to achieving postindustrial success. What this suggests is that rather than focusing on production- and knowledge-based relationships, the key to postindustrial economic prosperity lies in cultivating and strengthening the social and civic connectedness of companies in their regions. Doing so not only strengthens the community's ability to get things done; it also has important implications for the decisions that companies make and what impact those decisions have on local economies.

Summary of Findings

Chapter 3 began by establishing stark differences between the cities with respect to the configuration of their underlying social structures. In Allentown multiple elites emerged early on and competed for prominence. In Youngstown a single cohesive elite appeared which dominated social and economic spheres in the city. In both, similarities in geography led to the establishment of a cluster of iron mills, which formed the basis for the regions' emergence later in the nineteenth century as secondary centers of steel production. But the initial social structural differences affected the tenor of the cities' subsequent economic and social development, as was revealed by comparing how three exogenous events that struck both cities simultaneously played out within them.

In Youngstown a consistent pattern emerged: the core group of densely connected, elite actors formulated responses that drew on their cohesiveness, time and again, to circle the wagons in the face of uncertainty. Industrialization and the consolidation of industry was seen as posing a threat to local autonomy, and the city's elite banded together to establish a bulwark against it through the formation of the Youngstown Sheet and Tube Company. Subsequently, challenges were seen as coming from within as the influx of eastern European immigrants and workers was perceived as threatening the established social order. The elites' first response was to establish physical and geographical divisions within the emerging working class through their control over land use. Later they aligned themselves with the divisive politics of the Ku Klux Klan in an effort to reestablish "law and order." Finally, they used similar tactics in the 1930s in response to labor organizing activity, with bloody results. By the onset of World War II, Youngstown was a community that was deeply fragmented, containing pockets of cohesive—yet largely disconnected—factions.

In Allentown the community's earliest social structure was formed around four largely autonomous ethno-religious communities from which two major economic blocs emerged early on. One was centered on the Lehigh Valley Railroad and the Bethlehem Steel Company, and the other on the Lehigh Coal and Navigation Company and associated firms. For each, the locus of identity was fixed on the separate communities from which they hailed. Uncertainty associated with industrialization was therefore not interpreted as threatening the coherence of the region as a whole, but rather as part of the ongoing struggle for status within the community that had emerged out of the competition of these two groups. Indeed, industrialization for them ultimately served as a possible catalyst for establishing edifying institutions such as churches and universities that would enhance their status vis-à-vis other ethnoreligious groups of the region. Though possibly quixotic at the time, these institutions became a legacy of lasting value to the community. Eastern European immigration into the region followed this pattern, as local elites—by now composed of both original founding families and the managers of major companies—formulated a response that built identity that cut across working, middle, and upper classes, with the local community serving as the locus of identity building. In doing so, ties between the groups were strengthened within the various localities of the Lehigh Valley. Ironically, this made it easier for labor organizers to use a highly successful bottom-up organizing approach—an outcome that corporate leaders had hoped to avoid. (And this led directly to the organization of the steel industry nationwide.) Thus, by World War II Allentown was perhaps just as fragmented as Youngstown was, but the axes of its fragmentation differed in important ways.

Chapter 4 explored the significance of these underlying social structural differences during two moments in the cities' histories that had critical, direct implications for their postindustrial trajectories. The first was the realization in the 1950s that the shifting geography of the steel industry was likely to render the cities' existing economic foundations untenable into the future. This led actors in both cities to seek out advice on how address these concerns, and the advice they received was essentially the same. Yet the actions they took were different. In Youngstown the elites appeared to put forth a set of proposals to prop up the existing steel-based economic structure. But on closer inspection what becomes clear is that rather than circling the wagons, the elite had in fact grown largely apathetic to the future of the region, allowing others to pursue actions that were assumed to be in the elites' best interest but that ultimately lacked their active support. In Allentown a series of collective actions laid the groundwork for economic diversification and a shift toward higher ends of the value chain.

Chapter 4 also examined the immediate responses that emerged when the crisis foreseen in the 1950s finally arrived. In Youngstown the elite, who had been shown to be brittle in the 1950s, fragmented, leaving the community—so long centered on this set—leaderless at its most critical moment. The result was a deep partition, as labor and religious leaders, as well as urban and suburban politicians, all formulated separate responses to the crisis, responses that competed for public attention and support. Ultimately, none of these responses were implemented effectively. In Allentown, on the other hand, groundwork was in place to allow once-fragmented actors to find common ground toward formulating a set of consensus-driven responses to the crisis. These responses built on the latent capabilities of the region and quickly started showing results.

Finally, Chapter 4 introduced a network analysis of connections among local actors in the two cities to formulate a more specific explanation for how the structure of relationships in the two cities led to these two very different outcomes. Two relational axes within each city—one economic, the other civic—were identified. It was shown that in Youngstown these two networks were largely coincident with each other; actors who were connected economically were also likely to be connected through civic ties. In Allentown the two networks intersected but did not necessarily overlap. Indeed, it was shown that a few key civic organizations were particularly pivotal as focal points where actors from different communities and factions within communities came into contact. These civic organizations played critical roles as forums for sense making at moments of uncertainty. So two important theoretical points emerged from the network analysis. First is the importance of *multiplex independence*—the relative autonomy of different relational axes during moments of uncertainty. Second is the importance of having focal organizations within a social structure that can serve as unifying forums of interaction and engagement when needed.

Chapter 5 examined how these differences led to divergent evolutions of the cities' social structures in recent decades and how these differences affected organizational change processes. Three drivers of economic change were outlined: the transformation of large organizations, the emergence of new organizations, and inward investment. For each driver as matched pairs of representative organizations were identified and compared, stark differences emerged between the cities. In Allentown several large organizations have smoothly transformed themselves into globally competitive companies in ways that have brought resources and skills into the region. In Youngstown change processes within large firms have often been contentious. Firms that have transformed have done so in ways that leave the community—including workers within the companies themselves—in a weaker position.

Entrepreneurship followed a similar pattern. In Allentown the early efforts of local elites to develop an entrepreneurial infrastructure based on local capital and ties to universities proved successful. Later, as market opportunities emerged in high-tech industries, the infrastructure was in place to lend support. Youngstown also had efforts to encourage entrepreneurship. But these efforts lacked meaningful participation—either financial or in terms of mentorship and advice—from economic elites. Instead, a few very high-profile efforts emerged but were quickly revealed to be lacking substance, and in at least one case based on criminal acts of fraud, further undermining economic change efforts within the community. Finally, it was shown that inward investment policies in Allentown benefited from coordination among municipalities, which has allowed it to largely avoid the "race to the bottom" that can emerge as communities compete with each other to offer the most favorable terms to potential investors. Youngstown pursued several large investors over time but generally lost out to lower-cost regions that offered even more favorable terms. When economic development efforts did eventually materialize, communities squabbled among themselves for their fair share of the spoils. The targets of these efforts, however, were operations such as call centers and prisons—employers that bring little into the region in terms of skills or other resources.

To explain these differences, Chapter 5 presented data on the evolution of social networks within the two cities. In both places it was shown that the fairly well connected economic networks of the past had largely been decimated. Civic networks, however, remained dense in both. The differences between the two cities today have to do with who participates within those networks. In Allentown key economic actors—in particular, the CEOs of major companies as well as prominent local politicians—populate the upper ranks of local civic leadership networks. In Youngstown these leaders' counterparts were shown to be largely absent.

The remainder of the chapter linked organizational change processes to the observed differences in network structure. In Allentown it was shown that as organizations made sense of the challenges that emerged in the early 1980s, they were able to draw on various local resources in order to formulate their strategic response. By reaching out to other local actors during this period of uncertainty, new relationships were forged and others strengthened. With time these relationships coalesced into a new—reconfigured—social structure that included not only philanthropic support from large companies, but their active participation in local networks. In Youngstown the vacuum of leadership that emerged during the crisis gave way to an even more invidious social structure in which organized crime elements assumed a central role. This effectively pushed already poorly connected actors further away, intensifying barriers to collective action.

Revisiting the Framework

Chapter 1 laid out a framework that emerged as a response to the late Charles Tilly's call[11] for social scientists to use network analysis "to pinpoint the wide-ranging and recurrent causal mechanisms whose combinations produce the actual unique histories we observe." Its starting point is the idea that cooperation is not an anomaly to be explained; it is ubiquitous. Problems, challenges, and opportunities arise with regularity that are too complex for any one individual to tackle. People regularly reach out to make common cause with others in their day-to-day lives. So the question to ask is not whether cooperation, community, and collective action will happen, but rather with whom and according to what rules. When such challenges emerge during periods of relative stability, actors turn to well-worn—often taken-for-granted—patterns to inform how to behave. To the degree that a problem or challenge falls outside their normal experience, people bend existing rules and adapt them. But some challenges are more fundamental, calling for the redefinition of existing roles and rules.

These more fundamental crises have been at the center of our analysis. Drawing on the work of John Padgett,[12] David Stark,[13] and others, I have argued that actors presented with fundamental crises make do by reaching out to some subset of others around them in order to formulate a response. When they do, they are improvising—making the rules up as they go because the rules they had become accustomed to are no longer trustworthy.[14] But they don't engage in this process in a vacuum. Communities (like all mature societies) are thick with multiple intersecting layers of interaction and meaning. And when one layer is imperiled, people naturally fall back on these alternative layers of their social world to find partners and guide local action; and it is from these actions that new patterns of action emerge. As history progresses, the seeds of earlier periods of crisis and change influence and shape subsequent periods.

As it is argued, this framework places a great deal of importance on initial conditions, and this factor has proved vital throughout the narrative of the book: the initially subtle differences that marked the cities' early settlement patterns set the tone for interactions among various local actors that placed Allentown and Youngstown on paths that led ultimately to their divergence. However, I do not want to suggest that the cities' histories were entirely *determined* by these initial conditions. Their paths were not straight lines. Rather, consistent with Swidler's metaphor of the tool kit, there were many moments and places where socially aware actors had choices about what aspects of the social structure they chose to employ. Two mechanisms were outlined in the framework and were evident in *how* actors in the cities responded to external events. First, there were instances in which powerful actors drew on their resources—mainly social, but also financial—to actively shape social structure. This was the case with Charles Schwab's highly orchestrated efforts to bridge (both geographically and socially) the divisions that had emerged within Bethlehem in such a way as to insert his company into a key position to establish hegemony. We saw it also in the way that local elites in Youngstown—taking precisely the opposite tack—used their financial resources to divide ethnic communities streaming into the Mahoning Valley in a similar—but ultimately wrongheaded—effort to maintain control. We saw this too in the struggle to organize workers as the union—particularly in Allentown—drew on local social structure to achieve victory. Finally, in the period since the competitiveness crisis, powerful remaining actors in the Allentown and the Lehigh Valley have forged connections among themselves and key constituencies in the community. Yet again, we also saw its opposite in Youngstown and the Mahoning Valley as the actors who came to occupy a central place there—organized crime—used their social capital to maintain the divisions that sustained their aims.

The results lend support to Theda Skocpol's diagnosis of what may lie behind Robert Putnam's contention that generalized levels of social capital have been declining in the United States: what has changed is neither the overweening intervention of government nor the atomizing influence of television and cars, but rather the abandonment of civic responsibility among local economic elites. Indeed, we can push this further by looking into the data to develop new ways of thinking about the choices actors have with respect to the use of their social capital and how these might affect regional trajectories of change.

The results presented here have important implications for the argument: that "stocks" of social capital drive regional economic outcomes. This work suggests that it is not the amount of social capital that matters but rather how social structure shapes the ways in which actors use the social capital at their disposal. This is the view of social capital that has been most evident in research emerging from a historical institutionalist tradition. Scholars such as Peter Evans,[15] Patrick Heller,[16] Richard Locke,[17] Alejandro Portes,[18] Tilly,[19] Stark,[20] Saxenian,[21] and Sabel[22] show us how a richer, more contextually specific vision of social capital helps to explain not only outcomes but also trajectories of economic change. They show us how state and nonstate actors—be they workers, managers, small business owners, or corporate elites—interact and, in doing so, help us to pinpoint the mechanisms that produce unique economic trajectories among places (Tilly 1992; Emirbayer and Goodwin 1994).

Implications for Cities

In early 2004, the Eastman Kodak Company announced that it was eliminating fifteen thousand jobs at its headquarters in Rochester, New York, suggesting that older industrial cities continue to face difficult challenges adjusting to the global economy twenty years after the emergence of the terms *deindustrialization* and *rust belt*. The experiences of communities dealing with globalization and the decline of America's manufacturing base have provided important lessons, which should be informing a more substantive debate on what to do about the impact globalization is having on local economies. This book suggests that what is most vital is bridging the major divisions that remain within communities.

When Youngstown's steel manufacturing declined, non-steel-related companies were not included in the process of looking for solutions; neither was labor, nor many of the city's major suburban leaders. Each of these constituencies ended up developing their own plan of action in the wake of the city's decline and competed with each other to achieve their own narrow goals. There was no mechanism for them to engage each other's interests, no method for them to forge new relationships to the rest of the community. The result has been nothing short of catastrophic decline and hollowing out. Therefore, to succeed, leaders of mature industrial cities must take a hard look at the divisions that are the legacy of their industrial pasts—divisions between small companies and large ones, among identity groups, between suburbs and inner cities, and between labor and management—and find ways of bringing them together to craft effective responses.

Ultimately, the question that must be asked of this research is this: does it provide any lessons that might serve to head off the kind of disaster that happened in Youngstown or that might inform policies that would help to generate the positive outcomes that have occurred in Allentown? Several lessons are apparent.

Responding to Crises

The argument of this book suggests that some communities are in a stronger position to rebuild themselves in the aftermath of acute economic, political, and natural crises. And this difference comes down to whether mechanisms are in place to mediate relationships among and across various interest groups in the community. It is commonplace—indeed, I would suggest it is ubiquitous in the aftermath of acute crises—

to hear local officials decry one group or another's standing in the way of needed change. This is entirely understandable because acute crises—a hurricane or flood decimating a community, total war, or the collapse of a region's economic engine—undermine the very identities of those who are affected. After ensuring survival, a paramount concern is "What place will I have in this society once a new stable equilibrium is reached?" The responsibility of those in power is, of course, to address basic survival first. But subsequently, attention must turn to the sociological question of how identities and interests will sort themselves out.

This book provides some insight into *how* that sorting out happens and therefore points toward some concrete steps that policy makers and community leaders can take to facilitate it. First, the problem is too complex to be directly shaped. Actors take action to move toward an individual sense of security and certainty by taking local action. They improvise, but that improvisation does not happen in a vacuum. People grasp for that which is familiar and seek to rebuild relationships using the full range of multiplex ties at their disposal. At a minimum, this suggests examining the multiplex relationships—religious, educational, political and economic—that characterize a community to understand the complex but nevertheless observable ties on which people are likely to draw in taking action in the immediate aftermath of a crisis. Such an analysis will reveal that some communities are likely to fragment along disparate axes of affiliation and identity. Others may have mechanisms in place for bridging those divisions. Or analysis may point toward layers of a community or particular organizations that might serve as bridging vehicles. Smart government policy would target strengthening those bridging networks and provide incentives for potentially antagonistic members of the community to draw on those relationships—those identities—rather than on relationships that are more likely to lead to conflict.

On the Notion of Community Empowerment

In the specific case of mature industrial regions, one very clear implication of this research has to do with the role of economic leaders in these communities. Without question, one of the key factors that has contributed to Allentown's relative success is that top leaders of major companies and branches have devoted personal time and energy to participating in the region's civic leadership. This has had a number of important consequences. Of course, many are highly talented individuals, and the region has benefited from their experience and expertise. They also represent organizations that have far deeper reserves of resources—financial, physical, and social—which are extremely valuable when applied to the problems and opportunities facing the region.

But the importance of their participation goes beyond resources in two ways. First, because of those resources, the participation of a region's top economic leaders draws in the key leaders of other communities in the region. And the greater the concentration and focus of those leaders, the more ability they have to establish and facilitate bridges across other key constituencies that have a stake in the region's future.

Second, participation of this kind has important implications for how the companies themselves make decisions. The days when a company's decisions might be dictated by the personal connections its leaders have to a particular community are past. Companies that make decisions based on sympathy or sentimentality are not likely to last long enough to be of much benefit to the regions they inhabit. Nevertheless, direct personal participation by top company leaders gives them much useful information about how to compete most efficiently within a region, and provides opportunities for others (for example, universities and local government officials) to learn about how best to organize their activities in ways that create mutual benefit for companies and communities. Participation helps to create the kinds of communities that workers want to live in.

This participation must go beyond mere exercises in public relations. To be effective, leaders with real authority need to devote some portion of their personal time. And if the experience of Charles Schwab is an indicator, it makes a great deal of sense to concentrate those efforts where they are most effective. Rather than spreading out commitments across a wide range of organizations, top leaders should focus their participation on a few organizations that bridge important constituencies.

This points toward some specific things that government leaders can do. Incentives such as tax subsidies tied to job retention and the like have been shown to be ineffective. In part, this is because nothing is typically asked of the company other than token assurances. Incentives might be better directed to weaving company leaders into the local civil society. And in doing so, it makes sense to analyze the structure of that civil society and guide the leaders of key constituencies—economic, religious, social, and political—toward forms of participation that link up otherwise disconnected factions. One way to do this is to pay greater attention to the various advisory boards that mayors, county executives, and legislators control and to use those as opportunities to create connections among communities that need to be connected.

It would be a mistake to conclude from this book that what is needed are interventions to create more bridging-type organizations. The evolutionary approach taken in this book suggests at a minimum that a more dynamic approach is necessary: the emergence of forums that bridge salient divisions is an outcome of the processes by which those divisions emerged in the first place; it is an outcome of the specific ways in which actors resolve very specific, localized issues that emerge in the face of challenges. The Boy Scouts came to take on a central role in Allentown's networks, not because there was some intention of creating bridges between groups, but out of the more prosaic desire of individuals in that community to gain access to a powerful actor in the community. Its importance was sustained over time because it became a place where problems—far removed from the goals with which Boy Scout meetings were established—could be resolved. These were layered on as problems arose, and it became a natural place for those problems to be addressed.

Rather than simply providing mechanisms for conducting information and resources or even trust, the value of organizations like the Boy Scouts or its descendant—the Lehigh Valley Partnership—has to do with being sources of participative democracy.[23] That is, just as important as the ability to address issues and resolve conflicts is the fact that such organizations provide opportunities for *engagement,* the ability to interact, to have one's voice heard and one's identity as a citizen of a given community affirmed. It is this kind of dynamic interaction that has led to the continued participation of economic leaders in the social and civic life of Allentown as a community, and it is the *absence* of this kind of meaningful engagement that has led the disintegration of Youngstown's social fabric.

Youngstown is not hopeless. The action taken by individuals in the mid-1990s to wrest back control of local politics was a step in the right direction, not simply because it began to root out much of the corruption that had taken hold, but because—much more fundamentally—it gave at least a segment of that community the opportunity to take action. This has led to further efforts. The Youngstown Business Incubator is nevertheless drawing the participation of some of the key economic leaders of the community and has produced at least two successful companies. When the need arises, this group will potentially take on greater responsibility.

It is difficult to say at this point whether that will occur, but Allentown's experiences suggest that this is at least the right place to start.

We still live with the effects of the competitiveness crisis that emerged in the 1980s, a time in which economic institutions seemed antithetical to the purposes they were intended to perform, subsumed by an imperative of unfettered economic growth. Yet economic institutions remain as inevitable as they are necessary. They are a natural outgrowth of the conflict between our collective desire for change and our simultaneous need for stability. All societies are rife with conflict among those who hold opposing interests. Institutions are what keep us from lives that are nasty, brutish, and short. Policy makers, analysts, and scholars alike are therefore struggling to understand how we might come to a new understanding of what institutions are and how they work so that we might eventually design better ones. In its broadest sense, this book is intended to contribute to that effort.

What this work suggests is that moments of conflict-ridden crisis have the potential to fundamentally alter the structure of social networks— that is to say, the very ways in which individuals (and organizations) interact with each other in society. The ebb and flow of utilization, combination, and confrontation creates the unique patterns of relationships that are characteristic of a given community. This book shows that the *configuration* of social capital is the key in shaping these dynamics. It also suggests an important element of what makes civic society vibrant: particular organizations must bring together actors who are not otherwise well connected in order to serve as a focus of civic engagement. The results, therefore, move us closer to understanding that the interaction of agency and social capital explain divergent socioeconomic histories by highlighting the ways in which actors negotiate emergent social orders and adapt them in the process. This has important implications for policy. Rather than simply increasing the number of civic organizations or even participation in them, it suggests that what is most important is how social capital is deployed, called upon, and realized by actors within communities[24] in the context of the emerging global realities communities are increasingly forced to confront.

List of Interviewees

Allentown

Don Bernhard, PPL
Bill Billheimer, Bethlehem Steel
Glen Bresner, Mid-Atlantic Ventures
Lloyde Browne, Entopath
Donald Cunningham, Lehigh County
Burt Daday, PPL
Joe Daddona, City of Allentown (retired)
Gregory Farrington, Lehigh University
Don Fink, Acme Cryogenics
Aaron Fischer, T-Networks
Elmer Gates, Empire Bank
Mike Gausling, Orasure
Tom Hierl, IQE Epitaxial
Alan Jennings, Lehigh Valley Community Action Committee
Mark Lang, Ben Franklin Technology Partnership
James Molina, Akrion
Gordon Payrow, City of Bethlehem (retired)
Sal Salamone, Orasure
Bob Spellman, American Institute of Architects
Walter Stainbrook, Lehigh Valley Industrial Parks
C. J. Sutton, Air Products and Chemicals
Donna Taggers, Lehigh Valley Economic Development Corporation

Hap Wagner, Air Products and Chemicals and Agere
Bob Wendt, Lehigh Valley Economic Development Corporation
John Werkheiser, Lehigh Valley Labor Council

Youngstown

Dean Allen, Kent State University, Trumbull Campus
Bob Buss, Sovereign Circuits
Terry Buss, National Academy of Public Administration (formerly professor at Youngstown State University)
Don Cagigas, Youngstown/Mahoning Valley United Way
Tom Cavalier, Butler Wick Investments
Jim Coessler, Youngstown Incubator
Darwin Cooper, UAW Local 1112
Tom Croft, Steel Valley Alliance
Reid Duhlberger, Youngstown-Warren Regional Chamber of Commerce
Don French, Mahoning Valley Economic Development Corporation
Pat Gaughn, Youngstown Incubator
Frank Hiero, Sky Bank
Tom Leary, Youngstown State University
Betty Jo Licata, Youngstown State University
Stanton Lynd, Activist
Herman Maas, General Motors (retired)
Julie Michael, State of Ohio
Maureen Midglee, General Motors
Msgr. Robert Siffrin, Youngstown Diocese
George Ogletree, Treeman Industries
Dean Stevens, Youngstown State University
David Sweet, Youngstown State University
Deborah Taylor, Activist
Ralph Zirbonia, Zirbonia Systems

Chronology of Major Economic, Political, and Social Events, 1743–2003

		Youngstown	*Allentown*
1740s	1743		Members of the Moravian Church found the borough of Bethlehem.
1750s	1750		The City of Easton is established.
1760s	1761		Bethlehem's Moravians abolish the General Economy but remain closed to outsiders.
	1762		The city of Allentown is established.
1780s	1788	The State of Connecticut sells large tracts of land in the Mahoning Valley to the Connecticut Land Company.	
1790s	1796	Moses Warren settles in the Western Reserve, founding the town of Warren.	
	1797	John Young settles and lays out the town of Youngstown.	

		Youngstown	Allentown
1800s	1803	Iron ore deposits are found near Yellow Creek south of Youngstown. Hopewell Iron Furnace is constructed nearby, the first iron furnace east of the Allegheny Mountains.	
1810s	1819		Construction begins on the Lehigh Navigation Canal.
1820s	1820	Construction begins on the Ohio-Pennsylvania Canal.	
	1826		Lafayette College is established as a Presbyterian institution in Easton.
	1829		The Lehigh Coal and Navigation canal opens.
1830s	1830	The Ohio-Pennsylvania Canal opens, linking the Mahoning River to the Great Lakes.	
	1839		The Lehigh Crane Iron Company is established.
1840s	1840		The City of Bethlehem opens to non-Moravians.
	1846	The largest iron blast furnace east of the Appalachians, the "Eagle," is built near Youngstown.	
1850s	1851		Asa Packer announces plans to build a railroad on the south side of the Lehigh River to compete with the Lehigh Navigation Canal.
	1857		The Junction at South Bethlehem, establishing a direct link from the Lehigh Valley Railroad to Philadelphia, is established. August Wolle and Charles

		Youngstown	Allentown
			Broadhead establish an iron mill nearby, which later incorporates as the Bethlehem Iron Company.
	1858		Moravian College is established in Bethlehem.
1860s	1866		Lehigh University is established as an Episcopalian institution in South Bethlehem
	1867		Muhlenberg College is established as a Lutheran institution in Allentown.
1870s	1873		Bethlehem Iron Company installs a Bessemer furnace.
	1877		Bethlehem Iron wins a $4 million contract from the U.S. Navy to produce armor plate and gun forgings.
1880s	1880	Youngstown is a major railroad center served by four major trunk lines.	
	1880	The first waves of "new immigrants" from eastern Europe begin to arrive.	The first waves of "new immigrants" from eastern Europe begin to arrive.
1890s	1890	Packard Brothers found Packard Automobile Company and Packard Electric Company.	
	1891		Bethlehem Iron wins another $4 million contract from the U.S. Army to produce gun forgings.
	1891	The myriad small iron producers in the Mahoning Valley join forces to form the Mahoning and Shenango Valleys Iron Manufacturers Association.	

		Youngstown	*Allentown*
	1895	Alfred and Charles Harris found Harris Automatic Press Company.	
	1895	Ohio Steel Company forms after the failure of local industry group to secure lower rail rates. It installs the Mahoning Valley's first Bessemer furnace.	
	1898		Frederick Taylor arrives in Bethlehem to streamline operations.
	1899	Ohio Steel Company is sold to J.P. Morgan's National Steel Company.	
	1899	Beneficiaries of the Ohio Steel sale found Republic Iron and Steel Company.	
1900s	1900	National Steel Company—including Ohio Steel—is merged with Andrew Carnegie's interests to create the U.S. Steel Company.	
	1901	Former Republic Steel investors break off to create Youngstown Iron, Sheet and Tube Company (later renamed Youngstown Sheet and Tube).	
	1903		Charles Schwab purchases a significant stake in Bethlehem Steel.
	1908	Youngstown Association School is established by the YMCA (later YSU).	
1910s	1910		Workers at Bethlehem Steel go on strike, marking one of the first labor conflicts to bridge the interests of skilled and unskilled workers.

		Youngstown	*Allentown*
	1911		Two Hills Bridge Committee is established to explore linking Bethlehem and South Bethlehem.
	1914		Mack Truck moves from Brooklyn to Allentown.
	1916	Youngstown Sheet and Tube workers strike in East Youngstown. Rioting breaks out, and the central business district of the town is burned to the ground.	
	1917	Buckeye Land Company is established to build housing for Youngstown Sheet & Tube workers.	The boroughs of Bethlehem and South Bethlehem vote to consolidate, becoming the City of Bethlehem.
	1919	The first national steelworkers strike idles factories throughout the Mahoning Valley. Butler Art Institute is founded.	Bethlehem Steel workers sit out the Great Strike of 1919.
1920s	1923	Ku Klux Klan candidates win victories in municipal elections in Youngstown, Warren, and Niles.	
1930s	1932	General Motors acquires Packard Electric.	
	1937	The Little Steel Strike erupts. Six pickets are killed in violent clashes outside a Youngstown Sheet and Tube mill.	Bethlehem Steel workers sit out the Little Steel Strike.
1940s	1942	Other Little Steel companies—including Youngstown Sheet and Tube and Republic—follow Bethlehem's lead, recognizing the steel-workers union on the eve of World War II.	Workers at Bethlehem Steel vote to join the steelworkers union. Bethlehem Steel becomes the first Little Steel company to recognize the union.

		Youngstown	Allentown
	1943		Leonard Pool relocates Air Products from Detroit to Allentown
	1947	United Electrical (UE) Workers organize part of Packard Electric.	
	1948		Western Electric opens a manufacturing plant in Allentown.
1950s	1951	Mallory-Sharon Titanium (later RMI Titanium) Corporation is established in Niles.	Mass-produced transistor is introduced at Western Electric Allentown Works.
	1952	Edward DeBartolo builds America's first enclosed shopping mall in the Youngstown suburb of Struthers. Competitor William Cafaro begins building strip malls around this time as well.	Puerto Rican immigrants form the Puerto Rican Beneficial Society.
	1954	Kent State University opens a campus in Trumbull County near Warren.	
	1957	Youngstown Association School becomes Youngstown University. Also, Harris Automated Press merges with Intertype Corporation, becoming Harris-Intertype.	
1960s	1963	The city is dubbed "Crimetown USA" by the *Saturday Evening Post*.	
	1964	Arby's Restaurants is founded in Youngstown.	Community Action Committee of the Lehigh Valley is established.
	1965		Joe Daddona as president of the Allentown Jaycees

		Youngstown	*Allentown*
			initiates a project to study Allentown's form of government. With backing from the League of Women Voters and the Allentown-Lehigh County Chamber of Commerce, the community sets out to shift to a strong mayor form of government.
	1966	Fifteen hundred workers are hired, bringing the total working population up to 11,500 at Packard. GM—Lordstown plant opens.	
	1967	Youngstown State University (YSU) is incorporated into Ohio's state university system. Private YSU foundation has $9 million in endowments.	
	1968	Harris-Intertype acquires electronics manufacturer Radiation Inc. and later relocates to Melbourne, Florida. Radiation was an early entrant into the microelectronics business, and in 1963 developed its first working semiconductor for use in its digital communications equipment.	Spanish Apostolate and the Puerto Rican Beneficial Society combine to form the Council of Spanish-Speaking Organizations of the Lehigh Valley.
1970	Jan-70	Edward DeBartolo buys the San Francisco 49ers.	Mack Trucks opens a new headquarters building in Allentown.
1971	Jan-71		Air Products and Chemicals opens its Santa Clara nitrogen pipeline.
1972	Jan-72	Wildcat strike begins at Lordstown	

		Youngstown	Allentown
	Jan-72	Kent State's workforce development and continuing studies center opens.	
1977	Oct-77	Youngstown Sheet and Tube closes its Campbell Works plant, resulting in four thousand layoffs.	Bethlehem Steel announces the layoff of eight hundred headquarters employees.
1978	Jan-78	The Charles Cushwa Center for Entrepreneurship is established for the purpose of assisting inventors, innovators, and businesses in developing new products and processes for commercialization.	
	Jan-78	Packard begins manufacturing operations in Ciudad Juarez.	
	Jan-78	Mahoning Valley Economic Development Corporation is created.	
1979	Jan-79	Republic Steel closes Brier Hill works with three thousand layoffs.	Renault takes a 10 percent share in Mack Trucks.
1980	Apr-80	U.S. Steel closes McDonald works with one thousand layoffs.	Mack obtains exclusive North and Central American marketing rights to all commercial vehicles produced by Renault.
	Aug-80		Air Products receives grants from the U.S. government to pursue a $1.5 billion demonstration refinery to be built near Newman, Kentucky, to produce synthetic fuels from coal.
1981	Jan-81		Air Products, before investing more than $1 million in a new computer system, sends its managers to computer seminars at Lehigh University—the first such collaboration between the company and the university.

		Youngstown	Allentown
1982	Jan-82	County Sheriff James Traficant is indicted for taking $163,000 from rival gangs in exchange for protecting their rackets.	
	Jan-82	Affluent suburbanites with a financial stake in the region's image and reform-minded activists dedicated to "good government" found the anti-Mafia Citizen's League of Greater Youngstown.	
	Jan-82	Lordstown workers vote against quality of work life contract clause as well as concessionary national contract.	
	Jan-82	Monus and Shapira open first Phar-Mor store.	
1983	Jan-83		Mack Trucks has initial public offering. Renault increases its holding to 40 percent.
	Aug-83		Lehigh is one of four institutions in Pennsylvania selected to participate in the Ben Franklin Initiative.
1984	Jan-84	An agreement is reached between the IUE and GM's Packard Electric division. The company promises current workers at the Warren, Ohio, plant their jobs for life. The union agrees to a multitiered wage system with new workers earning 55 percent of the amount paid to veterans.	Breakup of AT&T occurs; Lucent spins off with Allentown's laboratory of 639 employees.
	Jan-84	Republic Steel merges with J&L Steel to become LTV.	Pennsylvania Power and Light experiences the first decline in demand for electricity in its history and begins shifting significant

		Youngstown	*Allentown*
			resources into economic development.
	Dec-84	Packard Electric workers approve the labor accord negotiated in January.	Dun and Bradstreet relocates six-hundred-person division to the Lehigh Valley.
1985	Jan-85		Lehigh Valley Partnership is founded.
	Jan-85	Lordstown management begins bimonthly labor-management meetings with the union	Ben Franklin applies for and receives a special $750,000 state grant to capitalize Mid-Atlantic regional Partners, a venture-capital fund.
1986	Jan-86		Contract negotiations with Mack Truck break down; two thousand layoffs follow.
	Jan-86	Regional Growth Alliance, a private not-for-profit group formed by leading business leaders under the auspices of the Youngstown Chamber of Commerce is created in order to play a more active role in the economic development of the Mahoning Valley.	Bethlehem Steel threatens to close primary steelmaking in Bethlehem if the union doesn't allow it to trim 550 from the workforce.
1987	Jan-87	The Charles Cushwa Center for Entrepreneurship is established at YSU.	
	Jan-87	Phar-Mor founder James Monus launches World Basketball League.	
	Jan-87	Youngstown developer J.J. Cafaro acquires Avanti.	
	Jun-87		Renault buys the rest of Mack Truck's outstanding shares. Mack closes its sixty-

	Youngstown	*Allentown*
		year-old main assembly plant and replaces it with an $80 million plant to be built in Winnsboro, South Carolina; eighteen hundred workers are laid off.
1988	Jan-88 WCI Steel (Warren Consolidated Industries), a subsidiary of New York–based Renco, takes over a former Republic steel mill in Warren, turning it into a mini-mill.	The Iacocca Institute is founded at Lehigh University to increase international competitiveness.
	Jan-88	Solid State Technology Center (now Agere's Opto-Electronics Center) is completed.
	Apr-88 Sovereign Circuits opens with $2 million in state and federal loans.	
	Jan-89 GM–Lordstown UAW Local 1112's leadership decides to reopen its collective bargaining agreement to consider changes in absentee policy, manning, and implementation of semiautonomous work groups. Several hours before a scheduled meeting on the contract, word leaks from GM top management officials that GM will likely shift van production, resulting in the loss of twenty-five hundred jobs at Lordstown.	
1989	Aug-89 RMI Titanium—a joint venture of USX and Quantum Chemical— issues an initial public offering.	

		Youngstown	Allentown
1990	Sep-90		Boston venture capital firm Advent International teams with Air Products and Chemical to launch an Air Products spin-off, Diamonex Inc.
	Sep-90		Mack Truck merges with a unit of Renault.
1991	Jan-04		Bethlehem Steel enters a joint venture with British Steel to produce rails.
1992	Aug-92	Twenty-four hundred workers at the Lordstown Fab plant engage in a nine-day strike that eventually shuts down six assembly plants and idles more than thirty thousand autoworkers nationwide.	
	Aug-92	Phar-Mor Inc., the drugstore chain, fires Monus after uncovering what it describes as an "incredible swindle."	
	Nov-92		Lehigh University announces it is "carving out a new industrial niche for itself as a partner with business in developing 'agile' manufacturing." A university spokesman states it "is in the technology-transfer business."
1993	Apr-93		Quantum Epitaxial Designs, a manufacturer of semiconductor materials, spins out of Ben Franklin and relocates to Bethlehem Technology Center on the former Bethlehem Steel site, investing $1.7 million in machinery and equipment and improvements.

		Youngstown	*Allentown*
1994	Jan-94	Four universities—the University of Akron, Kent State, Cleveland State, and Youngstown State—form a consortium to develop and jointly operate a graduate school of international business— the Ohio School of International Business	Bethlehem Technology Center receives $2.4 million in state economic development financing.
	May-94	Operating under the banner of "Mahoning Democrats for Change," reformist Democrats and the Citizen's League of Greater Youngstown win two-thirds of 409 Democratic precincts to win the chair of the county Democratic central committee, ending the sixteen-year tenure of the local Democratic machine's "boss."	PP&L forms a holding company and a for-profit subsidiary.
	Aug-94	Packard Electric announces it will open a manufacturing pant in Gadsden, Alabama, to produce wiring harnesses for GM's next generation of minivans.	United Way of Northampton County and United Way of Lehigh County merge to become the United Way of the Greater Lehigh Valley.
1995	Jan-95	Delphi Automotive Systems opens its Mexico Technical Center in Ciudad Juarez.	
	Jan-95	The new "supermax" Youngstown Penitentiary breaks ground. The $65 million facility will hold five hundred of Ohio's worst prisoners.	
	May-95	The proposed Ohio School of International Business dies after state officials reject it.	Bethlehem Steel ends hot steel production in Bethlehem. Officials promise quick redevelopment and community consultation on a

		Youngstown	Allentown
			plan for redeveloping a tract between the city's Minsi Trail and Fahy bridges.
1996	Jan-96	Lordstown starts making Chevy Cavaliers.	
	Nov-96	Delphi Automotive Systems announces plans to expand its Mexico Technical Center in Ciudad Juarez.	Lehigh Valley Economic Development Corporation is established with backing from the Lehigh Valley Partnership, taking over duties from various local EDCs throughout the region.
1997	Jan-97	A thirteen-month wiretap investigation culminates in the 1997 arrest of local mob boss Lenny Strollo. In the small city of Campbell, Strollo controlled at least 90 percent of the appointments to the police department.	
	Jan-97	Kent State University opens its Northeast Ohio Technology Education Center.	
	Jan-97	Kelly buys Avanti back from the Cafaro Company.	
	Feb-98	Youngstown State University completes a planned five-year campaign in three years after raising $26.3 million.	
	Aug-98		A $40 million joint venture of Air Products and BOC Gases will create seventy-five jobs in the Bethlehem Enterprise Zone.
1998	Sep-98	Six inmates escape from CCA prison facility.	
1999	Jan-99	Youngstown State University Foundation's assets exceed $130 million.	Air Products bids to acquire its main competitor, BOC, which eventually fails.

		Youngstown	*Allentown*

		Youngstown	*Allentown*
	Apr-99	United Community Financial Corporation—parent company of Home Savings and Loan—acquires financial services provider Butler-Wick Corporation.	
	May-99	Rep. James Traficant signs a "memorandum of understanding" with Doctor Crants, CCA's founder, agreeing to help the company site two more prisons in the district.	QED, Inc. joins forces with a manufacturer of compound semiconductor materials to complete a merger creating the industries' biggest group: IQE, Inc.
2000	Apr-00	The state's two-year capital budget provides $1 million instead of the $3 million requested to build a new high-tech business incubator.	
	Sep-00	The former president of Youngstown State University says campus trustees and public officials often pestered him for hiring favors.	
	Dec-00		Mack Truck is acquired by Volvo.
2001	Mar-01		Agere has a disappointing initial public offering of $3.6 billion.
	Apr-01	The last of 350 inmates will be out of the Northeast Ohio Correctional Center by August 18, the closing date for the company's contract to house prisoners for the District of Columbia.	
	May-01		Agere lays off two hundred from its Allentown plant.

		Youngstown	Allentown
	Oct-01	An investment company run by Bernie Kosar's family sets up an office in the Youngstown Business Incubator.	
2002	Jan-02	Caffaro pleads guilty to bribery in connection with the trial of U.S. Rep. James Traficant.	
	Apr-02	Traficant is convicted of bribery, racketeering, and fraud.	
	Aug-02	General Motors awards a new car—the Cobalt—to replace the Cavalier.	
	Sep-02	International Steel Group acquires LTV Corporation.	Lucent spins off Agere.
	Oct-02	Of the eleven tenants of the Youngstown Incubator, all but two are technology companies. They employ ninety-one and have a payroll of $3.4 million. They also receive four patents.	Bethlehem Steel files for Chapter 11 protection.
	Nov-02		Bethlehem and Allentown Chambers of Commerce combine to become the Lehigh Valley Chamber of Commerce.
2003	Jan-03		Agere sells optoelectronics business to Triquent.
	Aug-03		International Steel Group acquires Bethlehem Steel.
	Mar-03		Ailing microchip business IQE announces that it has parted company with two of its senior executives. Founder Tom Hierl and COO Steve Bayars will step down.

Notes

1. Cities That Worked

1. Bluestone and Harrison (1982).
2. Kochan, Katz, and McKersie (1986); Detrouzos, Lester, and Solow (1989); Womack, Jones, and Roos (1991).
3. Piore and Sabel (1984); Sabel and Zeitlin (1997).
4. Bluestone and Harrison (1982); Kochan, Katz, and McKersie (1986); Piore and Sabel (1984).
5. Throughout this book, references to Allentown and Youngstown pertain to each city's respective three-county Metropolitan Statistical Areas: Allentown-Bethlehem-Easton (PA) and Youngstown-Warren (OH). All statistics refer to data based on these definitions as well.
6. Deutch (1999).
7. Clines (2000a,b); see also Claiborne (2000).
8. On Youngstown's plans to shrink its footprint, see Nasser (2006) and Aeppel (2007).
9. Bureau of Labor Statistics, Metropolitan Areas at a Glance http://www.bls.gov/ro3/ro3_pa.htm.
10. Coleman (1984); Weinraub (1984).
11. Mouat (1984); Raines (1984).
12. DeGeer (1927).
13. Meyer (1989).
14. Bell (1976); Storper (1997).
15. The description of Fordism is related to a discussion about "varieties of capitalism." The American South, for instance, was largely—but certainly not completely—oriented toward agriculture and was not as integrated into the industrial hierarchy that existed in the North. The economies of Germany and Japan were organized differently than those in America and the United

Kingdom, with conglomerates centered on banks, rather than industrial oligopolies, serving as the most prominent way of organizing production along more elaborate systems for integrating interests of workers, communities, and government into the governance of industry. Further "varieties" have been elaborated on. On the concept of varieties of capitalism generally, see Hall and Soskice (2001), Dore, Lazonick, and O'Sullivan (1999), and Thelen (2004).

16. I use the term *variety* here advisedly. Fordism is in some ways a loaded term. Some consider it to be descriptive of any "industrial" economy and so would include different shades or varieties of Fordism prevailing in Northern Europe and Japan during the twentieth century. Even a list of reviews of that literature would not do it justice, but one good place to start is Amin (1994).

17. Lynd and Lynd (1929, 1937).

18. I do not claim to be the first to make such an argument; this delinking is a central tenet in the social theories of scholars such as Manuel Castells and Anthony Giddens, among others who have written on the emergence of modernity in the late twentieth century. More recently, Thomas Friedman (2002) invokes the memorable imagery of a "flat world" with goods, services, and information moving freely across geographic space conveyed by huge technological leaps in information technology and transportation and driving an increasingly sharp wedge between the institutions and processes governing communities and those governing the economy.

19. On the hub-and-spoke organization of industrial communities, see Romo and Schwartz (1985) and various essays in Markusen, Lee, and DiGiovanna (1999), particularly Markusen's chapters titled "Four Structures for Second Tier Cities" and "Studying Regions by Studying Firms," as well as Gray, Golob, and Markusen on Seattle's hub-and-spoke economy.

20. Whitford (2005:2).

21. Storper (1995); Cooke, Uranga, and Etxebarria (1997); Porter (2000).

22. See Fine (2006) and Osterman (2006).

23. On the consequences of the Reagan Revolution, see Pierson (1994) and Wier, Orloff, and Skocpol (1988).

24. This point speaks to a prominent argument among sociologists that explains the decline of industrial society as a result of *lock-in*. Proponents of the lock-in hypothesis argue that the very mechanisms that fostered economic efficiency during the period of the regions' growth and prosperity eventually came to constrain their ability to adapt. The rules and strictures of institutions and relationships that made it possible to cooperate effectively in a previous era became outdated, and individual actors found it difficult to shift to a different pattern of interacting even in the face of significant changes in the technological, social, or economic environment. As Gernot Grabher (1993, 1994) outlines it, lock-in revolves around three interrelated processes: (1) close interfirm relations founded on dense interpersonal ties generate echo chambers, amplifying information and understandings that already exist within a region while cutting actors off from new ideas; (2) high degrees of cohesion generate a totalizing worldview, generating narrow interpretive

frames and "groupthink"; and (3) a political culture of consensus produces cohesive political coalitions that block changes that might threaten the balance of power and influence among regional actors. Lock-in, in other words, is blamed on social structure, and specifically a tight interweaving of the social and economic relationships among community elites. Network sociologists who examine the actual structure of relationships in settings like this would use the term *density* to describe this tight interweaving, indicating strong social cohesion among a group of well-connected insiders. (On the relationship among inertia, density, and lock-in in social networks, see Burt 2000). But density is only one metric with which to describe relationships, and it is a fairly limited one at that. It is dichotomous: relationships are either dense or sparse. The tools exist to characterize the structure of relationships with much greater specificity, to examine the concrete *structure* of who is connected to whom and how. Doing so points toward the core empirical arguments developed in Chapters 3 and 4.

25. On institutions and institutionalism, see Hall and Taylor (1996), Nee (2005), Smelser and Swedberg (1994), and Thelen (1999). I draw particularly on the historical institutionalist tradition (see Clemens and Cook 1999, Fligstein 2001, Streeck and Thelen 2005, and Thelen 2003). My point of departure is a conviction that, while there may be a tendency in any community toward establishing and maintaining stability, communities are not inherently static. The constant evolution of new technologies, as well as the drive of other communities to survive and succeed, ensures a steady stream of externally driven events that confront and challenge communities to adapt. It is in the struggle to respond to these forces that communities evolve—through a constant push and pull between forces of decay, which push individuals away from cooperation, and forces of inertia, which pull individuals to maintain the status quo even in the face of an obvious need for change. Each change in the environment of a community presents a challenge to the established patterns.

26. This view draws more heavily on a path-dependent or "punctuated equilibrium" perspective on institutional change. See Fligstein (2001), Pierson (2000), and Pierson and Skocpol (2002).

27. The notion of "provisional moves" is related to Leifer's (1988) notion of "local action" and to Padgett and Ansell's (1993) notion of "robust action."

28. Powell, Koput, White, and Owen-Smith (2005) make a similar argument with respect to the emergence and evolution of San Diego's biotechnology sector: the industry in the region could have taken any of several paths; the one that emerged came out of early moves that then compounded over time to reinforce an emergent structure, which was eventually institutionalized.

29. The inspiration for this argument is found in John Padgett and Christopher Ansell's (1993) account of the rise of the Medici family to power in thirteenth-century Florence. As patrons and rulers, the Medici were vital to establishing Florence as the city that led Europe out of the Middle Ages and into the modern era, the site of myriad innovations as disparate as Michelangelo's

artistic genius and the methods of accounting and banking that continue to be used this day. But for my purposes, their importance is not in the role the family played in fostering innovation but in the circumstances that led to the Medici coming to power. In Padgett and Ansell's account, the ascent of the Medici was mainly a matter of occupying the right place in Florence's social structure at the right time. That time was a moment of crisis—akin to the collapse of the Soviet Union or the collapse of Fordism—which shook Florentine society to its foundations. Following a series of class revolts, the leading families of Florence had led the city into an ill-conceived war with neighboring city-states and ultimately suffered defeat. This humiliation undermined the hold of the elite enough to allow a new political pattern to emerge.

Padgett and Ansell were mainly interested in telling the story of the Medici themselves. Their focus is on how changes in the social structure benefited one particular actor within the social structure. But the effect of their rise to power was not limited to the Medici family; it fundamentally transformed the way that politics, economics, and culture worked in Florence. A deep crisis was the trigger, but the trajectory resulted from how the social structure shaped possibilities for action in its aftermath. Crucially, what led to the rise of the Medici was the fact that Florentine society was complex. It was organized in overlapping layers of identity and affiliation. When the political system was undermined, the Medici found themselves to be advantageously embedded within an underlying dimension of Florentine society. These alternative social structures as the platform led not only to the ascent of this one family, but to the fundamental reordering of that society.

30. Swidler (1986, 2001).
31. Molotch (1976, 1979); Molotch and Logan (1984); Logan and Molotch (1987).
32. See Marquis and Lounsbury (2007).
33. Dahl (1961).
34. Domhoff (1978).
35. See generally Storper (1995), Piore and Sabel (1984), Porter (1998), and Saxenian (1994).
36. The concept of multiplexity has a long lineage in social anthropology and in network analysis. Individuals interact on any number of dimensions with others. Expressed in terms of networks, one might have a particular group of contacts for work, a separate group of contacts with respect to religious expression, and a third with whom one engages in sports and recreation. Relationships are multiplex to the degree that a pair of actors has connections along more than one of those dimensions. Mitchell (1969) was among the first to identify the effect that multiplexity has on social change, observing that multiplexity among African villagers generates what he called "channel redundancy" with respect to communication, and therefore a tendency toward reinforcement of the status quo.

Density observed along one dimension will reinforce the density one finds elsewhere, which would suggest rigidity in the face of a change in the environment (Staber and Sydow 2002). But multiplex relationships need not overlap in such a way as to compound this among dimensions. Gould's provocative analysis of recruitment and commitment during the Paris Commune (1991, 1995) shows that overlapping ties between neighborhood and regiment significantly increased commitment to the cause, suggesting the role that multiplexity has within an explicitly political conception of change as well as the need to examine the particular dimensions on which multiplexity operates. Taken a step further, one can see how a pattern of multiplexity in which relationships among actors intersect but do not overlap can facilitate institutional and organizational change. To the degree that an individual, for instance, maintains separate networks of relationships in work, religious, and civic life, that individual then potentially becomes a link between those various realms; to the degree that different networks contain different meaning systems for interpreting and understanding the world, these nonoverlapping networks provide alternative sources of information and meaning from which new combinations of ideas or interpretations might emerge. Finally, access to multiple, separate networks provides a buffer in the event that one's position within one network—or the viability of the network itself—is jeopardized.

2. The Empirical Puzzle

1. On the rise of the American manufacturing belt, see Meyer (1983, 1989), Page and Walker (1991), Hudson (1989), and Teaford (1993).
2. Fordism refers to a particular macro-social regime of accumulation involving mass production, deskilling of work, and bureaucratic control over the means of production. Beyond the organization of the shop floor, the term extends to include modes of Keynesian macroeconomic policies as well as various means of international regulation. A full explication of Fordism and its role—if any—in the competitive crisis of the late 1970s and early 1980s is related to, but ultimately beyond, the scope of this endeavor. For discussions of Fordism in geographic context, see Tickell and Peck (1995), Goodwin and Painter (1996), and Jones and MacLeod (1999).
3. On the organization of industrial production during this period, see Hudson (1989) and Sabel (1992).
4. On the rise of industrial unionism in the United States, see Gutmann (1976), Montgomery (1979), Bernstein (1969), and Lichtenstein (1995).
5. On deindustrialization generally, see Bluestone and Harrison (1982), Magaziner and Reich (1982), Olson (1982), Piore and Sabel (1984), Markusen (1985), Scott (1988), Moore (1988), Storper and Walker (1989), Plunkert (1990), Walker (1981), Amin (1994), Romo and Schwartz (1995), and a review essay by Etzkowitz (1990). On the impact of deindustrialization on particular communities for Pittsburgh, see Hathaway (1993); on the Ohio Valley, see Brown et al. (1996); on Peoria, Illinois, see Uchitelle (1991); on

Syracuse, New York, see Short et al. (1993); and on Glasgow, Scotland, see Damer (1990).

6. Bluestone and Harrison (1982) is perhaps the best example.

7. On the divergence of outcomes among rust-belt cities since the early 1980s, see Magnet (1988), Harrison (1990), Florida (1995), Florida and Kenny (1992), Testa et al. (1997), Mayer and Greenberg (2001), and Faberman (2002).

8. Faberman (2002).

9. Amin and Thrift (1994) and Cooke (1995).

10. Bluestone and Harrison (1982:245–246).

11. Unpublished work by Howard Wial at the Brookings Institution has built on the analysis presented here to produce a similar—though admittedly superior—approach to examining the trajectory of cities in the rust belt. His analysis clusters 114 metropolitan areas in which manufacturing employment exceeded the national average in 1980 into five categories: low growth (defined as regions that lost large shares of durable manufacturing and which have not recovered), advanced services low growth (cities that lost manufacturing but kept pace with the national average in employment and wages), moderate growth (cities that lost manufacturing but gained in higher-growth industries accompanied by job and wage growth at the pace of the national average), advanced services moderate growth (above-average wage and job growth), and a final category identified as Southern growth clusters, which were marked by rapid gains in both wages and jobs. The results confirm the findings reported in this chapter: Youngstown, as one would expect, is located solidly in the low growth category. Allentown is situated in the moderate growth category. Allentown, in other words, has not excelled. It has essentially kept pace and done as well as might be expected under the circumstances. Youngstown, on the other hand, has fallen significantly behind.

12. Krugman (1993).

13. On the decentralization of economic policy following the election of Ronald Reagan, see Etzkowitz (1990).

14. On the concept of social capital and its intellectual heritage, see Portes (1998, 2000), Portes and Landolt (2000), Burt (2000), and Adler and Kwon (2002).

15. Putnam (2001).

16. Harrison (1995); Applebaum and Batt (1994).

17. For example, Leifer (1988) and Burt (1992).

18. Adler and Kwon (2002).

19. Breiger (1974).

20. Sewell (1992).

21. See Hirschmann (1958), Somers (1993), Locke and Thelen (1996), and Molotch, Freudenburg, and Paulsen (2000).

22. On the method of similarity in historical comparative analyses, see Skocpol and Somers (1980), Paige (1999), and Locke (1995).

23. This is drawn from Mill (1843/1976).

24. Page and Walker (1991).
25. Mizruchi (1996).
26. Laumann, Marsden, and Galaskiewicz (1977); Galaskiewicz (1979).
27. Burt (1980); Palmer and Barber (2001).
28. Mintz and Schwartz (1981).
29. Useem (1984); Davis (1991).
30. Kono et al. (1998).
31. Mills (1956); Mace (1971).
32. Domhoff (1967); Zeitlin (1974); Palmer (1983); Useem (1984).
33. Logan and Molotch (1987).

3. Historical Antecedents

1. On Moravian Bethlehem, see Mathews and Hungerford (1884), Levering (1903), Vadasz (1975), Yates (1978, 1992), Wolle (1972), and Folsom (2001).
2. On the early histories of Allentown and Easton, see Yates (1992) and Folsom (2001).
3. On the creation of Lehigh Coal and Navigation Company, see Parton (1986) and Folsom (2001). On Asa Packer, see Stuart (1938), Folsom (2001), and Venditta et al. (2003).
4. On the early history of the Lehigh Valley Railroad, see Vadasz (1975), Yates (1992), and Folsom (2001).
5. On the early history of Bethlehem Steel, see Cotter (1916), Vadasz (1975), Hessen (1974), Folsom (2001), and Venditta et al. (2003).
6. On the Fountain Hill elite and their activities (including the founding of Lehigh University), see Bowen (1929), Stuart (1938), Fister (1949), Hessen (1974), Ingham (1978), Yates (1992), Folsom (2001), and Venditta et al. (2003). On the founding of Lafayette and Muhlenberg colleges, see Swain (1967) and Ochsenford (1892).
7. On the history of the Connecticut Western Reserve, see Upton and Cutler (1910), Hatcher (1949), and Makowski (1973).
8. See Maharidge and Williamson (1985).
9. On the iron industry of the Mahoning Valley, see Kubik (n.d.), Butler (1921), Republic Steel Corporation (1943), and Youngstown Sheet and Tube (1950).
10. On the Mahoning Valley elite, see Upton (1909), Butler (1921), Girdler and Sparkes (1944), Aley (1974), Ingham (1978), Jenkins (1990), Stephens, Bobersky, and Cencia (1994), and Cart, Jagnow, and McFerren (2001).
11. On the introduction of the Bessemer process and the transformation from iron to steel generally, see Temin (1964) and Hogan (1971a,b).
12. Folsom (2001); Venditta et al. (2003).
13. Folsom (2001); Venditta et al. (2003).
14. On Frederick Taylor's time at Bethlehem Steel, see Nelson (1977), Hessen (1974), and Venditta et al. (2003).
15. Schwab is not related to the stockbroker Charles Schwab. On Charles Schwab and his years at Bethlehem Steel, see Grace (1948), Hessen (1974), and Venditta et al. (2003).

16. On the Fountain Hill elite and their activities, see Bowen (1929), Stuart (1938), Fister (1949), Hessen (1974), Ingham (1978), Yates (1992), Folsom (2001), and Venditta et al. (2003).

17. On the history of Lafayette College, see www.lafayette.edu/community/history.html.

18. When National Steel was incorporated into U.S. Steel Corporation in 1901, the Youngstown facilities eventually became the Ohio Works of U.S. Steel's subsidiary, the Carnegie-Illinois Corporation. See Hogan (1971b).

19. Although its largest production facilities were in Youngstown and Warren, its headquarters were located in New Jersey until 1930.

20. On the iron industry of the Mahoning Valley, see Kubik (n.d.), Butler (1921), Republic Steel Corporation (1943), Youngstown Sheet and Tube (1950), and Hogan (1971a).

21. On the community activities of the Wick Avenue elite, see Butler (1921) and Williams (1882).

22. On ethnic tensions and early organizing efforts in the Lehigh Valley, see Henry (1860), Pinkowski (1963), and Aurand (1991).

23. See Vadasz (1975), Illick (1989), and Yates (1992).

24. See Vadasz (1975) and Venditta et al. (2003).

25. See Vadasz (1975).

26. On the Bethlehem Steel Strike of 1910, see Cotter (1916), Brody (1960), Hessen (1974), Vadasz (1975), and Filippelli (1990).

27. On the hill-to-hill campaign, see Vadasz (1975).

28. Vadsz (1975).

29. On immigration patters of the Mahoning Valley, see Skardon (1983), Jenkins (1990), Stephens, Bobersky, and Cencia (1994), Bruno (1999), De-Blasio (2001), Cart, Jagnow, and McFerren (2001), and Linkon and Russo (2002).

30. Skardon (1983); DeBlasio (2001).

31. On the role of the YMCA in providing a bridge between old and new immigrants in Youngstown, see Skardon (1983).

32. On the steel strike of 1919 generally, see Brody (1965) and Gottlieb (1990). On its impact in the Mahoning Valley, see Skardon (1983) and Jenkins (1990).

33. Chicago-based Inland Steel was the fourth.

34. On industrial unions in the steel industry generally see Brody (1960), Bernstein (1969), Fine (1969), Montgomery (1979, 1987), Dubofsky (1984), and Hoerr (1988). On the Little Steel Strike of 1937, see Stolberg (1937), Blumenthal (1939), Silverberg (1941), Girdler and Sparkes (1944), Auerbach (1964), Sofchalk (1965), Speer (1969), and Baughman (1978).

35. On the implementation of the Mohawk Valley Plan in the Mahoning Valley, see Baughman (1978), Speer (1969), Sofchalk (1965), Girdler and Sparkes (1944), and Hogan (1971c).

36. Baughman (1978); Speer (1969); Sofchalk (1965); Girdler and Sparkes (1944); Hogan (1971c).

37. Baughman (1978); Speer (1969); Sofchalk (1965); Girdler and Sparkes (1944); Hogan (1971c).
38. Baughman (1978); Speer (1969); Sofchalk (1965); Girdler and Sparkes (1944); Hogan (1971c).
39. On the organizing of Bethlehem Steel, see Fones-Wolf and Fones-Wolf (1998), whose work provides much of the material for this section. See also Galenson (1960:107–116), Hogan (1971c), Lauderbaugh (1980), and Zeiger (1995).
40. Galenson (1960:107–116); Hogan (1971c); Lauderbaugh (1980); McCullough (1987); Zeiger (1995).
41. Galenson (1960:107–116); Hogan (1971c); Lauderbaugh (1980); McCullough (1987); Zeiger (1995).
42. Galenson (1960:107–116); Hogan (1971c); Lauderbaugh (1980); McCullough (1987); Zeiger (1995).

4. Two Critical Choices

1. Rodgers (1952a,b).
2. Walker (1981).
3. On the steel strikes of 1956 and 1959, see Hogan (1971c,d), Tiffany (1988), and Hoerr (1988).
4. On the steel crisis generally, see Hoerr (1988) and Tiffany (1988).
5. On the Ecumenical Coalition, see Buss and Redburn (1983), Lynd (1987), and Fuechtmann (1989).
6. Buss and Vaughan (1987).
7. An interesting challenge arose with respect to coding data pertaining to prominent wives. The data generally were coded in such a way that any two individuals with the same first and last names are assumed to be the same individual. However, in 1950 and 1975 many women took their husband's first and last names in formal settings. For instance, the wives of Sheet and Tube CEO Frank Purnell and Bethlehem Steel CEO Eugene Grace are generally listed as Mrs. Frank Purnell and Mrs. Eugene Grace, respectively. As John Strohmeyer (1986) makes clear in his book on Bethlehem Steel's rise and fall, these were not simply polite formalities. Wives' roles in the community were taken quite seriously:

> Conforming to the corporation's mores does not end with the executive. His wife (very few women have achieved executive status at Bethlehem Steel) is all but given a script to follow. Her wardrobe, topics of conversation, general appearance, drinking habits, skills as a hostess and certainly her devotion to her husband's career are carefully scrutinized. . . .
>
> The cloistered role for the wives back in the fifties and sixties reflected the cultural insecurity of the company's officials, then the highest paid industrial managers in the country. Although most were college graduates, the need to establish social credentials was paramount and the role models were eagerly sought. No woman sent tremors through ambitious

steel families more than that wife who came to the company with a Seven Sisters degree, a collection of heirloom silver and a lineage of old money. This type was home free. She could do as she pleased, join the organizations she chose, and always be accepted at the highest company level.

For the majority of wives, however, such license was an unavailable luxury. For them membership in even the non-partisan League of Women Voters was taboo (although they coveted and sought enrollment in the Junior League). The Ladies' Auxiliary of St. Luke's Hospital, church work, and family duties were the approved ways to use spare time. Later, during the seventies and assuredly in the eighties opportunities broadened to include working with youth services and health agencies. The right to pursue their own careers also became acceptable. Lucky was the organization that captured the attention of the steel chairman's wife. A whole retinue of eager volunteers was sure to follow. When Marge Foy, wife of Chairman Lewis Foy who headed the company from 1974 to 1980, plunged into volunteer work with the American Cancer Society, the local chapter became the biggest fund raiser in the state. This was due in part to the support she received from steel executives' wives." (Strohmeyer 1986:47–49)

This raises a difficult question for data collection, with a direct bearing on the outcomes we seek to gauge: to treat wives in the data as serving in their own right or as extensions of their husband's social obligations? I have chosen the latter—when a woman is listed using her husband's first and last name, the assumption is made that she is essentially acting in her husband's capacity. Where women are listed under their own names, they are counted as separate individuals. A dummy variable in the data notes wherever a civic tie is attributable to a wife's participation. In this way the data are included in all analyses that follow.

8. This grouping is slightly different from—though consistent with—Markusen's (1987:153) approach, which breaks local organizations into four categories: (1) economic institutions (union, business organizations), (2) political (local and regional governments and political parties), (3) cultural (churches, community groups), and (4) information-ideological institutions (the press and universities). Essentially, this research collapses categories 2, 3, and 4 into one.

9. Where necessary, data from the years either immediately before or after the target dates were substituted.

10. The quadratic assignment procedure is used in order to overcome the obvious colinearity of the data, which would lead to spurious correlation significance measures using conventional techniques. The procedure compares the observed correlation with a distribution of random correlations generated according to the null hypothesis of no relationship between the matrices. The p value is given by the proportion of random correlations that are as large as or larger than the observed correlation. The value does so by permuting the rows and columns (together) of the input matrices, and then cor-

relating the permuted matrix with the other data matrix. This process is repeated hundreds of times to build up a distribution of correlations under the null hypothesis.

5. How Allentown Got Its Groove Back

1. Interview, Tom Hierl, IQE.
2. For a detailed description, see Buss, Clebone, Stanley, and Mitchell (1990).
3. Thompson Financial, VenturExpert.
4. U.S. Department of Commerce data.
5. Harvard Cluster Mapping Project.
6. Several factors might explain these differences, including Allentown's geographic location within the highly entrepreneurial New York–Northern New Jersey–Philadelphia economic corridor. But the growth of the surrounding area cannot explain all of Allentown's successes. For example, over the course of the 1990s, new firms' growth in the New York–Northern New Jersey, Philadelphia–Southern New Jersey economies was 0.79 percent and 0.49 percent, respectively. The figures for Cleveland-Akron and Pittsburgh, major metropolitan areas located about the same distance from Youngstown as New York and Philadelphia are from Allentown, were 0.74 percent and 0.40 percent, respectively. Although the growth rate is slightly higher in Allentown's case, it is not high enough to explain the magnitude of the difference in new firm creation between Allentown and Youngstown.
7. Of course, given the findings of the previous chapters, we must question whether the dense core of economic leaders that has emerged in the Lehigh Valley is either sustainable or even a good thing in the long run, a question we will return to later.
8. As we saw earlier, there are several ways of measuring centrality within a network. Eigenvector centrality measures are appealing in this context because they take into account not only the network properties of the focal organization but also those of the organizations to which they are connected, resulting in a higher score for organizations that are connected to other high-status organizations.
9. On the transformation of American manufacturing in the postindustrial era, see Whitford (2005).
10. Data for 1960 are from Folger and Nam (1974:168). Data for 2000 were retrieved from the Internet via the U.S. Census DataFerret using a cross-tabulation of occupation and educational attainment for the following occupations: textile, apparel, and furnishings workers, all other (51–6099); miscellaneous plant and system operator (51–8090); chemical processing machine setters, operators, and tenders (51–901); packaging and filling machine operators and tenders (51–9111); cementing and gluing machine operators and tenders (51–9191); molders, shapers, and casters, except metal and plastic (51–9195); and tire builders (51–9197).
11. On the history of the transistor and AT&T generally, see Leslie (2001).
12. Leslie (2001).

13. It is interesting to note that another Lehigh Valley company—Air Products and Chemicals—had been (and remains) Allentown's primary supplier of industrial gases. Air Products was founded on the innovation of building and maintaining mini production plants directly at major customers' plants (rather than the usual practice of manufacturing gases at a central facility and then shipping them). The company thrived on this strategy as a supplier to large industrial firms with fixed assets—primarily steel and other metals manufacturers. But with the decline of heavy manufacturing, Air Products found itself looking for new directions in the late 1960s. Silicon Valley was just beginning to show signs that it would become a new industrial district centered on microelectronics at that point, and Air Products launched a new—and very risky—strategy of building centralized, fixed nitrogen-supply pipelines to facilities in the valley, which opened in 1971. In doing so, it built on skills and know-how garnered from supplying gases to Western Electric in Allentown. The companies maintain a close relationship—both economic and civic—today; the retired CEO of Air Products, Hap Wagner, serves as chairman of Agere Systems' board of directors.

14. In early 2003, Agere sold its optoelectronics business to TriQuint, a Portland-based semiconductor manufacturer

15. This section draws heavily from Helper (1998) and Rivero (2002).

16. Rivero (2002).

17. The Small Business Innovation Research Program (SBIR) and the Small Business Technology Transfer Program (STTR) are U.S. government programs that award seed grants to entrepreneurial companies based on a rigorous—peer reviewed—selection process. See Audretsch (2003) for a description and discussion of its use as an indicator of regional entrepreneurial performance.

18. Walter Dealtrey was cited by a number of interviewees as a particularly pivotal person in the Lehigh Valley's economic recovery. Many called him the driving force behind the success of the Lehigh Valley Industrial Parks. Dealtrey died in 2003.

19. The Ben Franklin Technology Partnership is an initiative of the State of Pennsylvania established in 1983. Charles Sabel (then a professor of political economy at Massachusetts Institute of Technology, who with Mike Piore coined the phrase "flexible specialization") sat on the organization's board of directors at the state level and was an important influence in articulating the Ben Franklin program's goals early on.

20. Baron (1985).

21. Associated Press, 2000.

6. Conclusions and Implications

1. See Whitford (2005).

2. Putnam (1995, 2001), but see also Etzioni (1993) and Fukuyama (1995). On social capital more generally, see reviews by Adler and Kwon (2002), Fine (1999), Portes and Landolt (2000), Chupp (1999), Woolcock (1998), and Portes (1998).

3. All of these scholars stands on the shoulders of Jane Jacobs (1961), who powerfully argued that it is the vibrant, diverse, messy, and cacophonous intermingling of people that brings cities to life.

4. Piore and Sabel (1984); Sabel and Zeitlin (1997).

5. Saxenian (1994).

6. Porter (1990, 1998, 2000).

7. Amin and Thrift (1994); Cooke, Uranga, and Etxebarria (1997).

8. Florida (2004).

9. Grabher and Stark (1997).

10. See Burt (1992, 2000); Merton (1957).

11. Tilly (1998).

12. Padgett and Ansell (1993); Padgett (2000).

13. Stark (1996); Grabher and Stark (1997).

14. By improvising, I mean something similar to Stark's use of the term *bricolage*; see Stark (1996).

15. Evans (1995).

16. Heller (1996, 2000).

17. Locke (1995).

18. Portes (1998).

19. Tilly (1992).

20. Stark (1996).

21. Saxenian (1996).

22. Piore and Sabel (1984); Sabel (1992); Sabel and Zeitlin (1997).

23. Skocpol (2001); Osterman (2002).

24. Bourdieu (1986); Emirbayer and Goodwin (1994); DeFilippis (2001).

References

Abbot, Andrew. 1997. "Of Time and Space: The Contemporary Relevance of the Chicago School." *Social Forces* 74(4): 1149–1182.

Abernathy, William J., Kim B. Clark, and Alan M. Kantrow. 1983. *Industrial Renaissance: Producing a Competitive Future for America*. New York: Basic Books.

Abernathy, William J., and J. Utterback. 1978. "Patterns of Industrial Innovation." *Technology Review* 50: 41–47.

Adler, Paul S., and Seok-Woo Kwon. 2002. "Social Capital: Prospects for a New Concept." *Academy of Management Review* 27(1): 17–40.

Aley, Howard C. 1974. *A Heritage to Share: The Bicentennial History of Youngstown and the Mahoning Valley, Ohio*. Youngstown, OH: Bicentennial Commission of Youngstown and Mahoning Valley.

Amin, Ash, ed. 1994. *Post-Fordism: A Reader*. Cambridge, MA: Blackwell Publishing.

Amin, Ash, and N. Thrift. 1994. "Globalization and Regional Development." *Ponte* 50(7–8): 67–81.

Amsden, Alice. 2003. *The Rise of "the Rest": Challenges to the West from Late-Industrializing Economies*. New York: Oxford University Press.

Applebaum, Elaine, and Rosemary Batt. 1994. *The New American Workplace: Transforming Work Systems in the United States*. Ithaca, NY: ILR Press.

Associated Press. 2000. "Ex-Youngstown State President Says He Was Pestered for Hiring Favors." *Associated Press State and Local Wire*, September 27.

Audrestch, David B. 2003. "Standing on the Shoulders of Midgets: The U.S. Small Business Innovation Research Program." *Small Business Economics* 20(2): 129–135.

Auerbach, Jarold S. 1964. "The LaFollette Committee: Labor and Civil Liberties in the New Deal." *Journal of American History* 51(3): 435–459.

Aurand, Harold W. 1991. "Anthracite Coal Strike of 1868." In *Labor Conflict in the United States: An Encyclopedia*, ed. Ronald L. Filippelli. New York: Garland Publishing.

Barley, Steven R. 1989. "Careers, Identities and Institutions: The Legacy of the Chicago School of Sociology." In *Handbook of Career Theory*, ed. Michael B. Arthur, Douglas T. Hall, and Barbara S. Lawrence. New York: Cambridge University Press.

Baron, James. 1985. "G.M. Getting Roses and Proposals from Suitors for Saturn Car Plant." *New York Times*, February 18, A1.

Baughman, James. 1978. "Classes and Company Towns." *Ohio History* 87: 175–192.

Bell, Daniel. 1976. *The Coming of Post-Industrial Society: A Venture in Social Forecasting*. New York: Basic Books.

Ben Franklin Technology Partners. 2003. *A Continuing Record of Achievement: The Economic Impact of the Ben Franklin Technology Partners*. Harrisburg, PA: Ben Franklin Technology Partners.

Bernstein, Irving. 1969. *The Turbulent Years: A History of the American Worker*. New York: Garland Publishing.

Blucher, Walter H. 1955. *Youngstown Comprehensive Plan: City Planning Administration in Youngstown*. Youngstown, OH: Pace Associates.

Bluestone, Barry, and Bennett Harrison. 1982. *The Deindustrialization of America: Plant Closings, Community Abandonment, and the Dismantling of Basic Industry*. New York: Basic Books.

Blumenthal, Frank H. 1939. "Anti-Union Publicity in the Johnstown 'Little Steel' Strike of 1937." *Public Opinion Quarterly* 3(4): 676–682.

Borgatti, S. P., and S. L. Feld. 1994. "How to Test Granovetter's Theory of Weak Ties." *Connections* 17(1): 45–46.

Bourdieu, Pierre. 1986. "The Forms of Capital." In *Handbook of Theory and Research for the Sociology of Education*. New York: Greenwood Press.

Bowen, Catherine Drinker. 1924. *A History of Lehigh University*. South Bethlehem, PA: Lehigh Alumni Bulletin.

Breiger, Ronald S. 1974. "Duality of Persons and Groups." *Social Forces* 53(2): 181–190.

Brody, David. 1960. *Steelworkers in America: The Nonunion Era*. Cambridge, MA: Harvard University Press.

———. 1965. *Labor in Crisis: The Steel Strike of 1919*. Philadelphia: Lippincott.

Brown, Lawrence A., Linda M. Lobao, and Anthony L. Verheyen. 1996. "Continuity and Change in an Old Industrial Region." *Growth and Change* 27: 175–205.

Bruno, Robert B. 1999. *Steelworker Alley: How Class Works in Youngstown*. Ithaca, NY: ILR Press.

Burt, Ronald S. 1980. "Models of Network Structure." *Annual Review of Sociology* 6: 79–141.

———. 1992. *Structural Holes: The Social Structure of Competition.* Cambridge, MA: Harvard University Press.

———. 2000. "The Network Structure of Social Capital." *Research in Organizational Behavior* 22: 345–423.

Buss, Terry F., Arnold Cleborne, Pamela Stanley, and Peter Mitchell. 1990. "Putting It All Together: Financing Sovereign Circuits." In *Financing Economic Development: An Institutional Response,* ed. R. D. Bingham, E. W. Hill, and S. B. White. Newbury Park, CA: Sage Publications.

Buss, Terry F., and F. S. Redburn. 1983. "Religious Leaders as Policy Advocates: The Youngstown Steel Mill Closing." *Policy Studies Journal* 11.

Buss, Terry F., and R. J. Vaughan. 1987. "Revitalizing the Mahoning Valley." *Environment and Planning C* 5(4): 433–446.

Butler, Joseph G., Jr. 1921. *History of Youngstown and the Mahoning Valley, Ohio.* 3 vols. Chicago: American History Society.

Cart, Sarah, Paul Jagnow, and Robert McFerren. 2001. *These Hundred Years: A Chronicle of the Twentieth Century as Recorded in the Pages of the Youngstown Vindicator.* Youngstown, OH: Youngstown Vindicator.

Castilla, Emilio J. 2003. "Networks of Venture Capital in Silicon Valley." *International Journal of Technology Management* 25(1–2): 113–135.

Chupp, Mark. 1999. *Investing in People through Place: The Role of Social Capital in Transforming Neighborhoods. A Literature Review of Social Capital and Neighborhood Transformation.* Cleveland, OH: Cleveland State University.

Claiborne, William. 2000. "A Rust Belt Democrat Will Not Go Gently; Facing Primary Challenge, Possible Indictment, Ohio's Flamboyant Rep. Traficant Remains Defiant." *Washington Post,* February 26, A3.

Clark, Paul F., Peter Gottlieb, and Donald Kennedy, eds. 1987. *Forging a Union of Steel: Philip Murray, SWOC, and the United Steelworkers.* Ithaca, NY: ILR Press.

Clemens, Elisabeth, and James Cook. 1999. "Politics and Institutionalism: Explaining Durability and Change." *Annual Review of Sociology* 25: 441–466.

Clines, Francis X. 2000a. "Fighting to Help an Ohio City Shed Its Image as 'Crimetown U.S.A.'" *New York Times,* April 16, A20.

———. 2000b. "Youngstown Reformers Seek Mob-Fighting Tips in Sicily." *New York Times,* November 21, A14.

Coleman, Milton. 1984. "Mondale Charges Reagan Is 'Hellbent' on Arms Race." *Washington Post,* September 18.

Cooke, Philip, ed. 1995. *The Rise of the Rustbelt.* New York: St. Martin's Press.

Cooke, Philip, Mikel Gomez Uranga, and Goio Etxebarria. 1997. "Regional Innovation Systems: Institutional and Organizational Dimensions." *Research Policy* 26(4–5): 475–491.

Cotter, Arundel. 1916. *The Story of Bethlehem Steel.* New York: Moody.

Dahl, Robert A. 2005. *Who Governs: Democracy and Power in an American City,* 2nd ed. New Haven, CT: Yale University Press.

Damer, S. 1990. *Glasgow: Going for a Song.* London: Lawrence and Wishart.

Davis, Gerald F. 1991. "Agents without Principles? The Spread of the Poison Pill through the Intercorporate Network." *Administrative Science Quarterly* 36(4): 583–613.

DeBlasio, Donna M. 2001. "The Immigrant and the Trolley Park in Youngstown, Ohio, 1899–1945." *Rethinking History* 5(1): 75–91.

DeFilippis, James. 2001. "The Myth of Social Capital in Community Development." *Housing Policy Debate* 12(4): 781–806.

DeGeer, Sten. 1927. "The American Manufacturing Belt." *Geografiska Annaler* 9: 233–359.

Deily, Mary E. 1991. "Exit Strategies and Plant-Closing Decisions: The Case of Steel." *Rand Journal of Economics* 22(2): 250–263.

Dertouzos, M. L., R. K. Lester, and R. M. Solow. 1989. *Made in America: Regaining the Productive Edge.* Cambridge, MA: MIT Press.

Deutch, Claudia H. 1999. "Lehigh Phoenix Rises from Big Steel's Ashes; Eastern Pennsylvania Region Recovers by Turning to Technology Companies." *New York Times,* October 7, Business/Financial Desk.

DiMaggio, Paul. 1997. "Culture and Cognition." *Annual Review of Sociology* 23: 263–287.

Domhoff, G. W. 1967. *Who Rules America?* Englewood Cliffs, NJ: Prentice-Hall.

———. 1978. *Who Really Rules? New Haven and Community Power Re-Examined.* New Brunswick, NJ: Transaction Books.

Dore, R. 1973. *British Factory, Japanese Factory: The Origins of National Diversity in Industrial Relations.* London: Allen and Unwin.

Dubofsky, Melvyn. 1984. *Labor in America: A History.* Arlington Heights, OH: N.p.

Emirbayer, Mustafa, and J. Goodwin. 1994. "Network Analysis, Culture, and the Problem of Agency." *American Journal of Sociology* 99: 1411–1454.

Emirbayer, Mustafa, and Ann Mische. 1998. "What Is Agency?" *American Journal of Sociology* 103(4): 962–1023.

Etzioni, A. 1993. *The Spirit of Community: The Reinvention of American Society.* New York: Touchstone.

Etzkowitz, Henry. 1990. "The Capitalization of Knowledge: The Decentralization of United States Industry and Science Policy from Washington to the States." *Theory and Society* 19(1): 107–121.

Evans, Peter. 1995. *Embedded Autonomy: States and Industrial Transformation.* Princeton, NJ: Princeton University Press.

Faberman, R. Jason. 2002. "Job Flows and Labor Dynamics in the U.S. Rust Belt." *Monthly Labor Review* 125: 3–10.

Fernandez, Roberto M., and Roger V. Gould. 1994. "A Dilemma of State Power: Brokerage and Influence in the National Health Policy Domain." *American Journal of Sociology* 99: 1455–1491.

Fernandez, Roberto M., and Doug McAdam. 1988. "Social Networks and Social Movements: Multiorganizational Fields and Recruitment to Mississippi Freedom Summer." *Sociological Forum* 3(3): 357–382.

Filippelli, Ronald L. 1990. "Bethlehem Steel Strike of 1910." In *Labor Conflict in the United States: An Encyclopedia,* ed. Ronald L. Filippelli. New York: Garland Publishing.

Fine, Ben. 1999. "The Developmental State Is Dead: Long Live Social Capital." *Development and Change* 31(1): 1–19.

Fine, Janice. 2006. *Worker Centers: Organizing Communities at the Edge of the Dream.* Ithaca, NY: Cornell University Press.

Fine, Sidney. 1969. *Sit Down: The General Motors Strike of 1936–1937.* Ann Arbor: University of Michigan Press.

Fister, Gordon B. 1949. *Half-Century: The Fifty-Year History of the Allentown Hospital, 1899–1949.* Allentown, PA: Board of Trustees of the Allentown Hospital Association.

Fligstein, Neil. 2001. "Markets as Politics: A Political-Cultural Approach to Market Institutions." *American Sociological Review* 61: 656–673.

Florida, Richard. 1995. "The Industrial Transformation of the Great Lakes." In *The Rise of the Rustbelt,* ed. Philip Cooke. New York: St. Martin's Press.

———. 2004. *The Rise of the Creative Class.* New York: Basic Books.

Florida, Richard, and Martin Kenney. 1992. "Restructuring in Place: Japanese Investment, Production Organization, and the Geography of Steel." *Economic Geography* 68(2): 146–173.

Folger, John, and Charles Nam. 1974. *Education of the American Population.* Washington, DC: Bureau of the Census.

Folsom, Burton W., Jr. 2001. *Urban Capitalists: Entrepreneurs and City Growth in Pennsylvania's Lackawanna and Lehigh Regions, 1800–1920.* Scranton, PA: University of Scranton Press.

Fones-Wolf, Elizabeth, and Ken Fones-Wolf. 1998. "Conversion at Bethlehem: Religion and Union Building in Steel, 1930–42." *Labor History* 39(4): 381–395.

Friedman, Thomas. 2002. *The World Is Flat: A Brief History of the Twenty-First Century.* New York: Picador.

Fuechtmann, T. G. 1989. *Steeples and Stacks: Religion and the Steel Crisis in Youngstown.* New York: Cambridge University Press.

Fukuyama, Francis. 1995. *Trust: The Social Virtues and the Creation of Prosperity.* New York: Free Press Paperbacks.

Galaskiewicz, J. 1979. "Structure of Community Organizational Networks." *Social Forces* 57(4): 1346–1364.

Galenson, Walter. 1960. *The CIO Challenge to the AFL.* Cambridge, MA: Harvard University Press.

Ganz, Marshall. 2000. "Resources and Resourcefulness: Strategic Capacity in the Unionization of California Agriculture, 1959–1966." *American Journal of Sociology* 105(4): 1003–1062.

Girdler, Tom M., and Boyden Sparkes. 1944. *Boot Straps: The Autobiography of Tom M. Girdler.* New York: Charles Scribner.

Goodwin, M., and J. Painter. 1996. "Local Governance, the Crises of Fordism, and the Changing Geographies of Regulation." *Transactions of the Institute of British Geographers* 21(4): 635–648.

Gottlieb, Daniel. 1990. "Steel Strike of 1919" and "Steel Strike of 1937." In *Labor Conflict in the United States: An Encyclopedia,* ed. Ronald L. Filippelli. New York: Garland Publishing.

Gould, Roger V. 1991. "Multiple Networks and Mobilization in the Paris Commune, 1871." *American Sociological Review* 56(6): 716–729.

———. 1995. *Insurgent Identities: Class, Community, and Protest from 1848 to the Commune.* Chicago: University of Chicago Press.

Grabher, Gernot. 1993. "The Weakness of Strong Ties: The Lock-in of Regional Development in the Ruhr Area." In *The Embedded Firm: On the Socio-Economics of Interfirm Relations,* ed. G. Grabher. New York: Routledge, 255–278.

———. 1994. "The Dis-Embedded Economy: The Transformation of East German Industrial Complexes into Western Enclosures." In *Globalization, Institutions and Regional Development in Europe,* ed. A. Amin and N. Thrift. New York: Oxford University Press, 177–196.

———. 2002. "The Project Ecology of Advertising: Tasks, Talents, and Teams." *Regional Studies* 3(1): 245–262.

Grabher, Gernot, and David Stark. 1997. *Restructuring Networks in Post-Socialism.* New York: Oxford University Press.

Grann, David. 2000. "Crimetown USA: The City That Fell in Love with the Mob." *New Republic,* May 10, p. 23.

Granovetter, M. 1985. "Economic Action and Social Structure." *American Journal of Sociology* 91: 481–510.

Gutmann, Herbert. 1976. *Work, Culture and Society in Industrializing America.* New York: Knopf.

Hall, Peter, and Rosemary Taylor. 1996. "Political Science and the Three New Institutionalisms." *Political Studies* 44: 936–957.

Hardin, Garrett. 1968. "The Tragedy of the Commons." *Science* 162(3859): 1243–1248.

Harrison, Bennett. 1990. "The Economic Perspective: Polishing the Rust Belt." *MIT Technology Review* 93(7): 74.

———. 1995. *Lean and Mean: The Changing Landscape of Corporate Power in the Age of Flexibility.* New York: Basic Books.

Harrison, Bennett, and Barry Bluestone. 1988. *The Great U-turn: Corporate Restructuring and the Polarizing of America.* New York: Basic Books.

Hassink, R. 2005. "How to Unlock Regional Economies from Path Dependency? From Learning Region to Learning Cluster." *European Planning Studies* 13(4): 521–535.

Hatcher, Harlan H. 1949. *The Western Reserve: The Story of New Connecticut in Ohio.* Indianapolis, IN: Bobbs-Merrill.

Hathaway, Dale. 1993. *Can Workers Have a Voice? The Politics of Deindustrialization in Pittsburgh.* University Park: Pennsylvania State University Press.

Heller, Patrick. 1996. "Social Capital as a Product of Class Mobilization and

State Intervention: Industrial Workers in Kerala, India." *World Development* 24(6): 1055–1071.

———. 2000. *The Labor of Development: Workers and the Transformation of Capitalism in Kerala, India*. Ithaca, NY: Cornell University Press.

Helper, Susan. 1998. "Lean Production and the Specter of Mexico: A Case Study of a U.S. Auto Parts Plant." In *Confronting Change: Auto Labor and Lean Production in North America*, ed. H. Juarez and S. Babson. Detroit, MI: Wayne State University Press.

Henry, M. S. 1860. *History of the Lehigh Valley*. Easton, PA: Bixler and Corwin.

Hessen, Robert. 1974. "The Bethlehem Steel Strike of 1910." *Labor History* 15(1): 3–18.

Hirschmann, Albert. 1958. *The Strategy of Economic Development*. New Haven, CT: Yale University Press.

Hoerr, John P. 1988. *And the Wolf Finally Came: The Decline of the American Steel Industry*. Pittsburgh, PA: University of Pittsburgh Press.

Hogan, William T. 1971a. *Economic History of the Iron and Steel Industry in the United States, 1860–1900*. Vol. 1. Lexington, MA: Lexington Books.

———. 1971b. *Economic History of the Iron and Steel Industry in the United States, 1900–1920*. Vol. 2. Lexington, MA: Lexington Books.

———. 1971c. *Economic History of the Iron and Steel Industry in the United States, 1920–1945*. Vol. 3. Lexington, MA: Lexington Books.

———. 1971d. *Economic History of the Iron and Steel Industry in the United States, 1946–1971*. Vol. 4. Lexington, MA: Lexington Books.

Hudson, R. 1989. "Labour-Market Changes and New Forms of Work in Old Industrial Regions: Maybe Flexibility for Some but Not Flexible Accumulation." *Environment and Planning D: Society and Space* 7(1): 5–30.

Illick, Joseph. 1989. *At Liberty: Story of a Community and a Generation*. Knoxville: University of Tennessee Press.

Ingham, J. N. 1978. *The Iron Barons: A Social Analysis of an American Urban Elite*. Westport, CT: Greenwood Press.

Jacobs, Jane. 1961. *The Death and Life of Great American Cities*. New York: Random House.

Jenkins, William D. 1990. *Steel Valley Klan: The Ku Klux Klan in Ohio's Mahoning Valley*. Kent, Ohio: Kent State University Press.

Jones, M., and G. MacLeod. 1999. "Towards a Regional Renaissance? Reconfiguring and Rescaling England's Economic Governance." *Transactions of the Institute of British Geographers* 24(3): 295–313.

Kirkland, Edward C. 1961. *Industry Comes of Age: Business, Labor and Public Policy, 1860–1897*. New York: Holt, Rinehart and Winston.

Knoke, David. 1993. "Networks of Elite Structure and Decision Making." *Sociological Methods and Research* 22(1): 23–45.

Knoke, David, Edward O. Laumann, Joseph Galaskiewicz, and Peter Marsden. 1978. "Community Structure as Interorganizational Linkages." *Annual Review of Sociology* 4: 455–484.

Kochan, Thomas A., Harry C. Katz, and Robert B. McKersie. 1986. *The Transformation of American Industrial Relations.* New York: Basic Books.

Kono, Clifford, Donald Palmer, Roger Friedland, and Matthew Zafonte. 1998. "Lost in Space: The Geography of Corporate Interlocking Directorates." *American Journal of Sociology* 103: 863–911.

Krugman, Paul. 1991. "Increasing Returns and Economic Geography." *Journal of Political Economy* 99: 483–499.

———. 1993. "First Nature, Second Nature and Metropolitan Location." *Journal of Regional Science* 33(2): 129–144.

Kubik, Maraline. n.d. "Industrialists' Legacies: Two Men Live On through Philanthropy." *Youngstown Business Journal,* www.business-journal.com/commom2000/comm_industrialists.html.

Lauderbaugh, Richard A. 1980. *American Steel Makers and the Coming of the Second World War.* Ann Arbor, MI: UMI Research Press.

Laumann, E. O., J. Galaskiewicz, and P. V. Marsden. 1978. "Community Structure as Interorganizational Linkages." *Annual Review of Sociology* 4: 455–484.

Laumann, E. O., P. V. Marsden, and J. Galaskiewicz. 1977. "Community-Elite Influence Structures: Extension of a Network Approach." *American Journal of Sociology* 83(3): 594–631.

Laumann, E. O., P. V. Marsden, and D. Prensky. 1992. "The Boundary Specification Problem in Network Analysis." In *Research Methods in Network Analysis,* ed. L. Freeman, D. White, and A. Romney. New Brunswick, NJ: Transaction.

Leifer, Eric M. 1988. "Interaction Preludes to Role Setting." *American Sociological Review* 53: 865–878.

Leslie, Stuart. 2001. "Blue Collar Science: Bringing the Transistor to Life in the Lehigh Valley." *Historical Studies in the Physical and Biological Sciences* 32(1): 71–113.

Levering, Joseph M. 1903. *A History of Bethlehem, Pennsylvania, 1741–1892.* Bethlehem, PA: Times Publishing Co.

Lichtenstein, Nelson. 1995. *The Most Dangerous Man in Detroit.* New York: Basic Books.

Linkon, Sherry Lee, and John Russo. 2002. *Steeltown USA: Work and Memory in Youngstown.* Topeka: University Press of Kansas.

Locke, Richard M. 1995. *Remaking the Italian Economy.* Ithaca, NY: Cornell University Press.

Locke, Richard M., and Kathleen Thelen. 1996. "Apples and Oranges Revisited: Contextualized Comparison and the Study of Comparative Labor Politics." *Politics and Society* 23(3): 337–367.

Logan, John R., and Harvey L. Molotch. 1987. *Urban Fortunes: The Political Economy of Place.* Berkeley: University of California Press.

Lynd, Robert S., and Helen M. Lynd. 1929. *Middletown: A Study in Contemporary American Culture.* New York: Harcourt, Brace, and Company.

————. 1937. *Middletown in Transition: A Study in Cultural Conflicts.* New York: Harcourt, Brace, and Company.

Lynd, Staunton. 1987. "The Genesis of the Idea of a Community Right to Industrial Property in Youngstown and Pittsburgh: 1977–1987." *Labor History* 74(3): 926–958.

Mace, M. L. 1971. *Directors: Myth and Reality.* Cambridge, MA: Harvard Business School Press.

Magaziner, Ira, and Robert Reich. 1982. *The Decline and Rise of the American Economy.* New York: Random House.

Magnet, Myron. 1988. "The Resurrection of the Rust Belt." *Fortune* 114(11): 116.

Maharidge, Dale, and Michael Williamson. 1985. *Journey to Nowhere: The Saga of the New Underclass.* Garden City, NJ: Doubleday.

Makowski, Karen. 1973. *Early Pioneers of the Western Reserve.* Boston: Lee and Shepard.

Markusen, Ann. 1985. *Profit Cycles, Oligopoly, and Regional Development.* Cambridge, MA: MIT Press.

————. 1987. *Regions: The Economics and Politics of Territory.* Totowa, NJ: Rowman and Littlefield.

————. 1994. "Studying Regions by Studying Firms." *Professional Geographer* 46(4): 477–490.

Markusen, Ann, Y. S. Lee, and S. DiGiovanna. 1999. *Second Tier Cities: Rapid Growth beyond the Metropolis.* Minneapolis: University of Minnesota Press.

Marquis, Christopher, and Michael Lounsbury. 2007. "Vive la Résistance: Competing Logics and the Consolidation of U.S. Community Banking." *Academy of Management Journal* 50(4): 799–820.

Mathews, Alfred, and Austin N. Hungerford. 1884. *A History of Bethlehem, Pennsylvania, 1741–1892.* Philadelphia: Everts and Richards.

Mayer, Henry J., and Michael R. Greenberg. 2001. "Coming Back from Economic Despair: Case Studies of Small- and Medium-Size American Cities." *Economic Development Quarterly* 15(3): 203–216.

McAdam, Doug. 1988. *Freedom Summer.* New York: Oxford University Press.

McCulloch, Mark. 1987. "Consolidating Industrial Citizenship: The USWA at War and Peace, 1939–1946." In *Forging a Union of Steel: Philip Murray, SWOC, and the United Steelworkers,* ed. Paul F. Clark, Peter Gottlieb, and Donald Kennedy. Ithaca, NY: ILR Press.

McDermott, Gerald A. 2002. *Embedded Politics: Industrial Networks and Institution Building in Post-Communism.* Ann Arbor: University of Michigan Press.

————. 2003. "The Political Foundations of Inter-Firm Networks and Social Capital: A Post-Communist Lesson." Manuscript, University of Pennsylvania, Wharton School, Philadelphia, Pennsylvania.

McGuire, Patrick, Mark Granovetter, and Michael Schwartz. 1993. "Thomas Edison and the Social Construction of the Early Electricity Industry in America." In *Explorations in Economic Sociology,* ed. R. Swedberg. New York: Russell Sage Foundation.

Merton, Robert K. 1957. *Social Theory and Social Structure.* Glencoe, IL: Free Press.

Meyer, David R. 1983. "Emergence of the American Manufacturing Belt: An Interpretation." *Journal of Historical Geography* 9(2): 145–174.

———. 1989. "Midwestern Industrialization and the American Manufacturing Belt in the Nineteenth Century." *Journal of Economic History* 42(4): 741–774.

Meyer, John W., and Brian Rowan. 1977. "Institutionalized Organizations: Formal Structure as Myth and Ceremony." *American Journal of Sociology* 83: 340.

Mill, J. S. 1843/1976. "A System of Logic." In *On the Logic of the Moral Sciences.* Indianapolis, IN: Bobbs-Merrill.

Mills, C. W. 1956. *The Power Elite.* New York: Oxford University Press.

Mintz, B., and M. Schwartz. 1981. "Interlocking Directorates and Interest Group Formation." *American Sociological Review* 46(6): 851–869.

Mitchell, J. 1969. "The Concept and Use of Social Networks." In *Social Networks in Urban Situations,* ed. J. Mitchell. Manchester, England: Manchester University Press, 1–50.

Mizruchi, Mark S. 1996. "What Do Interlocks Do? An Analysis, Critique and Assessment of Research on Interlocking Directorates." *Annual Review of Sociology* 22: 271–298.

Molotch, Harvey. 1976. "The City as Growth Machine: Toward a Political Economy of Place." *American Journal of Sociology* 82(2): 309.

———. 1979. "Capital and Neighborhood in the United States." *Urban Affairs Quarterly* 14(3): 289–312.

Molotch, Harvey, William Freudenburg, and Krista Paulsen. 2000. "History Repeats Itself, but How? City Character, Urban Tradition, and the Accomplishment of Place." *American Sociological Review* 65(6): 791–823.

Molotch, Harvey, and John Logan. 1984. "Tension in the Growth Machine: Overcoming Resistance to Value-Free Development." *Social Problems* 31(5): 483–499.

Montgomery, David. 1979. *Workers' Control in America.* New Haven, CT: Yale University Press.

———. 1987. *The Fall of the House of Labor: The Workplace, the State, and Labor Activism.* Cambridge: Cambridge University Press.

Moore, Thomas S. 1988. "Deindustrialization and the Dynamics of Local Employment Changes." In *Research in Politics and Society,* vol. 3: *Deindustrialization and the Restructuring of American Industry,* ed. M. Wallace and J. Rothschild. Greenwich, CT: JAI Press.

Mouat, Lucia. 1984. "America's Urban 'Rust Belt' Cinches Up for the Future." *Christian Science Monitor,* May 25, 16.

Nee, Victor. 2005. "The New Institutionalisms in Economics and Sociology." In *The Handbook of Economic Sociology,* 2nd ed., ed. Neil J. Smelser and Richard Swedberg. New York/Princeton, NJ: Russell Sage Foundation/Princeton University Press, 26–74.

Nelson, Daniel. 1977. "Taylorism and the Workers at Bethlehem Steel: 1898–1901." *Pennsylvania Magazine of History and Biography* 101: 487–505.

Ochsenford, S. E. 1892. *Muhlenberg College.* Allentown, PA: Muhlenberg College.

Olson, Mancur. 1971. *The Logic of Collective Action: Public Goods and the Theory of Groups.* Cambridge, MA: Harvard University Press.

———. 1982. *The Rise and Decline of Nations.* New Haven, CT: Yale University Press.

Osterman, Paul. 1988. *Employment Futures.* New York: Oxford University Press.

———. 2002. *Gathering Power: The Future of Progressive Politics in America.* Boston: Beacon Press.

———. 2006. "Community Organizing and Employee Representation." *British Journal of Industrial Relations* 44(4): 629–649.

Ostrom, Elinor. 1990. *Governing the Commons: The Evolution of Institutions for Collective Action.* New York: Cambridge University Press.

Padgett, John F. 2000. "Organizational Genesis, Identity and Control: The Transformation of Banking in Renaissance Florence." Paper presented at Santa Fe Institute, Santa Fe, New Mexico.

Padgett, John F., and Christopher K. Ansell. 1993. "Robust Action and the Rise of the Medici: 1400–1434." *American Journal of Sociology* 98(6): 1259–1319.

Page, Brian, and Richard Walker. 1991. "Settlement to Fordism: The Agro-Industrial Revolution in the American Midwest." *Economic Geography* 67(4): 281–315.

Paige, J. M. 1999. "Conjuncture, Comparison, and Conditional Theory in Macrosocial Inquiry." *American Journal of Sociology* 105(3): 718–800.

Palmer, Donald. 1983. "Broken Ties: Interlocking Directorates and Intercorporate Coordination." *Administrative Science Quarterly* 28(1): 40–55.

Palmer, Donald A., and Brad M. Barber. 2001. "Challenges, Elites, and Owning Families: A Social Class Theory of Corporate Acquisitions in the 1960s." *Administrative Science Quarterly,* 46: 87–120.

Parton, William Julian. 1986. *Decline and Fall of a Great Company: Reflections on the Decline and Fall of the Lehigh Coal and Navigation Company.* Easton, PA: Center for Canal History and Technology.

Pierson, Paul. 1994. *Dismantling the Welfare State? Reagan, Thatcher and the Politics of Retrenchment.* New York: Cambridge University Press.

———. 2000. "Increasing Returns, Path Dependence and the Study of Politics." *American Political Science Review* 94(2): 251–267.

Pierson, Paul, and Theda Skocpol. 2002, "Historical Institutionalism in Contemporary Political Science." In *Political Science,* ed. Ira Katznelson and Helen Milner. New York: Norton, 693–721.

Pinkowski, Edward. 1963. *John Siney: The Miner's Martyr.* Philadelphia: Sunshine Press.

Piore, Michael J., and Charles F. Sabel. 1984. *The Second Industrial Divide.* New York: Basic Books.

Plunkert, Lois M. 1990. "The 1980s: A Decade of Job Growth and Industry Shifts." *Monthly Labor Review* 113: 3.

Podolny, Joel, and Karen Page. 1998. "Network Forms of Organization." *Annual Review of Sociology* 24: 57–76.

Porter, Michael E. 1990. *The Competitive Advantage of Nations.* New York: Free Press.

———. 1998. "Clusters and the New Economics of Competition." *Harvard Business Review* 76(6): 77–90.

———. 2000. "Location, Competition, and Economic Development: Local Clusters in a Global Economy." *Economic Development Quarterly* 14(1): 15–34.

Portes, Alejandro. 1998. "Social Capital: Its Origins and Applications in Modern Sociology." *Annual Review of Sociology* 24: 1–24.

———. 2000. "The Two Meanings of Social Capital." *Sociological Forum* 15(1): 1–12.

Portes, Alejandro, and Patricia Landolt. 2000. "Social Capital: Promise and Pitfalls of Its Role in Development." *Journal of Latin American Studies* 32: 529–547.

Powell, W. W. 1990. "Neither Market nor Hierarchy: Network Forms of Organization." *Research in Organizational Behavior* 12: 295–336.

Powell, W. W., and Paul DiMaggio, eds. 1991. *The New Institutionalism in Organizational Analysis.* Chicago: University of Chicago Press.

Powell, W. W., K. W. Koput, D. R. White, and J. Owen-Smith. 2005. "Network Dynamics and Field Evolution: The Growth of Interorganizational Collaboration in the Life Sciences." *American Journal of Sociology* 110(4): 1132–1205.

Putnam, Robert D. 1993. *Making Democracy Work: Civic Traditions in Modern Italy.* Princeton, NJ: Princeton University Press.

———. 1995. "Bowling Alone: America's Declining Social Capital." *Journal of Democracy* 6(1): 65–78.

———. 2001. *Bowling Alone.* New York: Simon and Schuster.

Raines, Howell. 1984. "Debate Sets Stage of Hard Fighting on Trail to Nov. 6." *New York Times,* October 23.

Republic Steel Corporation. 1943. *Republic Steel: Known the World Over for Quality Steels.* Cleveland, OH: Republic Steel Corporation.

———. 1944. *Republic Goes to War.* Cleveland, OH: Republic Steel Corporation.

Rivero, Arturo A. Lara. 2002. "Packard Electric/Delphi and the Birth of the Autopart Cluster: The Case of Chihuahua, Mexico." *International Journal of Urban and Regional Research* 26(4): 785.

Rodgers, Allan. 1950. "Some Aspects of Industrial Diversification in the United States." *Economic Geography* 33(1): 16–30.

———. 1952a. "The Iron and Steel Industry of the Mahoning and Shenango Valleys." *Economic Geography* 28(4): 331–342.

———. 1952b. "Industrial Inertia: A Major Factor in the Location of the Steel Industry in the United States." *Geographical Review* 42(1): 56–66.

Romo, F. P., and M. Schwartz. 1995. "The Embeddedness of Business Decisions: The Migration of Manufacturing Plants in New York State, 1960–1985." *American Sociological Review* 60(6): 874–907.

Sabel, Charles F. 1992. "Studied Trust: Building New Forms of Cooperation in a Volatile Economy." In *Industrial Districts and Local Economic Regeneration*, ed. Frank Pyke and Werner Sengenberger. Geneva, Switzerland: International Institute for Labour Studies.

Sabel, Charles F., and Jonathan Zeitlin, eds. 1997. *World of Possibilities: Flexibility and Mass Production in Western Industrialization*. Cambridge: Cambridge University Press.

Saxenian, AnnaLee. 1994. *Regional Advantage: Culture and Competition in Silicon Valley and Route 128*. Cambridge, MA: Harvard University Press.

Scott, Allen J. 1988. *The New Industrial Spaces: Flexible Production Organizations and Regional Development in North America and Western Europe*. London: Pion.

Sewell, William H. 1992. "A Theory of Structure: Duality, Agency and Transformation." *American Journal of Sociology* 98(1): 1–29.

Short, J. R., L. M. Benton, W. B. Luce, and J. Walton. 1993. "Reconstructing the Image of an Industrial City." *Annals of the Association of American Geographers* 83(2): 207–224.

Silverberg, Louis G. 1941. "Citizens' Committees: Their Role in Industrial Conflict." *Public Opinion Quarterly* 5(1): 17–37.

Skardon, Alvin W. 1984. *Steel Valley University: The Origin of Youngstown State*. Youngstown, OH: Youngstown State University.

Skocpol, Theda. 1996. "Unravelling from Above." *American Prospect* 25: 20–25.

———. 2001. *The Missing Middle*. New York: Norton.

Skocpol, Theda, Marshall Ganz, and Z. Munson. 2000. "A Nation of Organizers: The Institutional Origins of Civic Volunteerism in the United States." *American Political Science Review* 94(3).

Skocpol, Theda, and Margaret Somers. 1980. "The Uses of Comparative History in Macrosocial Inquiry." *Comparative Studies in Society and History* 22(2): 174–197.

Slick, Max Harrell. 1967. "Manufactural Diversification in the Allentown-Bethlehem-Easton Standard Metropolitan Statistical Area: The 1915–1960 Period." PhD diss., Pennsylvania State University.

Smelser, Neil J., and Richard Swedberg. 1994. "The Sociological Perspective on the Economy." In *The Handbook of Economic Sociology*. New York: Russell Sage Foundation, 2–26.

Sofchalk, Donald. 1965. "The Memorial Day Incident." *Labor History* 6: 3–43.

Somers, Margaret. 1993. "Citizenship and the Place of the Public Sphere: Law, Community, and Political Culture in the Transition to Democracy." *American Sociological Review* 58: 587–620.

Speer, Michael. 1969. "The 'Little Steel Strike': Conflict for Control." *Ohio History* 78: 273–287.

Staber, Udo, and Jorg Sydow. 2002. "Organizational Adaptive Capacity: A Structuration Perspective." *Journal of Management Inquiry* 11(4): 408–424.

Stainbrook, G. H., and P. Beste. 2002. *Lehigh Valley Industrial Park: A 2002 Perspective*. Bethlehem, PA: Lehigh Valley Industrial Parks.

Stark, David. 1996. "Recombinant Property in East European Capitalism." *American Journal of Sociology* 101: 993–1028.

Stephens, David T., Alexander Bobersky, and Joseph Cencia. 1994. "The Yankee Frontier in Northern Ohio: 1796–1850." *Pioneer America Society Transactions* 17: 1–10.

Stinchcombe, Arthur. 1959. "Bureaucratic and Craft Administration of Production: A Comparative Study." *Administrative Science Quarterly* 4(2): 168–187.

———. 1965. "Social Structures and Organizations." In *Handbook of Organizations,* ed. James March. Chicago: Rand McNally.

Stolberg, Benjamin. 1937. "Big Steel, Little Steel, and the CIO." *The Nation* 145(5): 119–123.

Storper, Michael. 1994. "Specialization in the U.S. Film Industry: External Economies, the Division of Labor, and the Crossing of Industrial Divides." In *Post-Fordism: A Reader,* ed. Ash Amin. Boston: Blackwell Publishing.

———.1995. "The Resurgence of Regional Economies, Ten Years Later: The Region as a Nexus of Untraded Dependencies." *European Urban and Regional Studies* 2(3): 191–221.

———. 1997. *The Regional World: Territorial Development in a Global Economy*. New York: Guilford Press.

Storper, Michael, and Richard Walker. 1989. *The Capitalist Imperative: Territory, Technology, and Industrial Growth*. New York: Basil Blackwell.

Streeck, Wolfgang, and Kathleen Thelen. 2005. "Introduction: Institutional Change in Advanced Political Economies." In *Beyond Continuity,* ed. W. Streeck and K. Thelen. New York: Oxford University Press.

Strohmeyer, J. 1986. *Crisis in Bethlehem: Big Steel's Struggle to Survive*. Pittsburgh, PA: University of Pittsburgh Press.

Stuart, Milton C. 1938. "Asa Packer, 1805–1879: Captain of Industry, Educator, Citizen." Address delivered before the American Branch of the Newcomen Society of England, December 6, at the Union League Club. Bethlehem, PA: Lehigh University Archives.

Sull, Don. 2001. "From Community of Innovation to Community of Inertia: The Rise and Fall of the Akron Tire Cluster." Academy of Management Best Paper Proceedings.

Swain, James E. 1967. *A History of Muhlenberg College, 1848–1967.* Cambridge: Cambridge University Press.

Swidler, Ann. 1986. "Culture in Action: Symbols and Strategies." *American Sociological Review* 51(2): 273–286.

———. 2001. *Talk of Love: How Culture Matters.* Chicago: University of Chicago Press.

Teaford, John C. 1993. *Cities of the Heartland: The Rise and Fall of the Industrial Midwest.* Bloomington: Indiana University Press.

Temin, Peter. 1964. *Iron and Steel Industry in Nineteenth Century America: An Economic Inquiry.* Cambridge, MA: MIT Press.

Testa, William A., Thomas H. Klier, and Richard H. Mattoon. 1997. *Assessing the Midwest Economy: Looking Back for the Future. Report of Findings.* Chicago: Federal Reserve Bank of Chicago.

Thelen, Kathleen. 1999. "Historical Institutionalism in Comparative Politics." *Annual Review of Political Science* 2: 369–404.

———. 2003. "How Institutions Evolve: Insights from Comparative Historical Analysis." In *Comparative Historical Analysis in the Social Sciences,* ed. James Mahoney and Dietrich Rueschmeyer. Cambridge: Cambridge University Press, 208–240.

Tickell, A., and J. A. Peck. 1995. "Social Regulation after Fordism: Regulation Theory, Neo-Liberalism, and the Global-Local Nexus." *Economy and Society* 24(3): 357–386.

Tiffany, Paul A. 1988. *The Decline of American Steel: How Management, Labor, and Government Went Wrong.* New York: Oxford University Press.

Tilly, Charles. 1992. *Coercion, Capital and European States, AD 990–1992.* New York: Blackwell.

———. 1997. "History and Sociological Imagining." *Tocqueville Review* 15: 57–74.

———. 1998. "Political Identities." In *Challenging Authority: The Historical Study of Contentious Politics,* ed. M. Hanagan, L. P. Moch, and W. Brake. Minneapolis: University of Minnesota Press.

Uchitelle, Louis. 1991. "Trapped in the Impoverished Middle Class." *New York Times,* November 17.

U.S. Bureau of the Census 1951. *Statistical Abstract of the United States.* Washington, DC: U.S. Bureau of the Census.

———. 1952. *City and County Data Book.* Washington, DC: U.S. Bureau of the Census.

Upton, Harriet Taylor. 1909. *A Twentieth Century History of Trumbull County, Ohio: A Narrative Account of Its Historical Progress.* Chicago: Lewis Publishing Company.

Upton, Harriet Taylor, and H. G. Cutler. 1910. *History of the Western Reserve.* Chicago: Lewis Publishing Company.

Useem, M. 1984. *The Inner Circle: Large Corporations and the Rise of Political Activity in the U.S. and U.K.* New York: Oxford University Press.

Uzzi, Brian. 1996. "The Sources and Consequences of Embeddedness for the Economic Performance of Organizations: The Network Effect." *American Sociological Review* 61(4): 674–698.

Vadasz, Thomas P. 1975. *The History of an Industrial Community: Bethlehem, Pennsylvania, 1741–1920.* PhD thesis, College of William and Mary, Williamsburg, VA.

Venditta, David, Frank Whelan, Mark Frassinelli, Matt Assad, and Chuck Zovko. 2003. "Forging America: The Story of Bethlehem Steel." *Morning Call* (Allentown, PA). www.mcall.com/news/specials/bethsteel/all-bethsteel -c0p1,0,4389048.story?coll=all-bethsteel-nav.

Walker, J. E. 1981. *A City Tries to Save Itself: Youngstown, Ohio.* PhD diss., Claremont Graduate School.

Weinraub, Bernard. 1984. "Mondale, at Chicago Rally, Says 'Tide Is Turning in '84 Election.' " *New York Times,* October 31.

White, Harrison C., S. A., Boorman, and Ronald L. Breiger. 1976. "Social Structure from Multiple Networks: I. Blockmodels of Roles and Positions." *American Journal of Sociology* 81: 730–780.

Whitford, Josh. 2005. *The New Old Economy: Networks, Institutions, and the Organizational Transformation of American Manufacturing.* New York: Oxford University Press.

Wier, Margaret, Ann Shola Orloff, and Theda Skocpol, eds. 1988. *The Politics of Social Policy in the United States.* Princeton, NJ: Princeton University Press.

Williams, H. B. 1882. *History of Trumbull and Mahoning Counties with Illustrations.* Cleveland, OH: H. Z. Williams & Bro.

Wolle, Francis. 1972. *A Moravian Heritage.* Boulder, CO: Empire Reproduction and Printing.

Womack, James P., Daniel T. Jones, and Daniel Roos. 1990. *The Machine That Changed the World: The Story of Lean Production.* New York: Rawson Associates.

Woolcock, M. 1998. "Social Capital and Economic Development: Toward a Theoretical Synbook and Policy Framework." *Theory and Society* 27(2): 151–208.

Woolcock, M., and D. Narayan. 2000. "Social Capital: Implications for Development Theory, Research, and Policy." *World Bank Research Observer* 15(2): 225–249.

Yates, W. Ross. 1978. *Bethlehem of Pennsylvania: The Golden Years, 1841–1920.* Bethlehem, PA: Bethlehem Book Committee.

———. 1992. *Lehigh University: A History of Education in Engineering, Business, and the Human Condition.* Bethlehem, PA: Lehigh University Press.

Youngstown Sheet and Tube Corporation. 1951. *50 Years of Steel: The Story of Youngstown Sheet and Tube Company. This Is America.* Youngstown, OH: Youngstown Sheet and Tube Corporation.

Zeiger, Robert. 1986. *American Workers, American Unions, 1920–1985.* Baltimore: Johns Hopkins University Press.

———. 1995. *The CIO, 1935–1955.* Chapel Hill: University of North Carolina
Press.

Zeitlin, M. 1974. "Corporate Ownership and Control: The Large Corporation
and the Capitalist Class." American *Journal of Sociology* 79: 1073–1119.

Acknowledgments

I am most grateful to two people who have guided me through the writing of this book. Mike Piore has been a source of wisdom, humor, grace, and curiosity. Over the years, my intellectual relationship with Mike—prosecuted mainly over dozens of long, rambling, fascinating conversations in his office, messily eating lunch over a garbage can—has blossomed into a true friendship. There are too many things Mike deserves thanks for. Rick Locke has the ability to shine a very bright light on research. It can be a harsh light at times, but my work and intellectual growth have benefited vastly from being exposed to it. The bright and charismatic luminosity Rick shines on research comes from the same source as the warm and welcoming light he shines as a friend and mentor. Rick generously shined that light on me at several points in my journey here, which gave me the confidence to undertake work that was risky but ultimately extremely rewarding.

I benefited immensely from being associated with the Institute for Work and Employment Research at MIT early in the book's process. Paul Osterman served as a kind of conscience; whenever I got really befuddled, I turned to Paul for a sense of clarity. Before I came to MIT I had heard of Tom Kochan, who had achieved something of a legendary status by the time I was studying at Cornell. Tom's powerful sense of values and commitment have earned him high status in my mind and in those of others. Others from whom I have learned a tremendous amount in my time at MIT include Roberto Fernandez, Ezra Zuckerman, Maureen Scully, and Diane Burton.

Richard Lester spent hours puzzling through questions and brainstorming approaches (and also correcting my atrocious spelling!). Richard also provided generous financial and logistical support. He created a welcoming and open community of scholars at the IPC that made the research and writing that went into this book a much more enjoyable experience than it would have been otherwise. I cannot mention the IPC without also acknowledging the incomparable Anita Kafka. Anita has saved my butt more than once (including serving as my proxy in the cross-Atlantic final stages of producing the document you are reading).

I was also lucky enough to be at the IPC during Gary Herrigel's sabbatical—one of those serendipitous accidents that made being at MIT such a privilege. Gary became my colleague when I moved to the University of Chicago and has served on several occasions as a voice of encouragement. I have also absorbed a great deal from my other colleagues here at Chicago, including John Padgett, Ron Burt, Damon Phillips, Lis Clemens, and Matthew Bothner. They make for an extremely challenging—but rewarding—environment in which to engage ideas.

I benefited greatly from the friendships both personal and intellectual I have made along the way. Isabel Fernandez-Mateo, Forrest Briscoe, Matthew Bidwell, Corinne Bendersky, Sarah Kaplan, Andrew Von Nordenflycht, Henrik Bresman, Jordan Siegel, Brandon DuBroc, Kate Kellogg, Nils Fonstad, Emilio Castilla, Dan Beznitz, Carlos Martinez, Sachi Hatakenaka, Jean-Jacques DeGroof, and Céline Druilhe have all contributed greatly to making this book. Natasha Iskander deserves special thanks for much needed advice.

I am grateful to the benevolent librarians and researchers at the Bethlehem Public Library, the Lehigh County Historical Society, the Mahoning Valley Historical Society (who opened their archives to me on their day off!), the Museum of Labor and Industry in Youngstown, the Boston Public Library, Widener Library, and Dewey Library. Brian Corbin with the Youngstown Diocese provided an invaluable introduction to Youngstown. Peter O'Connor provided much-needed advice from the "real world," as did Carol Coletta of CEOs for Cities, whose thoughtful engagement with the (at times abstract) ideas in this book have brought it down to earth considerably. I am also grateful to Mike Aronson and his team at Harvard University Press. I appreciate their hard work and forbearance.

Finally, my family. I knew that I was telling a story that made sense when I was able to explain it to my parents, John and Irene Safford, without meeting a look of benign confusion. Lastly: Timothy Brian Doyle. My partner in every sense of the word, Tim has lent me his humor, compassion, humanity, humility, and sense of adventure. He listened to me as I worked through the confusion and has kept me honest to myself. I couldn't have done this without him.

Index

The letter *f* following a number denotes a figure. The letter *t* following a number denotes a table.

CPSIA information can be obtained
at www.ICGtesting.com
Printed in the USA
LVHW031508230621
690955LV00009B/740/J